My Sporting Life

My Sporting Life

Jimmy Deenihan

RED HEN PUBLISHING

First published in 2011 by

Red Hen Publishing
Duagh
Listowel
Co Kerry
Ireland

Email: redhen1@eircom.net
+353 (0)68 45942

Cover illustration by Carol Cronin, www.carolcronin.com

Typesetting and design by Kieran Nolan, www.oldtown.ie

Printed in Ireland
by
Walsh Colour Print, Castleisland, Co Kerry

ISBN 978-0-9570201-2-2

A catalogue record of this book is available from the British Library.

This book is dedicated to my parents,
Mick and Mary Ellen Deenihan.

Contents

The Lartigue Monorail

(Courtesy of Dominic Lee, Priory Studios)

Priory Studios

THE PROCEEDS from the sales of this book will be donated to the Lartigue Monorail Restoration Project in Listowel. Back in June of 1998, I paid a visit to Mick and the late Sheila Barry in Ballingown, Lisselton. They had reassembled 30 metres of the original Lartigue Monorail on their farmyard. I was fascinated by their achievement and decided there and then to examine the feasibility of doing a Lartigue project on the site of the former Great Southern Railway in Listowel.

With the help of an excellent and dedicated local committee, we achieved this objective, resulting in the provision of a replica of the original Lartigue locomotive, along with 550 metres of track, complete with turntables and switches and a state-of-the-art museum. Overall the project cost almost €2 million and we now owe the bank just €40,000.

I hope that the profits from this book will contribute towards clearing that debt and that the project, which is run by volunteers, will continue to expand and flourish, attracting visitors from all over the world to see and enjoy a rare piece of railway engineering heritage.

I would like to thank Patrick Trant,
chairman of Trant Construction, Southampton,
for sponsoring this book.

Book Patrons

Ned Bolger, Farm Managements Consultants, Listowel
Pats Carroll, Ardfert Quarry Products
Patricia Deenihan, Finuge
Pat & Jerry Galvin, Finuge
Brendan Griffin TD
Michael & Aine Guerin, Listowel
Pat Guiney, Coolaclarig, Listowel
Brendan & Bridie Harrington, Ballyheigue
Brendan Heaphy, Listowel Autos
Donie Horan, Horan's Centre, Tralee
Jackie & Davnet Hourigan, Ballybunion
Thomas Keane, Building & Civil Eng. Construction, Cahersiveen
Christy & Norita Killeen, Upper Church Street, Listowel
Michael MacWilliams, Paris
Sean McCarthy & Sons Ltd., Lixnaw
Helen Moran, Dublin
John Moriarty, Fenit
Paddy Mulvihill, Irish Wire Products, Limerick
Louis O'Connell, Bailys Solicitors, Tralee
Niall Ó Donnchú, Dublin
Ned & Maureen O'Hanlon, Tarbert
Con Lynch & Ann Marie O'Sullivan, Listowel
Danny O'Sullivan & Sons Ltd., London
Senator Ned O'Sullivan, Listowel
John Pierse, Listowel
Riobard Pierse, solicitor, Listowel
Cllr Liam Purtill, Main Street, Ballylongford
Pat Scanlon, Ballygrennan, Listowel
JJ Walsh, Lixnaw

Foreword

THERE WAS A KIND OF FOOTBALL in Ireland long before the coming of the GAA. It was especially strong in North Kerry. It was a primitive kind of game. The ball in use was mostly straw wrapped in leather. You couldn't kick it very far and you couldn't kick with any accuracy. A man whose name is forgotten revolutionised football, not only in Ireland, but all over the world. He was a veterinary surgeon in Belfast who, one day, got tired of seeing his small boy trundling around on a tricycle with rubber tyres. It dawned on him that rubber could be filled with air and this discovery made most of our modern field games possible.

When Michael Cusack founded the GAA in 1884, his big ambition was to revive hurling. He invented a game from the best elements of soccer and rugby and cleverly called it Gaelic football, thus giving the impression that it went back a long way. The ironic outcome of this was that Gaelic football almost wiped out hurling. It was a simple game to understand and, above all, it caused little injury. This was in an age when a man's hands were important to him. Hurling can be hard on the hands.

We are told that Gaelic football spread like wildfire. Soon there was a club in almost every parish in the country. People sometimes ask why the new game became so popular in Kerry. The answer may surprise you. There were many rugby clubs in Kerry and some of them turned over to the new game. Killorglin's Laune Rangers were an example: they were a famous rugby club but they were the first team to represent Kerry in an All-Ireland final. The new game attracted great crowds and soon the Kerry football team had a great following. They reached their peak in the late twenties and early thirties and again in the late thirties and early forties.

When Jimmy Deenihan was a small boy football was a great topic of conversation in Kerry. To get on the county team was the dream of almost every small boy and to captain Kerry in winning an All-Ireland would be a taste of heaven. Every man likes to achieve things that would guarantee to himself his own worth. He can turn to those memories in the depths of depression and they will revive him. He knows that he has done something good. Jimmy Deenihan achieved that mark not once, but several times. And when he captained Kerry in an All-Ireland winning final it was the height of any small boy's dream.

He was lucky in his birthplace, Finuge, just south of the river Feale, which is a dividing line between hurling and football in the region we call North Kerry, even though it isn't North Kerry at all. If he had been born a little to the south he most certainly would have been a hurler and no doubt a good one because he had the mentality to play in the sterling game. As it was, he made his way into Kerry's senior team by sheer dint of good displays and once he was there, his place was never in doubt. He was never a man to make the headlines but he was a footballer's footballer – in other words, his fellow players appreciated him more than most people.

He played most of his football at left corner-back; a difficult position because corner-backs are often meant to cover both a ball breaking in the goalmouth or a forward coming through from outfield. Jimmy Deenihan fulfilled those tasks consummately. He elevated commonsense into a kind of genius. Every team needs a man like him, especially in the defence, who will keep his head when all around are losing theirs. He retired full of honours and with honour.

His winning speech as captain of Kerry in an All-Ireland final was heard by Garret FitzGerald who marked him down as a young man with a future in politics. He nominated him as a senator and he stood for Fine Gael at the next general election. The party had lost their seat in North Kerry but Jimmy canvassed so intensely that he made certain of getting it back. On the night of the final rally in Tralee, the platform was in danger of collapsing from the weight of men who had won senior honours with Kerry. Some people said that it was not so much a Fine Gael election as a GAA election. He cruised into Leinster House and by hard work he nailed down his place and eventually, of course, he has become a member of the Cabinet.

I will give an example of his commitment. One night about five years ago he was having a quiet drink in a hotel with me and a girlfriend of mine in Castleisland on a bad night. It was very pleasant company but about 10 o'clock Jimmy said, 'I have to attend a party meeting in Fenit'. Fenit was about seventeen miles away and still is. It showed great commitment to part from pleasant company at that time of the night and in such bad conditions.

Left to right: Moss Keane (RIP), Donal Lenihan, Mick Galwey, Con Houlihan, myself and Mick Doyle (RIP) in Castleisland at the unveiling of a bust in honour of Con Houlihan in January 2004.

As Minister he is facing a huge task because not many people are interested in Arts, Heritage and the Gaeltacht. The new government has come into power with great promise and so far has behaved boldly. Its biggest task is to change the national mentality which, over the years, has come to accept dishonesty in politics and has become cynical. We cannot change this mental climate in one fell swoop but good behaviour at high levels will go a long way towards achieving it.

As far as I know this is a new ministry and Jimmy Deenihan will go about interpreting it in a bold and sensible way. As a footballer he has achieved the ultimate and he has the potential to leave a great mark in a bigger field. Jimmy has also run in a marathon: the biggest marathon of all is before him.

We wish him all the luck that he deserves.

Con Houlihan, journalist

Preface

IT IS A LONG WAY from Finuge to the heady heights of Croke Park and ministerial office. Jimmy Deenihan has travelled that road, showing considerable commitment and determination, sometimes concealed behind an affable exterior. He now tells the story in all its fascinating detail. It chronicles a changing Ireland as much as a personal journey.

The Deenihan story begins with a tranquil rural childhood dominated by traditional community values and Gaelic football. There was personal tragedy, too, with the death of a young sister in a car accident. His father's big ambition was that Jimmy would play for Kerry, while his mother literally started the ball rolling when she returned from Puck Fair with a brown rubber ball for her young son. He achieved his father's ambition in spades. The highlight was captaining Kerry to All-Ireland victory, and he writes with pride and affection about bringing the Sam Maguire back to Finuge Cross.

Although initially urging caution, his mentor, John B. Keane, encouraged him in his political career, first in the Seanad and then in the Dáil. He soon consolidated his political base, with the highlight being his appointment to ministerial office. Along the way, he has retained his interest in sport and has done much to promote North Kerry's remarkable literary heritage.

I was in Croke Park the day he lifted the Sam Maguire into the air, and I was in the Dáil when he was appointed to the Cabinet. The story is not over. His ministerial and political work, rooted in that sense of community he has never lost, will provide material for more chapters of progress in a remarkable personal, sporting, literary and political journey.

Michael O'Regan, correspondent with *The Irish Times*

Introduction

THIS BOOK is the story of my sporting life from the time my mother brought me a brown rubber ball from Puck Fair in Killorglin in 1957, to cycling the annual 110-mile Ring of Kerry Charity Cycle in July 2011 with An Taoiseach Enda Kenny. It traces my football-playing career with Kerry at all grades, from 1970 to 1983, my career with my local club, Finuge, and divisional club, Feale Rangers, from 1963 to 1990, my involvement with school and colleges football with Killocrim NS, St. Michael's College, Listowel, and with the National College of Physical Education in Limerick, as well as with Munster at inter-provincial level.

In this memoir, I set out the benefits to health and I emphasise the equally important role of sport in one's personal development. For too long the psychological benefits of involvement in sport, as well as the character-shaping influences, have been overlooked.

My sporting career, far from ending with retirement from competitive football, has branched out in new directions. Integrating it with my political career over the past 21 years, I have played several matches with the Oireachtas in rugby, soccer, Gaelic football and hurling, using sporting events to forge links, not only with TDs from other parties, but also with members of various overseas parliaments. I organise an annual Oireachtas charity hillwalking event and in 2010 I ran the Dublin City Marathon with ten Oireachtas colleagues.

Continuing to explore new sporting options, I have become a keen hillwalker and, when I have some free time, I enjoy the challenge of the Reeks and Slieve Mish Mountains in Kerry.

I have walked in the Alps, the Pyrenees and the Rocky Mountains in the US, as well as the breathtaking Lake District in England. However, for shorter, therapeutic, seaside walks with my wife Mary, Ballybunion remains my favourite place.

More recently I have taken up cycling and have participated in the past three Ring of Kerry Charity Cycles. I can think of no better way of enjoying that invigorating scenic route than on a bike. Keeping my sporting options open, I hope, from now on, to concentrate on walking, cycling and lifting light weights in the gym. I hope, too, to resume golf whenever I finish my career in politics.

Sport is about re-inventing oneself and staying young at heart and I aim to enjoy its challenge and its recreational bonuses for as long as I am able.

Finally, this book documents aspects of national sports policy that I have pursued since entering politics, including the promotion of physical education in schools, support for women in sport, access to land for walkers, the development of the greyhound industry, and the establishment of the National Lottery.

I hope that you will find this memoir interesting and at times informative.

Jimmy Deenihan

Kerry Football

A Unifying Tradition

GAELIC FOOTBALL holds a very special place in the hearts and minds of most Kerry people. For many it is more than a game, approximating at times to a religious mindset. Deeply ingrained in the Kerry psyche for generations, it has become an integral part of the heartbeat and soul of its followers at home and abroad. If horse racing is the sport of kings, Gaelic football is the sport of Kerry. Down through the decades, the game has become synonymous with the county in the same way as hurling has with Kilkenny, soccer with Brazil, and rugby with New Zealand.

Geographically, Kerry is a disparate county of marked contrasts. Segregated by three peninsulas, it is further divided by the Slieve Mish and the McGillycuddy Reeks mountain ranges. The northern part of the county, which is relatively fertile, supports a strong tradition of dairy and beef production while a pocket of cereal and tillage farming flourishes in the Ballyduff/Ardfert region. The southern part is mountainous and more conducive to sheep farming. Blessed with magnificent scenery and within easy reach of the sea, tourism and fishing are the backbone of the South and West Kerry economies.

Accents and dialects vary considerably across the county, with the Irish language still surviving in the West and South Kerry Gaeltacht areas. Due to the geographical division of the county, the rural population is rather dispersed. North Kerry people are likely to visit Limerick or Dublin more often than Kenmare or Cahersiveen, while East Kerry communities tend to gravitate towards Cork.

So what unites the dispersed communities of this sprawling, geographically diverse county? The answer must presumably be Gaelic football – a sport that brings together the people of Kerry under one banner and gives them a sense of collective identity more than any other single factor in the county.

The embracing network of the GAA clubs in Kerry, under the direction of the County Board, results in a shared ambition for the development of the game in Kerry, as well as the desire to keep the county at the helm of Gaelic football. Club competitions have proved to be a further factor in bonding disparate communities, bringing together players, fans and officials in the name of sport and entertainment.

Gaelic football has also contributed significantly to the nurturing of pride in the local community. Most Gaelic football clubs in Kerry are based on the parish entity and, in turn, have served to give the parish community a common identity. North Kerry writer Gabriel Fitzmaurice, in his book of essays, *Beat The Goatskin Till The Goat Cries*, vividly captures this connection between community and Gaelic football.

> One very obvious expression of the community is its football team. I often get the feeling that when a parish or a county team takes the field, for one hour it becomes the expression, the incarnation, of its parish or county. The boys and girls, the men and women who make up these teams, lose, as it were, their individual identity as they become a team – the visible expression of their community. And that is why we get so passionate about the game: because it is ourselves we see out there on the field. Our team, wearing our colours, are not just individuals: they are, in a mystical way, the physical expression of their community.
>
> This means the players and spectators are really one, that it's the community as an idea – the community's idea of itself – that takes the field. And when we win, the cup is not merely a trophy to be lost or won in the course of a game of football – it becomes a kind of grail, in the religious sense: in a very real sense, that cup is holy – something we have striven for, something we have hoped for, something which we may have prayed for, something for which we have given our very best; and that cup symbolises all that's good and beautiful in the game – the highest honour the game can bestow. Because when a cup comes to a county or parish, it flows with the heart's desire: the community celebrates – songs are made and sung, the deeds of the past are recalled, we rejoice in the present, and we face the future with joyful hope. And all because a group of individuals came together as a team.

To the extended Kerry diaspora, Gaelic football has a particular relevance. It provides them with an important connection with their communities and county. Over the past 40 years in the course of my travels in the UK, the USA and, occasionally, Australia, I have met with numerous Kerry people living abroad. Their interest in the fortunes of Kerry football and their knowledge of both club and county football at home never ceases to amaze me. In some instances, they were better informed than I would have been about the domestic football scene. Thanks to modern technology, they can now watch a match on the internet and tune into Radio Kerry for the commentary and reports on both county and club games.

Kerry emigrants have traditionally been very proud of their county's success in Gaelic football. It certainly boosts their self-esteem and raises their status in Irish communities abroad, while providing them with a bond of loyalty and affection with their native county and their respective parishes.

While in New York for the St Patrick's Day parade in 2010, I had the pleasure of marching with the Kerrymen's Association. I was hugely impressed with the degree of organisation it brought to the occasion and the effort it put into its dress code and its emblematic green and gold banner. As we marched down Fifth Avenue, led by the association's president, Tom Kennedy, I felt really proud of my fellow county men and women.

In 1989, I joined a Salvation Army soup run while in London on a fact-finding visit regarding homeless Irish people living rough in the city. The first homeless person I encountered was a North Kerry man sleeping in a cardboard box. He recognised me immediately from my football days and promptly asked, 'Are you Deenihan the Kerry footballer?' He didn't really want to discuss his plight and was only interested in Kerry's chances of winning the All-Ireland that year.

When playing with Kerry, especially at senior championship level, I always felt an extra sense of responsibility and desire to win; it was as if there was more at stake than the game of football itself, and that the team was carrying the hopes and aspirations of thousands of Kerry men and women, at home and abroad.

IF asked what I'd consider the most important contribution that Gaelic football has made to our county, I would, without hesitation, point to its healing effects on the bitterness and the wounds inflicted by the Civil War which raged from June 1922 to April 1923. According to Tom Doyle's book, *The Civil War in Kerry*, the fighting constituted 'a far more bloody, bitterly waged and protracted conflict in terms of lives lost, damage to property, disruption of people's daily lives and its impact on the local economy than the war waged against the British'. During August and September of 1922, 35 Free State soldiers were killed in Kerry, the equivalent of the Royal Irish Constabulary's entire death toll during the War of Independence in the county. In the 11 months of the Civil War, 73 anti-Treaty activists and 85 Free State soldiers, as well as about a dozen civilians, lost their lives. The GAA was split down the middle, with prominent activists like Austin Stack, Joe Barrett and John Joe Sheehy taking the anti-Treaty side,

The 1924 Kerry team.
Front row left to right: Jim Baily, J. Slattery.
Second row left to right: T. O'Connor, J. McCarthy, C. Brosnan, Miss Farrington (Barry's Hotel), Phil O'Sullivan (Capt.), Mrs. J. McCarthy, J. Barrett, J.M. Collins, J. Hannafin.
Third row left to right: Dr. E. O'Sullivan (Trainer), J. Sheehy (Goal), J. Walsh, J. Murphy, W. Landers, D. O'Connell, P. Russell, J.J. Sheehy, Jer McEllistrim (Sel Comm), Dr. D.J. O'Callaghan.
Fourth row left to right: D.J. Baily, T. Costelloe, J. Prendergast, E. Moriarty, R. Stack, J. Ryan, E. Fitzgerald, Jer Moriarty, M. Galvin, John Baily, M.J. Hannafin, P. Foley.

while Con Brosnan and Dick Fitzgerald sided with Michael Collins and the pro-Treaty supporters.

In his book, *In the Name of the Game*, JJ Barrett gives a moving account of the healing effects of Gaelic football on divided family members, neighbours and friends in the aftermath of that bloody conflict.

> The terrible animosity which this war created severely tested the multi-factioned nationalist membership of the GAA. But the great majority controlled their more extreme political tendencies in the name of the game. After the Civil War, in late 1923 and early '24, a group of young Kerry men were released from the internment camps at Hare Park and Tintown in the Curragh Camp. My father was one of those released. A number of them won an All-Ireland senior football medal within slightly over a year, after losing the postponed 1923 All-Ireland final to Dublin in the meantime. On that Kerry team were IRA members, Free State Army soldiers and other players who sympathised with the ruling Cosgrave Government but would not have been actively involved in politics.
>
> After captaining Kerry to All-Ireland victory in 1929 Joe Barrett handed over his next captaincy in 1931 to Captain Con Brosnan, a Free State Army officer, who was a member of the Army which had incarcerated Barrett in various locations for almost a year and a half. Brosnan and Barrett played on opposing sides in the famous Ex-Internees versus Kerry match in 1924, which was to set the foundation stone for Kerry's successes of the 1920s and even further ahead.

In 1953 there was another notable healing gesture in Kerry football. Tralee historian, Ryle Dwyer, in an article in the *Irish Examiner*, describes how John Joe Sheehy, a prominent Republican and one of the Kerry selectors, dropped his son Paudie, the reigning captain, on the eve of Kerry's clash with Armagh in the All-Ireland final, and handed the captaincy to Jas Murphy whose father was one of the two RIC men who had escorted Roger Casement from Ardfert to Tralee on Good Friday in 1916.

The following quotation from Reverend Liam Ryan, former Professor of Sociology at Maynooth College, in a celebrated article in *The Furrow* in

December 1984, confirms the significant role that Gaelic football and the GAA played in helping our county pull through this dark and divisive period.

> The GAA has been highly influential in healing the many rifts that had threatened to disrupt and fragment families and communities in Ireland through the years. In this task, common membership of the GAA has been a more powerful healing factor than common membership of the Catholic Church. Men who were deeply divided over Parnell, neighbours who shot at one another in the Civil War, families who had squabbled over grievances, great or small or imagined, all soon displayed a greater willingness to forgive and forget when gathered round the goal posts than when gathered around the altar.

This fraternal spirit still prevails, and, when it comes to electing officers at club or county levels, party politics is rarely a factor. The job normally goes to the most competent candidates who are judged by their performances rather than by their political affiliations, underpinning one of the key strengths of Kerry football.

MANY observers and sports journalists have tried over the years to identify the reasons why Kerry became such a dominant force in Gaelic football; the reasons are manifold and I will try to identify the ones I believe to have made the greatest contribution, starting with our schools.

In the early days of the organisation, Gaelic football was vigorously promoted in the Christian Brothers schools of Tralee, Cahersiveen and Dingle. Diocesan schools like St Brendan's College in Killarney and St. Michael's College in Listowel were equally enthusiastic and would become noted nurseries for future Kerry footballers. The game was also strongly encouraged in vocational schools when they were established under the 1930 Education Act. In addition, many primary schools throughout the county played a prominent part in fostering the game despite their limited playing area which was confined to the half acre sites on which the schools were built.

Since the foundation of Comórtas na mBunscol in 1971, primary school competitions have been better organised and have served as a nursery for all Kerry teams from underage to senior. The emphasis on skill development by Comórtas na mBunscol in Kerry is very much reflected in the ball handling and kicking skills of players who participated in the competitions and who went on to play for the county. The promotion of Gaelic football in Kerry at both primary and post-primary levels has always gone hand in hand with education, confirming the value and importance of the game to Kerry society.

The standard and quality of the County League, sponsored by Lee Strand Co-op, makes a huge contribution to the depth of talent available to the county selectors. There are five divisions, each comprising 12 teams. Games are well organised and the standard and consistency of refereeing is generally good. Games are played irrespective of whether or not county players are available for their clubs. The fact that most clubs in Kerry possess a good playing pitch with good changing and spectator facilities also helps. Thankfully, success at county level has never overshadowed the status and appeal of club football which is the very lifeblood of the game, as well as the place from where future stars emerge.

Since the introduction of the National Lottery in 1988, there has been major investment in the playing pitches of Kerry. Between 1998 and 2008, €11.225 million was allocated to GAA projects in the county, €8 million of which was invested during the period 2002–2007 when John O'Donoghue was Minister for Sport.

The level of physical conditioning and coaching has also improved considerably and most senior teams now have a manager who usually acts as trainer and coach. The majority of these trainers/coaches have attended coaching courses, and are capable of designing a well-structured fitness and coaching session that includes warm-up and warm-down exercises.

Apart from the County League, there are junior, intermediate and senior County Championships which are of a very high standard. The County Senior Championship is usually won by a divisional team representing a district board. Tralee's John Mitchels dominated the championship in the late 1950s and early 1960s, winning five successive County Championships. South Kerry dominated the championship in recent years, eventually conceding to Feale

Rangers and to Mid Kerry, who won titles in the past three years. In 2010 Dr. Crokes won the title for the first time since 2000. They consolidated their position as County champions by taking the title again in 2011. Other strong club sides, like An Ghaeltacht, Austin Stacks, Kerins O'Rahillys and Laune Rangers, have all figured in the roll of honour of County Championship winners over the past 20 years. These intensely contested competitions have been the launching pad for aspiring county players and a window for county selectors in quest of new talent. It is also important to acknowledge the success of Bord na nÓg in Kerry and its many volunteers who both officiate at matches and provide transport for the participants.

The Kerry County Board has been blessed over the years with competent officers, notably the many chairpersons, secretaries and treasurers who served their county unselfishly. During my time playing with Kerry, the County Board benefited from the services of excellent chairpersons like Jim Brosnan, Ger McKenna and Frank King, as well as from outstanding secretaries like Tadhg Crowley, Andy Molyneaux and, for a short period, the late Tim Lenihan, and subsequently Gerald White. Since 1987, Seán Kelly, Seán Walsh and Jerome Conway have served with distinction as chairpersons, while Anthony O'Keeffe, Eamonn O'Sullivan and Peter Twiss provided indispensable service as county secretaries. The officers, at all levels of the GAA in Kerry, deserve immense gratitude for their outstanding commitment and their contribution. They have all, in one way or another, contributed to our 36 All-Ireland victories.

Since the glorious era of the iconic Dr. Eamonn O'Sullivan, who trained Kerry to win eight All-Irelands, Kerry has been fortunate to have had the service of some very gifted managers, notably Mick O'Dwyer, arguably the greatest manager of all time. Other successful helmsmen were Jackie Lyne, who managed Kerry to All-Ireland success in 1969 and 1970; Páidí Ó Sé in 1997 and 2000; Pat O'Shea in 2006 and 2007; and Jack O'Connor in 2004 and 2009. Managers such as Johnny Culloty, Mickey Ned O'Sullivan and Ogie Moran, while not winning All-Ireland finals, made a very important contribution to the development of the county senior team.

Since the foundation of the GAA, the Kerry media has also served to promote Gaelic football. In the early years of the Association, the *Kerry Sentinel* gave extensive coverage to GAA matches. Since *The Kerryman* was established in 1904 it has given, along with *Kerry's Eye* (established in 1974), similar coverage to Gaelic games, both at club and county level. The advent of local radio in 1991 added a new dimension to the reporting of Gaelic games in Kerry, resulting in commentators such as Weeshie Fogarty and the late Liam Higgins becoming household names, both within the county and further afield. Thanks to the internet, Kerry people everywhere can get a direct commentary on club and County Championship games.

Weeshie's chatshow, *Terrace Talk*, also attracts widespread participation and comment, while Murt Murphy, who featured for some time on the *Kerry Today* programme, emerged as an excellent, if at times controversial, analyst. *Weekend Sport* on Saturdays and Sundays, presented by Gary O'Sullivan and produced by Joe O'Mahony, provides extensive coverage of all GAA matches throughout the county. Such programmes, along with affording fans their say, make an invaluable contribution to sporting culture and to the promotion of the game.

The cost of training county teams is now considerable for all grades. Kerry Group PLC has made a significant investment in Kerry football, especially in the senior team, since it became involved with Kerry team sponsorship in the early 1990s. This sponsorship, together with church gate collections and other fundraising initiatives, has provided the team with the necessary medical and rehabilitation support personnel who have proven invaluable in extending the inter-county playing careers of a number of key players.

Another factor which has contributed significantly, in my opinion, to the success of Kerry football, has to be the esteem in which players who wear the Kerry jersey are held. To be selected for the county is a singular distinction. A glamour and mystique traditionally surrounds the wearers of the green and gold. Great players are revered, their feats and skills celebrated in song and story, earning them an enduring place in sporting folklore. For younger aspirants, they assume, in time, mythic stature, making for endless recollections and reinventions of their heroics. The Kerry production line has never failed to deliver its quota of such inspirational heroes in every generation.

Success, undoubtedly, begets success. It certainly breeds confidence and self-belief, which are indispensable ingredients in winning. Croke Park, with its daunting atmosphere on All-Ireland final day, has rarely failed to bring out the best in Kerry teams adept, on those nail-biting occasions, at snatching victory from the jaws of defeat. In a sense, it has become our sporting habitat where each successful team puts down a fresh marker for its successors to emulate.

In his celebrated book, *Gaelic Football*, published in 1941, Pádraig Mehigan, who wrote under the pseudonym 'Carbery', attributes the success of Kerry in Gaelic football to certain qualities of 'brain and brawn'. I'm sure most sports analysts would readily disagree with him that Kerry footballers are more intelligent or more macho than their counterparts in other counties. Perhaps, what Carbery had in mind was footballing IQ. However, I'm sure many hurling fans feel the same about the current Kilkenny team.

The ability of Kerry teams to bounce back down the years from lean periods and achieve stunning strings of victories, certainly gives pause for thought. Few counties, however promising, recover from defeat, and fewer still manage to remain for long at the top. Great teams, for some reason, seem to come and go all too quickly, while dogged Kerry teams, somehow, continue to defy the odds.

The inspirational effect of Kerry's unique landscape as a contributory factor in the county's footballing success merits some consideration. I am convinced that players' pride in their county springs from their love of its spectacular mountains, valleys and coastline. That connection to landscape and attachment to county always influenced me as a footballer.

When all the reasons for the success of Kerry football have been debated, perhaps tradition is the real key. In his ballad, 'Dúchas', the late Garry McMahon, a former Kerry player on the All-Ireland winning teams in 1959 and 1962, captures the essence of what tradition means:

You say tradition counts for naught when two teams take the field,
I fear you are mistaken, lad, but the years will make you yield,
And when your hair's as grey as mine, and time had made you old,
Then you'll invoke the truth I spoke of the Kingdom's green and gold.

You cannot box or bottle it, not grasp it in your hand,
But pride of race and love of place inspire love of the land.
Time honoured is our birthright, we'll never break the mould,
It's deep within the soul of us who wear the green and gold.

Garry McMahon and myself in October 2006 with, from left to right, the McCarthy Cup, the Sam Maguire and the Heineken Cup.

Grey lakes and mountains soaring high, Mount Brandon's holy hill,
The little church at Gallarus, our language living still,
The Skellig Rock, stout football stock, they can't be bought or sold,
For our county's fame, we play the game in the Kingdom's green and gold.

And when the battle's fiercest and fortunes ebb and flow,
We're still alive, we can survive, and still we won't let go,
For the spirit of our fathers and of stories yet untold,
Will lead us on to victory, in the Kingdom's green and gold.

We savour Kerry victories, we salute a gallant foe,
And when we lose, there's no excuse, we pick up our bags and go,
So raise your glass each lad and lass to our warriors brave and bold,
Who again aspire to the Sam Maguire in the Kingdom's green and gold.

Me with Jack Walsh, May 1980. Jack was corner-back on the first Kerry four-in-a-row team, 1929–1932.

As a young lad growing up in Finuge, I couldn't help but be inspired as I listened to my father and his friends reminiscing about former Kerry greats and famous Kerry victories. He introduced me to sporting legends like Con Brosnan, Bob Stack, Johnny Walsh, Jack Walsh and Eddie Dowling before I ever played competitive football. In my teen years I also got to know other notable North Kerry footballers, like Dan McAuliffe, Eddie Walsh, Paud and Eamonn O'Donoghue, Garry McMahon, Gerdie O'Connor, Bernie O'Callaghan, Mick Finucane, and Tony McAuliffe. Even then I wanted to follow in their footsteps and match their achievements. No doubt the present generation of Kerry footballers are similarly influenced by players of the '70s and '80s, while the youngsters of today look up to the likes of Colm Cooper, Paul Galvin, Kieran Donaghy, Declan O'Sullivan, and the Ó Sé brothers – Marc, Tomás and Darragh.

Formative Years

1952–1970

THE FINUGE I WAS BORN INTO in 1952 was a wonderful place in which to grow up. I realise that you can view the past through rose-tinted glasses but, nevertheless, I can honestly claim to have had a very happy childhood. There was a great spirit of neighbourliness and a keen sense of community in Finuge; the people were caring and came to one another's help in times of need.

Me at age two.

I was the only son in a family of girls. I had five sisters – Nora Mary, Annette, Eileen, Madeleine and Patricia. Madeleine was killed in car accident in September 1959 and this tragedy had a traumatic impact on our family at the time. To this day, whenever I pass the scene of the accident, I think of her and pray for her. I often try to imagine the kind of person she would have become, being a very intelligent child and possessed of a most pleasant and endearing personality. Since then, my heart goes out to families who have lost a loved one in a traffic accident.

A crossroads rather than a village, Finuge was a hive of activity when I was growing up. It consisted mostly of small farmsteads with a few larger farming units in the surrounding area. The farms were predominantly mixed enterprises of dairying, tillage, poultry and pigs. Almost every house had an orchard and a fishing rod, as the local River Feale teemed with sea trout and salmon during

Nora Mary, Eileen, Annette, myself and Madeleine.

the fifties and sixties. Both my parents worked hard on our 27 acre farm. My mother, Mary Ellen, took care of the cows and calves and reared turkeys for the Christmas market while my father, Mick, looked after the garden, the hay and turf, some of which he sold. At the time, Finuge was the market garden for Listowel and supplied eggs, poultry, vegetables and fruit to the hospital, convent, restaurants, grocers, hotels and guesthouses of the town. I remember that whenever I went to the market in Listowel with my father, there was always a strong presence of Finuge people there selling their produce.

Like all other young people growing up in the village, I pulled my weight at home, especially during the summer holidays. In the morning I took the milk to the creamery for us and our neighbours. One neighbour, Kit Lane, gave me half a crown a week (a lot of pocket money back in the 1960s) to take their milk. Kit – who was like a second mother to me – died, sadly, at a very young age in October 1966.

During the day I usually worked in the bog or on the farm and whenever free I played football in Ned Seward's haggard with my friends Christy O'Sullivan, Red Timmy Sullivan and Liam Hayes. We also played every evening with other local lads in Paud Sullivan's and Jim Galvin's fields. When the sea trout were running, I fished the Feale River at twilight with my father and his close friends, Moss Lyons and Steve Whelan. Life continued like that for several years until the summer of 1970 when I went to work in Ballybunion for Jackie Hourigan who owned Harty Costello's bar. This was my first time away from home.

With Jackie Hourigan in his bar in Ballybunion, 1970.

I WAS fortunate that my boyhood predated the advent of television and that I was thereby given an opportunity to develop an appreciation of the fascinating oral tradition and folklore of Finuge and North Kerry. In those days there were a number of rambling houses in the village where neighbours congregated during the winter evenings to pass the long nights with storytelling and other activities. It was in these homes that stories were passed on and local folklore and legends were preserved. Due to the large number of elderly people in the village at the time, my mother often referred to Finuge as *Tír na nÓg*.

Many of these elders visited our house or those of our neighbours, Willie Joy and my father's first cousin, Paddy Regan. This was not an insular, parochial world: in Willie Joy's house the discussion could range from the state of Ireland's economy – especially the price of agricultural produce – to the Cold War and the Space Race between the US and USSR. There could be hours of debate concerning which country would put a man on the moon first. We also played chess and draughts there and I was one of six chess players in Finuge who could hold our own with any outside competition at that time. In Paddy Regan's, apart from the usual storytelling, we played darts, rings and cards, with 31 being the most popular card game. For me, study took second place to visits to those rambling houses over the winter months. I don't regret this unduly as these houses, from my experience, provided a liberal education in themselves.

Willie Joy's wife, Bridie, and her brother, Mikey Cussen, who also lived with them, were my godparents. They took this responsibility very seriously and always had a genuine interest in what I was doing, either at school or in sport. It was an interesting house to visit and while I didn't fully realise it at the time, it was here that I got my early political education. It was a divided house politically: Willie was an avid Fine Gael and Michael Collins supporter, while Mikey was an ardent Republican and de Valera follower. Every day, Willie bought the *Irish Independent* and Mikey the *Irish Press*, with the result that I got to read both papers daily, especially the sports pages.

Mikey, who was also an avid reader, had a great collection of books in his loft to which I and a privileged few had access. One of these books was *Kerry's Football Story* by Paddy Foley (P.F.), the renowned GAA reporter with *The*

Mikey Cussen, Dora Joy, Willie Joy and Bridie Joy.

Kerryman newspaper. I read this book, which was published in 1945, from cover to cover and it gave me an insight into the history of Kerry's All-Ireland championship victories from 1903 to 1941 and the players who were part of them. Mikey gave me a permanent loan of this book which I still have. It's a book that should be reprinted as it gives a very accurate and authentic account of Kerry football from its formative years to 1941.

Tracy and Lester Piggott with Willie Joy, September 1999.

Willie was a fanatic on horse racing. He had a daily bet on the horses well into his nineties. He was an expert on betting combinations and would often have a windfall out of a small wager. He was thrilled when I brought Lester and Tracy Piggott to visit him in September 1999. Although he gave them both a great welcome he reminded Lester when he was leaving that Scobie Beasley was also a great jockey.

Willie was the perfect neighbour who could turn his hand to almost anything. He was, in turn, a mechanic, watchmaker, tailor, electrician, a farrier with his own forge, a shoemaker, fisherman, fowler and a farmer. He often mended my football boots in my early years when a pair of boots had to last a few years and, right up to the end of my playing days, he would ensure that my cogs were tightly adjusted for big matches, using the vice-grip in his forge.

Willie died tragically in a house fire on 28 May 2001 at the age of 102. My wife, Mary, was on her way to school when she saw smoke billowing from his front door and immediately sped back to our house to alert me. I managed

Left to right: Jim Kennelly, Timmy O'Sullivan, myself, Dan Lyons, and Liam Buckley at Finuge Cross in 1967.

to extinguish the blaze before it completely engulfed the house but it was too late to save Willie. That same day the President of Ireland, Mary McAleese, was visiting Lixnaw to open the Ceolann, a local traditional music centre, and I had arranged that she would stop at Finuge Cross to meet Willie. He had been really looking forward to meeting the President; sadly, it wasn't to be.

During the summer the locals usually congregated at Finuge Cross, especially on Sunday evenings. At that time of year, discussions about farming, gardening and fishing would inevitably digress to football and the fortunes of the Kerry or Finuge football teams. Many of the older men could recall Kerry's first All-Ireland victory in 1903 and could name the members of every Kerry team that won an All-Ireland final up to the 1960s. They would recall great games that Kerry pulled out of the fire in the dying moments and the stars of these victories. Listening to these recycled heroics, I became inducted into a sporting culture that, in time, would fire me with a burning ambition to play for Kerry.

With that overriding ambition in mind, I consequently spent most of my time at both primary and post-primary school developing my fitness levels

Taken on the day I kicked the ball over the bar for the first time.
Front left to right: Myself, Danny Lane, Paul Kennelly, Johnny Lyons, Gerald McCarthy (RIP).
Back left to right: Leo Kennelly (RIP), Christy O'Sullivan, Maney Enright.

and Gaelic football skills. I just did enough study to get me through the various exams. Maybe it sounds a little crazy now, but that's how it was. No one, least of all my father, tried to steer me in a different direction. Since my childhood, he, too, had one ambition for me – to play for Kerry – and he did everything possible, until his death in 1974, to help me achieve that end.

The toy I most treasured was a brown rubber ball which my mother bought for me in 1957 during a visit to Puck Fair in Killorglin where she went annually with her parents. Her father, Mike Horgan, who was a great lover of horses, enjoyed the horse fair aspect of the festival while she preferred to browse around the stalls with her mother and enjoy the funfair. At that time, a ball of that kind was a treasure, and playing with it with the local lads made for hours of happiness. I still recall the sense of achievement I derived from kicking a football for the first time over the bar in Paud Sullivan's field in 1959. For me it was a defining moment in my development as a footballer and I remember running home excitedly to tell my father about it.

I ATTENDED Dromclough national school which was about a mile away from our house from 1957 to 1965. I walked to school and I usually ran home in the evening which, no doubt, helped to build up my stamina for the future. As there was limited space around the school building, it was impossible to play football in the schoolyard. We played a form of Olympic handball – with a paper ball usually – but instead of throwing the ball, we palmed it or hand passed it. I got a special dispensation, along with other pupils, to play with nearby Killocrim national school in the Listowel Primary School League. The late Bernie Long, who was principal of the school, was instrumental in making this arrangement. At the time, the huge interest in this competition in Listowel and the surrounding areas attracted large attendances to the games. One of the organisers of the league was the late Bryan McMahon, writer and teacher. During the two years that I played in the competition I developed a friendship with him that continued for the rest of his life.

John B., Joe Murphy, Bryan McMahon and myself in Listowel in 1992.

(Photo: Ruth Rogers)

Left to right: Myself, Billy Keane and Jeremiah O'Carroll in Dublin before the 1984 semi-final between Kerry and Galway.

I also met Billy Keane for the first time during the competition. Billy is now a well-known writer and sports journalist. John B., his father, asked me to show my medal to Billy and his brothers, Conor and John, when we won the final in 1965. I had long known John B. who was a close friend of my father's with whom he shared a similar outlook on football and politics, and I remember them often meeting up for a drink in McCarthy's bar in Finuge. This, however, was the first time I met Billy and we have remained close friends ever since.

The school league was a great breeding ground for future footballers. There was intense rivalry between the various parts of the town – the Boro, the Gleann, the Ashes, and the Country, a team comprising country lads attending Listowel boys' national school. Some of the spectators were fanatical and pitch invasions were not uncommon. During my two years in the school league I played at centre-forward or centre-field.

In the first year of the competition we lost the opening match by 20 points to the Gleann. After the game, I called the boys together and advised them that, if we trained and got organised, the Gleann would not beat us by the same margin should we meet up again in the later stages of the competition. When we did meet them in the final, they beat us by only a single point with

Kilocrim, winners of the Listowel Primary School League in 1965.
Front row left to right: Brendan Kelly, James Hennessy, Jimmy Buckley, Joe Kelly, Willie Thornton, John Beasley,
Joe Buckley, Tosh Beasley, Noel Sullivan, PJ Hennessy.
Back row left to right: John Murphy, John Barrett, myself, Timmy O'Sullivan, Jim Cronin, Pat Hayes,
William Hennessy, Johnny O'Connor.

a late goal. It proved to me, even at such a young age, that with preparation and the right attitude, it was possible to improve a team's performance. The following year, 1965, we won the final.

WHEN I left Dromclough national school in 1965, I went to St. Michael's College in Listowel. My father and uncles had gone there so it was natural that I would follow in their footsteps. I spent six memorable years at St. Michael's where, under the guidance of teachers like John Molyneaux and Johnny O'Flaherty, students with an interest in sport were exposed to the most modern training methods practised at that time. Among these were

Jerry Kiernan (who became one of Ireland's greatest marathon runners and came 9th in the 1984 Olympics in Los Angeles), the late Tim Kennelly and, some years later, future Kerry stars Páidí Ó Sé, Gerard Leahy, Johnny Mulvihill, Robert Bunyan, Liam O'Flaherty, Eamon Breen, Stephen Stack, Brendan Guiney, and Noel and Tadhg Kennelly. Another pupil, John O'Connell, won the All-Ireland Colleges Long Jump Championship in 1970.

A typical training session in my time would include 6 x 100 metres, 4 x 200 metres and 2 x 400 metres, all timed. The training mostly took place in the town park and we often used the hill in the park for resistance training. The two teachers were advised by Jack Sweeney who was a maths teacher in Catholic University School in Dublin and who trained Ronnie Delaney before he went to Villanova University in the USA. However, training did not end on the field. We were introduced to weight training, including bench pressing, curling and squatting, before it was fashionable for athletes in Kerry to do this kind of conditioning. Our football practice always involved

The Kerry youth cross country team that competed in the National Championship at Mallow Race Course in February 1968. This was the first ever BLE national cross country race. Left to right: Brian Carmody, Paul Carmody, Mike Sugrue, myself, Hugh Murphy, Mike O'Connor, Tony Falvey, Pat O'Riordan, Cornelius O'Donnell.

ball drills, with particular emphasis on 'give and go' and moving the ball at speed. Most drills ended on shooting for a score. Apart from participating in college football at both county and Munster levels, we competed at county, provincial and national levels in both cross country and athletics for both college and club.

We were also introduced to Paarlauf and Fartlek training methods; I recall vividly those long distance runs along that scenic stretch of the River Feale, better known as the Spa, on Sunday mornings with springtime emerging in all its glory.

During my time at St. Michael's, we won the County Cup for the first time in 1970, giving football in the school a great boost. That year, the college also won the Kerry Colleges U16 Championship (Dunloe Cup). In November

After winning the County Cup with St. Michael's College, Listowel, in 1970.
Front row left to right: Kieran Fitzgerald, Maurice O'Sullivan, Mick O'Connell, Tom Lyons (RIP), David Kissane.
Second row left to right: John Hines, Tadhg Moriarty, PJ Browne, Tim Shanahan, myself, Pat Stack.
Back row left to right: Eamonn Carroll, Maurice O'Connor, Pat Stack, Tommy O'Flaherty, John O'Connell, Jerry Kiernan, Paddy Quilter.

1970 we lost the Kerry Colleges Senior Championship final (O'Sullivan Cup) to St Brendan's College in Killarney by just one point, which was a major disappointment as it would have been the first for St. Michael's. Playing on the St Brendan's team that day were John Long, one of the finest high fielders in my experience, and Páidí Ó Sé, who later transferred to St. Michael's and was instrumental in winning the first O'Sullivan Cup for the school in 1974. He went on to win eight All-Ireland medals with Kerry and to successfully manage Kerry to two All-Ireland Senior Championships, in 1997 and 2000.

We were also introduced to rugby in St. Michael's which we played in the town park during our games' period on Wednesdays from time to time, despite the fact that the divisive Ban on foreign games was still in place. O'Flaherty believed that the body contact in rugby would help us to be more physical and to cope with heavy tackles in Gaelic football. The Ban, although it may have served a purpose when introduced in the late 19th Century, had no place in the Ireland of the 1960s. Regrettably, many young GAA players were deprived of the opportunity to play competitive rugby as a result.

Thanks to the tireless campaigning by Tom Woulfe of the Civil Service GAA club in Dublin, and originally from Beale, Co. Kerry, the Ban was eventually removed from the constitution of the GAA at the 1971 annual Congress. The ending of the Ban did not lead, as feared, to the flight of players from the GAA to rugby and soccer. Instead, it brought the GAA into a modern, pluralist Ireland. It also provided an opportunity for Kerry county players like Moss Keane, Mick Galwey and the Doyle brothers – Mick and Tom – to play rugby for Ireland and for the British and Irish Lions.

I would like to acknowledge my personal indebtedness to Johnny O'Flaherty and John Molyneaux, two exceptional men. John Molyneaux was a great Latin teacher and often used Latin idioms in his pep talks before and after matches. I still recall some of those that he used regularly: *Carthago delenda est* (Carthage must be destroyed) from the wars between Rome and Carthage; *Nil mortalibus ardui est* (There is nothing that cannot be conquered); *Pelago decurrunt aperto* (They coast to victory) from the end of the boat race in Virgil's *Aeneid*; *Nunc est bibendum* (Now is the time to celebrate); *Veni, vidi, vici* (I came, I saw, I conquered). His favourite quote was *Primus inter pares* (First among equals). He was a great tactician and a shrewd reader of the game.

Left to right: Tim Kennelly, Johnny O'Flaherty, John Molyneaux, Páidí Ó Sé and myself.

Johnny O'Flaherty was a tremendous coach and trainer and I was delighted for him when Feale Rangers, which he trained, won the County Senior Championship for the first time in 1978. A number of that victorious team passed through his hands at St. Michael's College. Many successful footballers who went to the college, I am sure, would share my admiration and respect for both men. They devoted so much of their time to us in after-school training and transporting us to matches and athletic events all over Munster.

Club Football with Finuge

1963–1990

WRITING IN THE BROCHURE to mark the opening of the Frank Sheehy Park in Listowel in May 1960, the renowned novelist and short story writer, Maurice Walsh, makes the following reference to the existence of Gaelic football in Finuge in the early days of the GAA:

> I mind as a mere lad playing in a famous game at Kiltean; our side of the river – the Galey – a combination of Ballydonoghue and Ballyconery – played the other side, including Finuge. The sidelines were the hedges; the goalposts piles of jackets and, of course, the goals grew narrower as the game proceeded. Everyone played that could play – or couldn't – and thirty-five aside took the field. There was no referee and the rules were rough and tumble – nothing barred and nothing foul. The game lasted two hours. It would have lasted longer only the bladder burst and the winning goal by Finuge was scored with an empty leather and thirty men went through with it. The remarkable thing – the fine thing – is that during these two hours, not a hand was lifted in anger.

As Maurice Walsh was born in May 1879, that game most likely took place in the early years of the GAA and, from his description, was more like *caid*, the forerunner of Gaelic football. In the early days of the Association, the local team was called Irremore, named after the townland adjacent to Finuge. This may have been because the local church was in the townland of Irremore or because Irremore was recognised as a parish at that time. According to Pat O'Shea's book, *Records of the Kerry County Senior Championship, 1889-1998, Face the Ball,* Irremore had a team in the football championship from 1889–1905, reaching the final on two occasions, 1894 and 1897.

In 1894, Irremore conceded the final to Ballymacelligott who won the championship without playing a game. The only game that was played in that year's championship was between Irremore and Lixnaw in the quarter-final, Irremore winning by 0-8 to 0-1. The fact that only six teams took part in the County Championship in 1894 was probably due to the Parnellite split, which was very bitter in Kerry at that time. In 1898, Irremore defeated Tralee Mitchels in May by 0-8 to 0-7 in the final. However, Mitchels raised an objection and the County Board ordered the match to be replayed. Irremore refused to participate and conceded the match. My grandfather, Jim Deenihan, played in goals for Irremore for a period of time.

For whatever reason, the Irremore club ceased to exist after 1905 and hurling seems to have taken over in Finuge. Although it never fielded a team in the County Hurling Championship it did participate in the North Kerry Hurling League up to 1937, according to minutes of the meetings of the North Kerry Hurling Board. Writer Bryan McMahon, in a contribution in the programme to mark the opening of the Finuge sportsfield in May 1980, was glowing in his praise of the Finuge hurlers of the 1920s:

> I have the liveliest and loveliest memories of Finuge and its hurlers of old! Every Sunday in summer when I was a boy, we ate a hurried dinner, crossed the racecourse, moving out of Iraughticonnor into Clanmaurice, and made our way along the river bank to Finuge to see a hurling match. And what mighty hurlers there were in the village at that time. First and foremost there was full-forward Donal Treacy, that stalwart man who could be counted on to neutralise the greatest full-back, a man who has passed into legend both as a hurler and a personality. I recall a famous incident in Listowel Sportsfield where, having broken all the hurleys available, he tore a lath from the front of the stand and finished the game to resounding applause.

The first football club was formed in the village in 1937. Joseph Joy (former chief of the Special Branch) in another contribution in the same souvenir programme, wrote:

> For some years prior to 1937 there was no adult football team in Finuge. In that year the teenagers from Finuge who had kept the flag flying for the game decided to do something about forming an adult football team in Finuge.

A meeting was called at Finuge Cross which was the regular meeting place at that time, and Mick Deenihan, Jim and Ned Seward found ready acceptance to the proposal to enter an adult football team in the North Kerry League.

This was the beginning of the Finuge football club and allowing for a seven-year break from 1954–1961, arising from the introduction of the Parish Rule, it has survived and enjoyed considerable success for a small club. The club won its first competition, the North Kerry Junior Championship, in 1943. My father, Mick, played at full-back on that team. In 1945, the club lost the North Kerry Senior Championship final after a replay against a star-studded Ballydonoghue team which included notable players like Gus Cremins, who captained Kerry to win the 1946 All-Ireland final, Eddie Dowling and Mick Finucane. Many of the Ballydonoghue team were members of the Shannon Rangers team that brought the County Senior Championship to North Kerry for the first time in 1942, repeating this achievement in 1945. The club won the North Kerry Junior Championship in 1948 and 1949.

With the introduction of the Parish Rule in 1953, Finuge was unable to field a team for a number of years as it straddled the parishes of Listowel and Lixnaw. The Listowel side of the village played with Clounmacon or Listowel, and the Lixnaw side with neighbouring club, St. Senan's, from 1953 to 1960. In 1961 the club was revived following the introduction of a by-law by the Kerry County Board which deemed the Listowel side of Finuge village to be in Lixnaw parish for GAA purposes. This was another demonstration of the pragmatism of the Kerry County Board. The North Kerry Board, under the chairmanship of Leo Stack, also played a pivotal role in this decision.

I was present at the first meeting of the club fifty years ago in Jack Kennelly's workshop at Finuge Cross. My father was elected chairman and Paul Kennelly secretary.

The club entered the North Kerry Intermediate Championship, with the first game away to Tarbert. I remember travelling to the game with my father, the players and a few supporters in Dave Allman's green school bus. The match was played on the site of Tarbert Comprehensive School, where I was later to work as a teacher from 1975 to 1983. Finuge won and went on to beat Listowel in the final but the win was disallowed following an objection by Listowel against Finuge for playing an illegal player. Listowel were subsequently declared winners.

In 1962, Finuge stormed back and won the North Kerry Intermediate Championship: they went senior in 1963 and 1964 without success. In 1965 the club reverted to intermediate football and won the championship and, as a result, was promoted to senior grade again in 1966. It made history, winning the 1967 North Kerry Senior Championship by defeating Ballylongford in the final which was played on Easter Sunday 1968.

The team was trained by Listowel man, the late Andy Molyneaux, who later became secretary of the Kerry County Board. The club had arrived and, arising from that victory, grew in confidence to become both feared and respected in North Kerry football. I was just arriving on the scene and probably could have made the panel for the final, but I felt I was too young for North Kerry senior football, although I did make the team a few months later.

The 1967 team was remarkable for the number of brothers who featured on it – Jerry, John and Patsy Galvin; Tom, Timmy and Christy Sullivan; James and Danny Lane; Tom and Richard Carey; Johnny and Noel Lyons. The other members of the panel were Haulie Costelloe, Liam Hayes, Tod Nolan, Frank Murphy, Brendan Twomey, Gerard McCarthy, Eddie Enright, Jim Corridan, and Martin Whelan. Tom Sullivan was an inspirational leader both on and off the field. Finuge, over the years and to the present day, has had a huge reliance on the input of brothers for the success and survival of the club. Brothers, from my experience, bring a spirit of camaraderie to a team. There are seven sets of brothers on the present Finuge senior team, maintaining the tradition.

Since our first victory in 1967, the club has won three North Kerry Senior Championship titles (1987, 1996 and 2001), two North Kerry Leagues (1970 and 2011), two County Junior Championships and two Munster Junior Championships (2002 and 2004) and the inaugural All-Ireland Junior Championship (2004), as well as several underage competitions at both county and divisional levels.

I PLAYED my first competitive game with Finuge in the 1963 North Kerry Juvenile Championship against Listowel Emmets in Listowel sportsfield. I was selected at corner-forward and scored a goal with my first touch of the ball. My football career with Finuge had kicked off and continued for 27 years until I retired after losing to Beale in the quarter-final of the North Kerry Championship in November 1990. My other enduring memory of that game is of my father's reaction when I scored that goal. I can still recall the pride and delight in his expression afterwards. It meant so much to him that he had a son who could hold his own on the football field.

Nowadays, whenever I see a father getting excited when his son is playing, I understand. Kerry parents, in general, harbour an ambition for their sons to play, not only for the local club, but also for the county. Their support and encouragement, especially during the formative years when young lads are susceptible to parental influence, is vital.

Our next game in the championship was against Ballybunion and we won it rather easily. I remember that match for one reason: I was involved in a clash of heads with an opponent and was lying prostrate on the ground being attended to by our team manager – local chemist, David McMahon – when my father ran in from the sideline and ordered me, in the strongest language, to get back on my feet immediately. After the match, he explained to me the importance of staying on your feet at all costs. I always remembered his advice and rarely went down injured in a match subsequently, irrespective of how I felt. I have passed on this advice to several players over the years, having seen so many going to the ground and taking themselves out of the game for very little reason. It puzzles me at times to watch them rolling and groaning on the pitch and then to see them on their feet seconds later with no apparent injury. They fail to realise that while they are on the ground, their opponents can get vital scores that can decide the outcome of a game.

Finuge went on to win the North Kerry Juvenile Championship that year, beating Tarbert in the final. At 11 years of age, this was a great start to my football career. On that Tarbert team was Patsy 'Skin' O'Connell, who later played on the same Feale Rangers side with me. Tarbert were managed by Brendan Scannell, later to become secretary of the INTO and a very good friend of mine when I was teaching in Tarbert. His son, Brendan, now Irish

The St. Senan's team, 1965.
Front row left to right: Jackie O'Sullivan, Denis Kelleher, Kevin Somers, Patrick Connolly, Sean Fuller, Willie Fuller, myself.
Middle row left to right: Timmy Leen, Frank Buckley, Liam Relihan, Micky Fuller, Paul Twomey, Tom O'Brien,
John Sullivan (RIP), John Galvin (RIP), John Callaghan, Mundy Hayes.
Back row left to right: John Fitzmaurice, Dan McCarthy, Jeremiah O'Carroll, Pat Hayes, Vincent Twomey,
Declan Lynch, Lar Shanahan (RIP), Vincent Cashill, Tom Stack.

ambassador to Denmark, played on that team too. Finuge also won the North Kerry Minor Championship that year and both the successful juvenile and minor teams provided the backbone of Finuge teams for many years to come.

Finuge had no juvenile team in 1965 so I played with neighbouring club, St. Senan's, who lost the North Kerry Juvenile Championship final to Ballylongford.

In 1968, I played with Listowel Emmets U16 team, which went on to win the North Kerry Championship. Jerry Kiernan, later to become one of Ireland's greatest marathon runners, and Tim Kennelly played with me on the team. I played minor with St. Senan's in 1969 and 1970, losing the North Kerry Championship finals to Ballylongford and Listowel respectively. Because I played with both my neighbouring football clubs, I never felt any sense of rivalry when playing against them afterwards during my career at senior level.

Football by now had become the love of my life. It made for close bonding with team-mates and great rivalries with other clubs as we competed in various competitions and tournaments. At this stage I was becoming more conscious of my prowess as a footballer; I was physically stronger and faster than most of my peers and I was growing in confidence as my skills developed. Football too, was throwing open new vistas for me as I travelled with the team to play matches in places that would otherwise have been out of reach for me then. I was now deriving immense satisfaction and pleasure from the game.

I played my first senior match with Finuge in July 1968 against Ballylongford in the Frank Sheehy Memorial Tournament, a highly regarded competition in those days. I remember that game for one particular reason – a fair but crunching shoulder tackle I received from Darby O'Sullivan of Ballylongford. It was the hardest physical contact I had with any opponent during my entire football career and it took months for my shoulder to recover. Darby was a wiry, teak-tough defender. Sadly, he passed away at an early age in 2007.

Front row left to right: Johnny Lyons, Tom Carey, Christy O'Sullivan, Todd Nolan (RIP), Timmy O'Sullivan, James O'Sullivan (RIP), Patsy Galvin, Liam Hayes, Danny Lane.
Back row left to right: Gerard McCarthy, Gerry Galvin, Eddie Enright, Pat Cronin, James Lane (RIP), Haulie Costelloe, Tom O'Sullivan (RIP), myself, John Galvin.
The two men to the left are Johnny Sheehan (RIP) and Martin Whelan (RIP).

James O'Sullivan after the Athea game; I am visible on the upper left.

We went on to defeat Athea in the final of the tournament on the Sunday after they won the Limerick County Senior Championship. That game will be remembered for the three goals scored by the late James O'Sullivan, who worked locally with the Galvin family and was killed in a traffic accident outside Tralee in 1974. The club honoured him by naming the local pitch in his memory in 1980.

We lost the 1968 County Inter-mediate Championship final by just one point to Kenmare in Fitzgerald Stadium in Killarney in April 1969. We got a late penalty but Christy O'Sullivan was tripped as he was about to take the free. As a result, he didn't strike the ball properly and the opportunity was missed. The referee ignored all appeals to have it re-taken and we lost the match. I was in goals for Finuge while Mickey Ned O'Sullivan, later to become my team-mate on many a Kerry team, was a key forward on the Kenmare team.

My first major victory with the Finuge seniors was in the North Kerry League final against Ballylongford in 1970. I was again playing in goals. The first match ended in a draw and we won the replay after an exciting game. Ballylongford was powered by the late Paudie and Eamonn O'Donoghue and Jackie Walsh, all of whom won All-Ireland Senior Championship medals with Kerry. My abiding memory from the match was saving a penalty from Eamonn O'Donoghue at his second attempt. He drove the first penalty wide but the referee ordered it to be re-taken because one of our players, the late Todd Nolan, threw a glove at Eamonn as he was running up to the ball. One of our players shouted to Todd, 'You'll eat that glove before the night is out if we lose the match'. Luckily for Todd, I saved Eamonn's second attempt and we went on to win our first North Kerry Senior League in the history of the club.

Finuge defeated Ballybunion in the semi-final of the competition. I was unable to play in that game as I couldn't get time off from my job in Harty

Costello's bar in Ballybunion. My replacement in goals, John Joe Somers, suffered a serious knee injury as a result of a heavy tackle on the goal-line. As he said himself afterwards, his knee was 'bent around the goalpost'. He never recovered from the injury and the accident marked the end of a very promising football career. I could have suffered the same fate had I been in goals that evening. John Joe is now a very successful businessman in Boston and a great supporter of everything Irish in that city.

The 1970s were generally a lean period for the club. We lost the North Kerry Championship final to Listowel in 1972 and the league final to Ballylongford in 1974 and, for a while, it was a struggle to field a senior team. The 1980s proved to be a more fruitful period. We won the Mart Cup, a competition for teams that were knocked out in the first round of the North Kerry Championship, in October 1981.

I had to wait until 1987 to win another major trophy with Finuge – the North Kerry Senior Championship. I was 35 years old at that stage and felt that I had to win a North Kerry Senior Championship medal, which is the

Mart Cup winners, 1981.
Front row left to right: Pat Lyons, Maurice Lyons, Jimmy Horgan, Tom Lyons (RIP), myself, Liam Hayes, Joe Kelly, Denny Sullivan, Ger McEnery.
Back row left to right: Christy Killeen, Seán O'Rourke, Moss McElligott, Tom Kelly (RIP), Johnny O'Connell, Timmy O'Sullivan, Pat Daughton, Frankie Bowler, Paddy O'Sullivan, Denis McElligott, Patrick Stackpoole.

(Photo: Tom Fitzgerald)

Finuge/St. Senan's minor team, 1983/84.
Front row left to right: Paudie McAuliffe, Aidan Falvey, Martin Conway (RIP), Denis O'Mahony, Gerry Keane, Gerry Behan (Capt.), Sean O'Rourke, Kenneth Hayes, Johnny Buckley, Tom Finnerty.
Back row left to right: Robert Barry, Dan McNamara, Paul O'Donoghue, Alan Hayes, Pat McCarthy, Aidan Behan, Jimmy Horgan, Pat Stackpoole, Donal Hunt, Johnny McElligot, Paudie Horgan, Richard McKenna (RIP), Moss McElligott, myself.

flagship of North Kerry football, before I retired. For years, the local publican, Gerard McCarthy, affectionately known as 'Sikes', reminded me on most visits to his bar – especially if there were any visitors present from outside Kerry who recognised me – that he had a 'little medal' that I would never win!

A number of the team who played in the final against Moyvane in 1987 were members of an U12 Finuge team that I started when I returned to Kerry to teach in Tarbert Comprehensive School in 1975. I established that team with Dora Joy, who was teaching in Lixnaw boys' primary school at the time. She did the secretarial work and I trained and coached the team. From 1976 to 1987, the team won a number of competitions at both county and North Kerry underage levels. Following an initiative by myself and Robert Barry of neighbouring club St. Senan's in 1983, both clubs came together to play as Finuge/St. Senan's. The arrangement lasted for two years, during which time they won the Division 1 North Kerry League, the North Kerry Minor Championship and the County Minor Leagues Divisions I and 2.

A number of the Finuge/St. Senan's team played on the Feale Rangers divisional minor team of which I was coach and which won the County Minor Championship in 1983. Finuge, on their own, won the North Kerry Under 21 Championship in 1986, beating Listowel in the final. I stayed with them all the way, despite my inter-county career and later, my political commitments, as they were an exceptional bunch of lads. Unfortunately for the club, many of them left Ireland for various parts of the world in the late eighties because of the lack of job opportunities at home.

Winning the North Kerry Senior Championship was one of the high points of my football career. I was joint trainer, coach and manager of the team with fellow team-mate, Joe Kelly. We had thrilling victories over St. Senan's in the first round, Tarbert in the quarter-final, Castleisland Desmonds in the semi-final, and Moyvane in the final.

The semi-final win over Desmonds in a replay must go down in our club's history as one of the greatest victories Finuge ever had. Desmonds were All-Ireland club champions in 1985 and runners-up in 1986. They were powered by All-Ireland senior medal-holders Charlie Nelligan, Dermot Hannifin and Willie Dom O'Connor, Cork star Christy Kearney, and one of the legends of Kerry club football, midfielder Mikey O'Connor, Donie Buckley (current skills' trainer of the Kerry senior football team), Donal 'Duke' O'Connor, and many more high profile players. We played them in two of the most competitive matches I've ever played for either club or county, and we prevailed in the replay by 0-8 to 0-5.

Our victory in the final against Moyvane was one of the most important in my career given the status of a North Kerry Championship medal. Moyvane had a top class team at the time consisting of the five Mulvihill brothers – Johnny, Paddy, Mike, Donal, and Tom – as well as Seán Walsh, who was later to become chairman of Kerry County Board and is presently chairman of the Munster Council and a possible future president of the GAA.

After waiting for almost 20 years to win a North Kerry Championship medal, I realised that it would take a special effort to beat Moyvane. The team responded enthusiastically, doing everything that Joe and I asked of them in training and on the pitch on match day. During that 1987 championship campaign I played at centre-forward, my favourite position. As the play-maker

59

(Courtesy of The Kerryman, www.kerryman.ie)

The Finuge team that won the North Kerry Championship in 1987.
Front row left to right: Aidan O'Connell, Paul Wallace, Seán O'Rourke, Eamon Breen, Paddy Sullivan, Johnny McElligott (Capt.), Joe Kelly, myself, Johnny Buckley, Martin Conway (RIP).
Back row left to right: Tommy Stackpoole, Paul Breen, Denny Sullivan, Timmy Sullivan, Johnny Joy, Richard McKenna (RIP), John Fealy, Tom Kelly (RIP), Paudie Horgan, Liam Hayes, Denis McElligott, John Barrett, Con O'Connell.

I orchestrated most of the attacks and when we were under pressure, I played as an extra defender. Our tactics worked a treat.

I continued to play with Finuge until November 1990 when I decided to retire after losing to Beale in the North Kerry Championship quarter-final. I could have played for another few years but I didn't wish to deprive younger players of a place on the team. I also found it very difficult to combine training with my political commitments. As you get older it is essential that you devote more time to training at a lower intensity. I was not in a position to give the time required to be competitive on the pitch. On my way to the quarter-final match I met local photographer, Brendan Landy, at Mass in Listowel. I told him that if Finuge lost that I would hang up my boots. I pulled a hamstring during the second half of the game and retired early to the dressing room.

I subsequently continued to work with the club in various capacities. In the later stages of the 1996 North Kerry Senior Championship campaign I was asked to train the team by manager Gerry Galvin. We drew with Moyvane in the final and afterwards we did intensive match analysis from the video

Hanging up my boots in the Listowel dressing room, November 1990.

of the game where we identified our mistakes and players' weaknesses. I am convinced that this was a major contributory factor to our winning the replay.

I was again involved in training the team in 1997 and 1998. In 1998 we lost to Listowel after a replay in the North Kerry final. We were leading by a point in the dying moments of the match; Listowel, however, succeeded in equalising with the last kick of the game. In the dressing room after the match I asked the players to make a serious commitment to training over the Christmas period and promised in return that I would forego a skiing trip to Austria immediately after Christmas.

I received an enthusiastic response to this request from the lads but not from my wife, Mary, who was not at all pleased when I told her that evening. We haven't gone on a skiing trip since! Before the replay, a reporter asked the late John B. Keane who he thought would win the game. His response was, 'The team that drank least over Christmas'. Regrettably, some of our lads overindulged during the festive season and it showed on the day.

(Courtesy of Don MacMonagle, www.macmonagle.com)

John Coleman (captain) and myself pictured after Finuge won the Munster Junior Club Championship final on 19 December 2004.

Listowel got two early goals, which didn't help us, and they ran out easy winners in the end.

I got involved again with the senior team from 2004 to 2006 as a selector, with former Kerry hurling star, Maurice Leahy, as manager. Tony McCarthy, a former Finuge footballer and Lixnaw hurler, was the other selector. The team won the County Junior Championship, beating Lispole in the final after extra time. We went on to beat Aghabullogue of Cork in the Munster Junior final and Tulsk of Roscommon in the All-Ireland semi-final. We beat Stewartstown of Co Tyrone in the inaugural All-Ireland Junior final in

Finuge, All-Ireland Junior Club champions, 2005.
Front row left to right: Riobard Thornton, Declan McCarthy, Rayond Galvin, Enda Galvin, Aidan Galvin (chairman),
John Coleman (Capt.), Liz Thornton (secretary), Eoin Galvin, Michael Quilter, Mike Cronin, Maurice Corridan.
Middle row left to right: Maurice Leahy (manager), myself (selector), Jack Corridan, Jimmy Galvin, Paudie Lyons,
Michael Conway, Eamonn Fitzmaurice, Ger Lovett, Chris Allen, Fergus Fitzmaurice, Pat Corridan, Trevor McKenna,
Tony McCarthy (selector).
Back row left to right: Paul Galvin, Eamon Breen, Ger Galvin, John Griffin, Eoin McCarthy, David Corridan,
Paudie Galvin, Darren O'Sullivan, Conor Galvin, Cillian Fitzmaurice.

Portlaoise on 28 March 2005 in what was perhaps the greatest achievement ever by the club. The fact that we had four All-Ireland senior medal-holders – Eamon Breen, Eamonn Fitzmaurice, Paul Galvin and Enda Galvin – on our team, no doubt helped. Maurice Corridan, who was a substitute on the All-Ireland winning Kerry team in 2009, was also a member of the team, as was his brother, Pat, who was a county senior panellist in 2008 and 2010. Most of the remaining members of the team represented Kerry at some level, either in football or hurling.

In 2005 we lost the final of the County Intermediate Championship to Legion of Killarney and in 2006 we were very unlucky in the semi-final of the same competition against Ardfert, losing by just two points. Ardfert went on to win the All-Ireland. Finuge again lost the County Intermediate Championship final to Gneeveguilla in 2010. Since 2007, I have taken a back seat in the club.

In Lixnaw sportsfield after training in 2010, left to right: Enda Galvin, Eamonn Fitzmaurice, myself, Paul Galvin, Eamon Breen.

Thanks to so many individuals who, since 1976, have looked after its underage teams, Finuge has continued to produce top class players, many of whom have played for the county at different levels. Since 1975, Kerry has won 14 All-Ireland Senior Championship Football finals. The Finuge club was represented on the field in 11 of these victories. I figured in 1975, '78, '79, '80, and '81. Eamon Breen played at wing-back in 1997, Eamonn Fitzmaurice at centre-back in 2000 and 2004, Paul Galvin at wing-forward in 2004, 2006, 2007 and 2009, and Enda Galvin came on as a substitute in the 2000 semi-final. The club missed out in Kerry's three-in-a-row from 1984 to 1986. Were it not for my change of career to politics, I might have figured in these wins.

I have nothing but the fondest of memories of my 28 years playing with Finuge. I played with some great footballers and characters. I never missed a match because of inter-county commitments as the club was always very precious to me. I appreciated the respect that my team-mates gave me, both in the dressing room and on the playing pitch, even if, at times, I made excessive demands on them.

Aidan Galvin, who was chairman of the club for most of my playing career, deserves special mention. He was totally committed and frequently devoted more time to the club than to his farm.

The club is presently functioning extremely well under chairman Denis McElligott. It has one of the best playing pitches in the county and over the years I was delighted to have been in a position to successfully apply for National Lottery funding for the club to provide lights, a new playing surface and an upgrade of the dressing rooms. The club will always mean a lot to me and no doubt I will continue to be involved with it in some capacity for the rest of my life, especially with the younger age groups.

In 1980, I wrote the following words as a 'Focal Scoir' – 'A Final Word' in the match programme to mark the opening of Finuge sportsfield, and my views have not changed in the intervening time:

The phrase 'small is beautiful' is now in vogue and it could well be said to apply to our efforts which have reached their culmination in the opening of the new field today. We do not claim to be big, representing, in essence, only a few hundred people; but in the sense of being typical of a thousand similar small places in Ireland, we are not without importance. And we believe that if other Irish villages, almost as nameless in the national sense, made a similar effort, the fabric of Irish life would be considerably enhanced. For, above all, we are concerned with deed, not thought; with action, not with idle dreams, and we do claim to have achieved something tangible upon which future generations shall build. Beag uile is atáimíd tá traidisiún againn mar is léir do gach léitheoir a léann na haltanna atá sa chlár seo. Sé ar naidhm na traidisiúin chéanna a choinneál beo ins na glúinte atá romhainn.

I am glad that tradition has survived and continues to thrive over the past 30 years since I wrote these words.

College Years

1971–1975

HAVING COMPLETED the Leaving Certificate in 1971, I went to St. Mary's College in Strawberry Hill, London, to study physical education and history. I was influenced to go there by Mickey Ned O'Sullivan, who was a team-mate on the 1970 minor team and who had started there the year before me. I was very taken by the stories he told me about the training facilities and coaching expertise available at the college. At that time, before the National College of Physical Education opened in Limerick, the Department of Education awarded a number of scholarships for males to attend St. Mary's College in 1969, 1970 and 1971. A number of prominent sports people in Ireland availed of this opportunity, among them Kevin Kehilly and Billy Morgan (both Cork), the late Dermot Earley and Tom Donnellan (both Roscommon), and rugby international Johnny Moroney.

I re-sat the Leaving Certificate in 1971 to get the necessary honours to apply for one of these scholarships. I also had to pass a skills test and an interview. Thankfully I did, and was offered one of the twelve places on the programme in September 1971.

The year and a half I spent at the college was a memorable experience. At St. Mary's we were exposed to world class coaches like Vaughan Thomas and Bill McLoughlin, both members of the British Olympic coaching team. Thomas coached the Olympic team in basketball and McLoughlin coached the gymnastics team. Rugby was the most popular sport in the college and there was a good coaching set-up. Most of the Irish students took up rugby; a few had already played in school competitions in Ireland. I started in the thirds and graduated to the firsts after a while.

I was lucky to play with some outstanding players and developed a great love and understanding of rugby while I was there. I still have contact with some of the people I played with, including second row John O'Connor who later played with the London Irish firsts. I spent most of my time in Strawberry Hill either in the weights room or on the playing pitches where I was able to build on the fitness I had developed at St. Michael's College.

We were introduced by expert professional coaches to a wide range of sports, including rugby, soccer, basketball, volleyball, gymnastics, racket sports, athletics, swimming, and water sports. Our swimming coach was Mick Jagger's father, Joe. He was an excellent teacher and taught me how to swim a very good breast stroke. It was the ideal environment to develop my skills and physical fitness and was a period of intense activity with the odd social event in the college bar, especially after playing some physically taxing rugby matches.

During my time at Strawberry Hill, I played with the Kingdom football club in London and had the honour of marking the great Offaly footballer, Tommy Greene, who was a veteran at that stage, in a London Intermediate Championship final. On the following Sunday, I played on the winning Kingdom senior team when they won the London Senior League. The club went on to win six London Senior Championships in a row afterwards and two All-Ireland seven-a-side finals in Belfield.

In London with the Kingdom Football Club in November 1971.
Front row left to right: Donal Enright, John O'Mahony (RIP), Michael Moran, John Doody, Gerry O'Mahony, Johnny 'Porridge' O'Connor, Pat Cronin, Dan Aherne, Fongo Diggins, Donal Ó Sé.
Back row left to right: Paudie Casey, myself, Mick Aherne, John Keating, Bernard Dennehy, Gerry Donoghue, Seamus O'Driscoll, Tony Flavin, Mick Murphy, Jimmy Thompson, John Fenton, Mickey Joe O'Sullivan.

On match weekends Mickey Ned O'Sullivan and I used to go into London on Friday evenings. We were well looked after by the club over the weekend, which usually included a visit to the Crown Bar in Cricklewood and the Galtymore dance hall on Friday and Saturday nights, and a few bob for pocket money before we left on Sunday evening. While in Strawberry Hill I continued to play with Finuge and Kerry at junior, U21 and senior levels. I often played a rugby game on a Saturday afternoon in London, and a club or county game in Ireland on Sunday.

I was over and back to London so often that I attracted the attention of the police at Heathrow Airport and was taken in for questioning one Monday morning on my way back from Ireland. I had difficulty convincing them that I regularly travelled over and back to play Gaelic football matches for both my club and county. When I felt I wasn't getting anywhere, I requested permission to call the Irish embassy in London to intervene on my behalf. The matter was quickly resolved and I was allowed to leave in time for a rugby practical at Strawberry Hill that morning.

Generally it was a tense time for Irish people in London because of the Northern Troubles. I remember the events of Bloody Sunday on 30 January 1972: after seeing the report on the BBC that evening I went to the college bar with some of the other Irish lads and drank a number of bottles of Newcastle brown ale to suppress my disgust and anger at the actions of the Parachute Regiment of the British Army. It was obvious then that it was an act of murder of innocent, unarmed people. The following Saturday, to protest against the killings, Mickey Ned O'Sullivan, Rory Kinsella (Wexford), Tom Donnellan (Roscommon) and myself went on a march from Cricklewood to Westminster which ended in a riot at Westminster.

Years later, in 1997, I was delighted to be a Minister of State in the John Bruton-led Rainbow Government which provided the British government with information that led to the re-opening of the Bloody Sunday files. This resulted in the Saville Inquiry, the report of which was published in June 2010 and which confirmed that the events on that day constituted an act of murder.

In September 1972 the second year students of Sion Hill and Ling Colleges in Dublin joined us at Strawberry Hill. Both colleges trained female physical education teachers and this move was in preparation for our planned return to Limerick in January 1973 to the newly opened National College of Physical Education (NCPE).

Moving from St. Mary's was a traumatic experience; I remember arriving in Limerick on a cold and miserable day in early January. A few of us went to see our new college and, to our dismay, it was only in the early stages of construction and was little more than a building site. There was also little suitable accommodation for students in Limerick at the time, resulting in almost all the male members of the class staying in the same flat for the first few weeks until we were sent packing by the landlady. The first year students were accommodated in the Brandon Hotel in Tralee, which was far from a satisfactory arrangement. They were probably the only students ever to begin their third level education in a hotel.

While the provision of a physical education college in Ireland was visionary, the college buildings and facilities should have been ready for the influx of first and second year students before we returned from England. When we

NCPE classmates from college, Colm Honan, Tom Donnellan, myself and Frances Brennan in 1976 at classmates Rory Kinsella and Geraldine Kiely's wedding.

arrived in Limerick there was also very little continuity regarding the courses we had already been studying while at Strawberry Hill; staff were still being recruited and, in fairness, as a number of them were not from Ireland, they found it difficult to adjust to the unusual circumstances in which they found themselves. The sensible thing would have been to allow us complete our degree course at Strawberry Hill and start a first year class in Limerick when the facilities were up and running and the staff recruited. At Strawberry Hill we had access to well-established courses, internationally respected coaches and lecturers in PE on a campus with top class facilities. There was also a very good history department in the college which I found beneficial as history was my second subject.

We all gradually settled down in Limerick and were made to feel very welcome there. In the early, difficult days of 1973 when I started in NCPE, I played a few games of rugby with Garryowen at junior and U20 level. Unfortunately, as my inter-county Gaelic football career was taking off at U21 and senior level, I was unable to devote much time to the club as match fixtures clashed. In any case, it would have been impossible to commit to club football with Finuge, county football with Kerry, and rugby with a serious club like Garryowen. I regretted this very much as I was very impressed with the club from my brief contact with it. I continued to play the odd rugby game in the college, winning the Webb Cup in 1975 which was considered a good achievement back then for a group of students. We had a number of talented rugby players in the college at the time, including Tony Ward, who became one of the greatest fly-halfs Ireland ever produced.

A game that still stands out in my memory in that competition is the semi-final against St. Mary's, better known locally as the 'Parish'. They were specialists in the competition and had a number of seasoned rugby players on their team. The game got rather physical but my team-mates, many of them teenagers, met fire with fire and, although conceding stones in weight in the pack, we prevailed, much to the dismay of the St. Mary's team and supporters.

Because of the large number of inter-county Gaelic footballers that entered the PE college at that time, Gaelic football became the dominant game on campus. In 1974, under my captaincy, we won the second division Higher Education Football League, beating St Patrick's Training College, Drumcondra,

Front row left to right: Dennis O'Boyle (Mayo), Eddie Mahon (Meath), Éamonn Ó Riordáin (Dublin), Richie Bell (Mayo, RIP), Brendan Lillis (Monaghan), Gerry Dillon (Kerry), Dick Dunne (Laois), myself (Kerry), Fran Ryder (Dublin), Ted Owens (Cork), John Tobin (Galway), Jimmy Dunne (Offaly), Dave Weldrick (manager). Absent: Pat Spillane and Ogie Moran. Back row left to right: Seán O'Shea (Longford), Larry McCarthy (Cork), Andy Shorthall (Laois), Mick Spillane (Kerry), Paud Moriarty (Wexford), Tom Donnellan (Roscommon), Hugo Clerkin (Monaghan), Joe Mulligan (Offaly), Declan Smith (Galway), Brian Talty (Galway), Tony Harkin (Donegal), Liam Fardy (Wexford), Brian Mullins (Dublin).

in the final. Their team included Ritchie Connor, who captained Offaly to beat Kerry in the 1982 All-Ireland Senior Championship final. Under my captaincy again in 1975 we won Division I, having despatched a star-studded UCD team in the final. This team, who were Sigerson Cup-holders and All-Ireland club champions in '74 and '75, included players like John O'Keeffe (Kerry), Jackie Walsh (Kerry), Ivan Heffernan (Mayo), Eamonn O'Donoghue (Kildare), Gerry McCaul (Dublin), PJ O'Halloran (Meath), Mick Carty (Wexford), Benny Wilkinson (Sligo), John P. Keane (Mayo), Barry Walsh (Kerry), and Pat Duggan (Dublin).

Many of our outstanding panel of players would become well-known inter-county stars in later years, among them Brian Mullins, Fran Ryder (Dublin), Ogie Moran, Pat Spillane and Mick Spillane (Kerry), John Tobin and Brian Talty (Galway), Brendan Lillis and Hugo Clerkin (Monaghan), Ritchie Bell (Mayo, RIP), Liam Fardy and Rory Kinsella (Wexford), Tom Donnellan (Roscommon), and so many more.

Brian Mullins was the type of player that I'd prefer playing on my team than against me. He was very competitive and inspirational on the playing pitch and was a great man to rally the team when under pressure. In my experience, he was one of the best high fielders and distributors of a ball. He was always prepared to go forward and have a shot for a score; he just exuded confidence and this permeated right through the team. I knew that the clash between himself and John O'Keeffe would decide the match so I psyched Brian up for the week before the final by taunting him about the beating that Johnno would give him. It worked and Brian rose magnificently to the challenge.

I devoted most of my time to fitness and Gaelic football training while at NCPE. The college had a multi-stationed weights machine of which I made great use. I used to train with Rusty Keane, an army captain and fitness fanatic who played second row for Garryowen. Together we devised our own programme to develop speed and strength and exercises to aid in leaping for a high ball.

We were fortunate to have had outstanding players, but even more so to have a trainer/coach of the calibre of Dave Weldrick. Dave was one of the first of the modern trainers. His training methods differed from the norm at that time; he used small-sided games to place players in pressurised situations and put major emphasis on power and speed endurance training. He stressed the importance of feedback and match analysis; we videoed most of our games and spent considerable time analysing them afterwards to identify team and individual weaknesses.

Dave had a marked influence on the development of new approaches to skill training and physical conditioning in this country. His training methods were replicated all over the country at that time and I am convinced that people like Eddie O'Sullivan and Liam Hennessey, who played a very important role in raising the fitness and technical levels of Irish rugby, learned a lot from him during their years at the college in Limerick.

Dave believed in making our training sessions as game-specific as possible and his drills were very much tailored to game situations. We worked a lot on one-on-one drills to improve our tackling and blocking techniques. For shooting practice, he had us work equally hard on technique in unopposed

(Courtesy of the Irish Examiner, www.irishexaminer.ie)

Dave Weldrick and myself, February 1974.

practice drills, being adamant that a player didn't develop technique under pressure. He always stressed that technique was the foundation of skill. The player would be fed several balls at a high tempo and he would knock them over the bar from different angles. On defence, Dave always emphasised that every team member became a defender the moment possession was lost. He discouraged fouling and constantly reminded us that fouling puts points on the scoreboard for the opposition.

He emphasised the need for width and depth in attack and would often remark to wing half-forwards and corner-forwards that he wanted to see the lime of the sidelines and end lines on their boots after the match. He drummed into midfielders and half-backs the importance of playing the ball quickly to the frontline players who must always be showing for the ball. Dave's advice was to inflict as much damage as possible when you had the ball and to treat it as your friend and not give it away cheaply.

Passing drills invariably involved the use of both hands and both feet as Dave believed that there was no point in excluding fifty per cent of your body from such exercises. He emphasised the importance of first touch and would lose his cool if the ball went to ground in a hand passing drill. Dave got us thinking about our game, about learning from our mistakes and the importance of video analysis. He often reminded us that the most important part of the anatomy was the brain and that we should use it.

Dave is now retired and over the years since 1974, he has passed on his training and coaching techniques to hundreds of students who have passed through his hands at NCPE and later at Thomond College, now part of the University of Limerick. Several of his students who went on to become club and inter-county coaches introduced many of his ground-breaking innovations in training and coaching methods to the teams they were involved with. His contribution deserves generous recognition.

Inter-County Years

1970–1983

1970

MY INTER-COUNTY FOOTBALL CAREER started in June 1970 at the age of 18 when I was selected at corner-back against Waterford for the first round of the Munster Minor Championship in Askeaton. It could have started earlier as I had been invited by Cormac O'Leary from Moyvane, then a selector for the Kerry minor team, to join the panel for the Munster final in 1968, following a number of good performances with Finuge in the North Kerry Minor Championship. However, I felt that I was too young and, in any case, I hadn't participated in the trials beforehand. Grateful though I was to Cormac, a close friend of my father's, for his encouragement at that time and throughout my playing career, I could picture the reaction I'd have received in the dressing room had I been parachuted into the team in that fashion. In 1969, the then minor trainer, Dan Kiely, called to my house to take me to a trial game for the Kerry minors. Again, I declined, as I felt my time had not yet come.

In 1970, I was certainly ready. I now had two years of North Kerry senior football experience with Finuge behind me. John B. Keane always said that if you could survive one season in North Kerry senior football, you would survive in any competition in Gaelic football. I had undergone an intensive physical conditioning programme at St. Michael's College for the previous five years. The coaching techniques employed by Johnny O'Flaherty and John Molyneaux really helped develop my Gaelic football skills and technique. As a result, I had no fear of any opponent.

As I played all of the trial games at either centre-forward or midfield, I was hoping that I would be selected in one of those positions. However, when it came to the team announcement I was picked at left corner-back. I had rarely played in that position so I was somewhat disappointed at not having been selected in one of my favourite positions. However, I was relieved that I had

(Courtesy of Tom Burke)

Humphrey Kelleher and myself in front of the Dáil, November 2010.

achieved my childhood ambition of playing with the Kerry minor team and wearing the green and gold county colours. For the next thirteen years I generally played at either left or right full-back for Kerry, with the odd appearance at full-back and as goalkeeper for one National League match in 1981 against Mayo and again for a brief period in the 1978 final against Dublin.

We beat Waterford rather easily in the semi-final of the championship at Askeaton. I was marking Humphrey Kelleher who later became manager of the Dublin hurling team and a radio sports commentator.

We then faced a star-studded Cork minor team in the 1970 Munster final in Killarney. Cork had dominated the minor champ-ionship since 1965, easily defeating Kerry in the 1966, '67, '68 and '69 finals, and were clear favourites to win another Munster minor final. They had some excellent players, notably Dinny Allen, Billy Field, Gerry Lynch, Martin Doherty, Seamus Coughlan, and Brian Murphy, but we emerged victorious and the seeds were sown for future success. I would regard this victory as the launching pad for the 1975 senior team. Names that were to become permanent fixtures on Kerry senior teams from 1973 to 1983 emerged and, in the case of Ger Power and John Egan, even further on. John Barry's report of the match in *The Kerryman* summed up this future promise:

Cork's monopoly in Munster minor football was decisively broken by an enthusiastic and highly accomplished Kerry fifteen at Killarney on Sunday last. Beforehand, Cork were installed as firm favourites but by the end of the hour their talented team was reduced to a shambles by the power football of the Kerry boys. It was the first time since 1965 that Kerry had succeeded in winning the Munster minor title and it was only natural that the victory was greeted with much elation.

Cork came storming back into the game in the second half and gradually pulled back their arrears. With thirteen minutes left, there were only three points between the sides. But Kerry managed to shake off the lethargy that had beset them and, after a tense six minute period, they regained control and finished well on top at the end. Their whirlwind performance in the first twelve minutes was a decisive factor in sweeping Cork to defeat. John Egan made it 2-4 to nil when he landed his second point and at this stage one could hardly be blamed for wondering how Cork had managed to gain their high rating.

At midfield Kerry were very well served by Paudie Lynch and John Long and by Lynch and Michael O'Sullivan. Lynch and Long controlled mid field right through the first half and although Cork came much more prominently into the picture in the second half, Lynch and Long emerged from the game as two of the outstanding figures of the hour. Centre-half Michael O'Sullivan, who was involved in a switch with Long in the second half, was another to impress. He played excellent defensive football and also lent valuable support to Lynch while he was at midfield. In the full-back line, Jimmy Deenihan, at

(Courtesy of The Kerryman, www.kerryman.ie)

The Kerry minor team, Munster champions, 1970.
Front row right left to right: G. Browne, T. McEllistrim, G. Dillon, M. Burns, Leo Griffin.
Middle row left to right: R. Casey. D. Moore, C. O'Connell. M. O'Sullivan, G. Murphy, G. Power, myself, G. O'Keeffe, J. Egan, M. O'Connor.
Back row left to right: D. Sheehan, (-), D. Kiely, J. Clifford, D. Healy, P.B. Brosnan, P. Lynch, J. Long, P. O'Mahoney, J. Cahill, D. O'Connor, S. Fitzgerald, B. O'Shea, S. Mason.

The Kerry minor team that defeated Derry in the All-Ireland semi-final in Croke Park in 1970.
Front row left to right: S. Fitzgerald, D. Moore, J. Daly.
Middle row left to right: G. Dillon, C. O'Connell, J. Murphy, G. Power, B. O'Shea, M. O'Sullivan, J. Egan, G. Browne, J. Cahill.
Back row left to right: G. O'Keeffe, D. Healy, R. Casey, D. O'Connor, B. O'Shea, P. Lynch, myself, P.B. Brosnan, M. Burns, J. Long, P. O'Mahoney, T. McEllistrim.

left full, showed that he has great potential, whilst Gerard O'Keeffe was very competent at full-back. Batt O'Shea batted gamely at right full before being replaced by John Clifford who proved an excellent replacement. Paudie O'Mahoney proved quite competent between the posts.

I remember that game for a number of reasons, but mostly for an observation made by a local football analyst, the late John Buckley, after the game. He remarked on the fact that I had fisted the ball out of defence on a number of occasions and that this was clever use of the ball; defenders generally kicked the ball as far as possible out of the danger zone at that time and he liked the idea of holding possession and playing it short to an

Left to right: Maurice Burke, Peter Silke, John Clifford and myself in the All-Ireland Minor final replay in 1970.

unmarked team-mate. As a defender for the next twelve years, I always tried to find an unmarked team-mate with a clearance out of defence and I used a fisted pass as much as possible to ensure accuracy.

In the All-Ireland semi-final we beat Derry. I had a lot of sympathy for the Derry players as the Northern Ireland Troubles had started and this resulted in huge disruption of the team's preparation for the match; they really needed the win more than we did as a morale boost for their county. The turning point in the game came when Derry were awarded a penalty. Martin O'Neill, who later became a top class soccer player and a successful manager, took the penalty and it was saved by Paudie O'Mahoney.

In the All-Ireland final we played a highly rated Galway team. Galway equalised in the final minute of the game and subsequently beat us by a last-minute point in the replay. Reporting on the replayed game, John Barrett wrote in *The Kerryman*:

At left full-back Jimmy Deenihan had a thundering game, his aggressive tackling and dashing clearances earning him the respect of many a Galway forward. The switch which sent him to left half-back in the closing stages unsettled the defence at a crucial time.

It was a huge disappointment after all the effort that had been put into the preparation, but it set the stage for future success as I and eight members of that team were part of the Kerry panel in the 1975 senior final. These included Paudie O'Mahoney (goalkeeper), Ger O'Keeffe, Ger Power, Paudie Lynch, Mickey Ned O'Sullivan, John Egan, John Long, Batt O'Shea, and myself.

We had a charismatic trainer in Dan Kiely from Tarbert, who later became a county councillor and senator and with whom I subsequently had several political battles. Dan was a great motivator and he introduced new football drills that made his training sessions interesting. He also introduced a new stimulant for players at half time – hot tea with a small portion of brandy; it seemed to work for some players. After the Munster final victory that year, he held a huge banquet – with an up-and-coming Gay Byrne as special guest – at his dance hall, the East End in Ballybunion. To his credit, he was a progressive thinker in Gaelic football and was responsible for the first-ever tour to the United States by a North Kerry team.

1971

1971 WAS a relatively uneventful year for me on the inter-county scene. I was selected to play for the Kerry junior team to play Cork in Charleville in the first round of the Munster Championship in May. The one incident I remember from that game was buying a dummy from Dinny Allen – which never happened again! As I wasn't playing well, I was substituted in the second half. Cork won the match rather easily.

I was a substitute on the Kerry U21 team against Cork in the Munster final at Killarney later in the summer and came on in the second half of a very exciting match, which ended in a draw. I had arranged to go to London the following day to work for the summer holidays and on my way via Dublin I stayed with Christy O'Sullivan, Martin Whelan and Jack Stack, who were from Finuge. They persuaded me to stay in Dublin and arranged a job for me in Bachelors factory on Bannow Road in Cabra through Brian Brady from Cavan, who was a supervisor in the factory. Brian later went on to become president of the Leinster rugby branch.

I worked on the night shift, from 8pm to 8am, and was given the plum job of making the tea and sandwiches, much to the annoyance of some of the lads from Sheriff Street who didn't approve of a country lad getting such an easy number. They tested me out the first night but I stood my ground and following that we developed a friendly working relationship.

I went on to spend three wonderful summers in Bachelors where I met some great characters. It gave me an invaluable insight into working class Dublin people and a first-hand experience of the working conditions on the factory floor.

During my stints there I stayed at Hardiman Road in Drumcondra and at North Circular Road with the Finuge boys. I ran to and from work and occasionally trained in the Phoenix Park during the day. Fran Ryder, later to play with Dublin and winner of three All-Ireland Senior Championship medals, worked in Bachelors at the time and we struck up a good friendship. We spent many hours doing press-ups and pull-ups to pass away the nights and later played together on the NCPE team, from 1973–1975.

In the replay of the Munster U21 final I was selected at corner-back. Cork won rather easily but I was very happy with my own display considering I came off night shift that morning and drove straight to Cork – not the best preparation for a Munster final. John Barry's report in *The Kerryman* was very reassuring: 'For Kerry, corner-back Jim Deenihan turned in a splendid performance.' I also got very positive encouragement after the game from selector Joe Keohane (RIP) who said that he liked my style of defending. Coming from a legend like Joe, this gave me a considerable lift and boosted my confidence no end. Joe was one of the true legends of Kerry football. He was selected at full-back on the GAA football team of the century and was a selector for our four-in-a-row team.

1972

1972 REPRESENTED another milestone for me: I began my senior inter-county career with Kerry. In April I was selected on the Kerry team at corner-back to play Limerick in the first round of the Munster Junior Championship in Moyvane. Moss Keane, later to become one of the greatest second row forwards ever to play for Ireland and a British and Irish Lion, was at full-back. Pat Hartigan, who won an All-Ireland senior hurling medal with Limerick in 1973 and numerous All Star awards, was on the Limerick team. We beat Limerick but were beaten by Cork in the final which was played in Kenmare in May.

That summer I was selected at full-back on the U21 team that beat Cork in the Munster final in Killarney. I had the experience of marking three different Cork players – Seamus Coughlan, Declan Barron and Jimmy Barry-Murphy – during the course of the match. This was my first experience of marking Jimmy Barry-Murphy whom I would mark on ten occasions in total in competitive football. Martin Ferris, who also represents Kerry North in Dáil Éireann, played on that team, scoring a vital goal that evening.

In the All-Ireland semi-final in Naas, we beat a highly rated Kildare team 0-13 to 0-6. This was undoubtedly one of my best performances ever in a Kerry shirt. John Barry wrote in *The Kerryman*:

> Without a doubt, Jim Deenihan was the star of the hour. Showing tremendous dash and anticipation, he was simply unbeatable in front of the goal, often beating two and three men before clearing his lines. It was a performance that did much to break the morale of the Kildare team as a whole and followers of the Leinster champions were not slow to express their admiration of his display afterwards.

On foot of my display against Kildare, I was added to the Kerry senior panel for the 1972 All-Ireland final against Offaly. This was a special honour and I thoroughly enjoyed the excitement of the build-up to the All-Ireland, along with training with Mick O'Connell, Mick O'Dwyer and many of my boyhood heroes. Jackie Lyne was the trainer of the Kerry team at the time. He was a man of immense stature and was widely respected. What impressed me most about him was his authority, both in the dressing room and on the training pitch.

I flew back from Strawberry Hill for the match with Mickey Ned O'Sullivan, who was also a substitute on the team for the All-Ireland final. I remember the game for a number of reasons; sharing the same dressing room on All-Ireland day with my boyhood heroes was a special experience and, on an embarrassing note, I discovered that there was no gear provided for me, despite the fact that I was on the panel. As I had only brought my boots along, I had to borrow a jersey, socks and togs from a number of players in the dressing room to look in some way presentable when we went out on the field.

The match was a draw and the replay took place some weeks later, resulting in an easy victory for Offaly. I felt that for the replay the Kerry selectors should have introduced some of the younger players. We were in no way overawed by the reputation of the strong men from Offaly and we might have made a difference with our youthful exuberance and speed.

The following Sunday, 22 October, Kerry played Galway in the All-Ireland U21 final and I was again at full-back. We led at half time, having the benefit of a very strong wind. However, we didn't put enough points on the scoreboard. In the second half we contained Galway right up to the last few minutes when they got two goals. It was a bitter disappointment; Galway had now beaten us in an All-Ireland minor final replay and an U21 All-Ireland final. It looked like they were going to be the team of the '70s but it wasn't to be. Galway did contest the All-Ireland senior football finals of 1973 and 1974, losing to Cork and Dublin respectively. Oddly, very few of the All-Ireland winning U21 or minor teams made it at county level afterwards.

I played my first senior game for Kerry against Roscommon in the National League on 29 October 1972 in Roscommon. I travelled from London the previous day and stayed with John O'Keeffe and Ger Power in Dublin. They shared a house with sports journalist Eugene Magee who drove us to the game. Eugene later managed UCD to both the Sigerson Cup and the All-Ireland club titles in 1974 and 1975, and in 1982 he managed Offaly to their historic victory in the All-Ireland senior football final against Kerry.

Apart from it being my first senior game for Kerry, the one incident I recall from the game was a well-timed block I made on Dermot Earley as he was about to kick the ball into an open goal. Dermot was one of the greatest footballers of that time, a superb athlete and totally dedicated to his county.

I met him on a regular basis in his capacity as Chief of Staff of the Defence Forces during my term as my party's spokesperson on defence. He was a great ambassador for both the GAA and his country. Unfortunately, he was forced to take early retirement due to health reasons in March 2010 and sadly passed away in July of that year.

We lost our next league game to Longford in Tralee. The headline in *The Kerryman* was 'Kerry slide to defeat against lowly Longford'. The one incident I remember from that game was the collapse of a section of the playing pitch in Austin Stack Park which necessitated a brief delay before the game resumed. Our subsequent game in the league was against Cork at the Athletic Grounds. Kerry won by 1-13 to Cork's 1-8. I remember Mick O'Dwyer whispering to me as we were leaving the changing room before the start of the game, 'It's important to win this game and keep these buggers down'. He went on to play an outstanding game himself that day.

It was the first of many games I played against Cork over the next ten years. I always felt a greater sense of rivalry between Kerry and Cork than between Kerry and any other county, be it in league or championship matches. There was a fair bit of needle between both counties, with tempers sometimes boiling over, but it was mostly a healthy rivalry making for full-blooded encounters which continue to the present day.

Despite three good performances, I was not selected for the next league game against the All-Ireland champions, Offaly, in December, which Kerry won. So ended 1972 – a very important year for me: I had begun my senior inter-county career with Kerry which was to last for ten years, and I achieved a childhood ambition of playing with sporting icons like Mick O'Dwyer and Mick O'Connell.

The experience of losing an All-Ireland U21 final and being on the losing senior panel against Offaly made me appreciate the importance of winning in Kerry and served to make me even more determined to achieve success in the future.

1973

I APPROACHED 1973 with considerable enthusiasm. During the Easter period I was selected at full-back against Limerick in the Munster U21 Championship at Castleisland. The same evening I was asked to play for Garryowen in the Munster U20 Cup final and had no choice but to opt for the Kerry game. That was the end of any aspirations I had to pursue a serious rugby career. Following a good performance in the U21 match, I was selected for the Kerry senior team at corner-back to play Derry in the replay of the National League semi-final. The previous game ended in a riot and an invasion of the pitch as the match ended. It was very scary, as emotions ran high and a number of missiles were thrown onto the pitch and the roof of our dugout. Two Derry players had been sent off by referee Paul Kelly and a number of Derry supporters took exception to this and attacked him after the game. He was lucky to escape without serious injury. As he said himself: 'They came at me like wild animals, not like human beings; only for the guards I would have been torn asunder.'

I always liked to mark well-known, high profile players in my early years playing with Kerry, so I was really looking forward to playing Derry as I was to be marking Anthony McGurk, who was one of the top forwards in the country at the time and an All Star in 1971. However, as the Kerry team assembled on the platform at Tralee railway station, we got word that Derry had pulled out of the game because they refused to play under Paul Kelly as referee. I went home very disappointed but, a few weeks later, I got my opportunity to play my first game for the Kerry seniors in Croke Park when I was selected to play against Offaly in the National League final.

I was marking Murt Connor from the well-known footballing family which also included his brothers Ritchie and Matt, from Walsh Island. The previous year he had scored five points from play in the All-Ireland final so I knew that I had to mark him very closely. I managed to do this and kept him scoreless. Kerry had a four-point winning margin, 2-12 to 0-14. It was some consolation for the defeat by Offaly the previous year in the All-Ireland final. Brendan Lynch, who captained the team, had an outstanding game, scoring 2-3.

We followed this victory over Offaly with a very exciting win over the Carroll's All Stars in the annual Wembley Tournament. Not only was it a unique experience playing in a world-famous stadium where the greatest

The Kerry team celebrating our win over the All Stars at Wembley.
Front row left to right: Liam Higgins, Paudie O'Shea (Waterville), Mickey Ned O'Sullivan, Eamonn Fitzgerald, Timmy Doyle.
Back row left to right: Ger Power, Jackie Walsh, John Coffey, Phil Horan, Seamus O'Donovan, Eamonn O'Donoghue,
myself, Mick O'Dwyer, Seamus Fitzgerald, Dan O'Keeffe, John O'Keeffe, Frank Russell.

soccer players had played, but it was even more special because I was marking Seán O'Neill of Down, a boyhood idol of mine. He was at full-forward and I was at full-back. *The Kerryman* report was rather flattering about my performance. John Barry said that I 'put no less a man than Seán O'Neill in the shade' with my display. I recall vividly the pep talk given by County Board chairman, Ger McKenna, which was included in *The Kerryman* report on the match:

> You must play with all the spirit, determination and skill at your command; nothing less will suffice. I know you can win this game, and I want you to go out there and prove me right. Show the All Stars what you are really made of, what fifteen men in Kerry jerseys are made of.

Hopes were really high after the victories over Offaly and the All Stars that we would go all the way in the championship that year. Following an easy victory over Tipperary in the Munster semi-final in Tralee, winning by 3-11

Jimmy Barry-Murphy scoring his goal.

to 0-5, we headed for Cork full of confidence for the final. However, for those of us playing in our first Munster senior final, it would be a baptism of fire. In the first twenty-five minutes Cork scored five goals and led by 16 points. Goals by Jimmy Barrett (2), Declan Barron, Billy Field (from a penalty) and Jimmy Barry-Murphy put Cork almost out of sight. Jimmy Barry scored a spectacular goal that day. The ball appeared to be going wide but came back off the upright, whereupon Jimmy trapped it with his right foot and slid it into the net with his left foot without putting a hand on the ball. It taught me one lesson about marking him: never take your eye off him for a moment. He just needed half a chance and was undoubtedly one of the most lethal finishers in the game at that time.

The positive outcome from that game was that we managed to cut the deficit to five points with twenty minutes to go and, but for a superb save by Billy Morgan from Jackie Walsh, it would have been closer. In the end, Cork ran out easy winners, 5-12 to 1-15, and went on to win the All-Ireland final that September.

The 1973 Munster final: Declan Barron punches Cork's first goal. Also in the photograph are Paudie O'Donoghue (3), J.B. Murphy, myself and Donie Sullivan.

Although it was a bitter disappointment to lose my first Munster final, I was very happy with my own performance. Apart from that flash of genius by Jimmy Barry when he scored a brilliant if opportunistic goal, I felt I had a good game on him. This was confirmed by the distinguished *Irish Times* sports journalist, Paddy Downey, in his report on the match.

With the sole exception of Deenihan, who played lion-heartedly all through, Kerry's stars failed to shine ... but all the others will remember the Munster Final of 1973 only with remorse. With the subjection of Kerrymen in all sectors it was clear that Kerry had lost the battle from an early stage. The whole attack, with the exception of John Egan, when he moved to centre-forward in the second quarter, was no match for the tenacious Cork backs,

Attempted block on a kick by Jimmy Barry-Murphy.

they never gained parity at midfield and their defence, with the sole and honourable exception of Jim Deenihan, had few answers to the clever movements and excellent fielding of the winner's forwards.

I went back to work at Bachelors the following Monday and started preparing on my own for the Munster U21 final against Cork in Skibbereen a few weeks later. Because of the defeat in the Munster senior final, this match was now of even greater importance. There was a view in Kerry – and beyond – that Cork would have the edge over Kerry for the foreseeable future.

There are few games that stick out more in my mind during my 13-year career with Kerry than the game in Skibbereen. I was all fired up for that match and felt that both the team and I had something to prove because there was so much negativity in Kerry after the Munster final defeat. I was selected at full-back and during the course of the game I marked three Cork players – Seán O'Shea, Jimmy Barry-Murphy and Seamus Coughlan – keeping all three scoreless. After the defeat in the Munster senior final it was a very sweet victory and we sent out a message that Kerry football, far from being in the doldrums, was on the way back. It's worth noting that eleven of the 1975 winning All-Ireland senior team played that evening.

Sports journalist Michael Ellard gave the following account of the game in the *Cork Examiner*:

> Cork's hopes of adding the Munster U21 Football Championship to their senior and minor titles ended at Skibbereen last evening when they were conclusively beaten by a far more decisive Kerry side. Their slick forward movements had the Cork defence in trouble all through. In defence, Jimmy Deenihan was master of everything that happened around the square.

The following day I left for America with the Kerry senior team to play in the Cardinal Cussen Charity Series against Roscommon, with games scheduled for Boston, Hartford and New York. We played three very competitive games and, in the process, built up a strong rivalry – along with many friendships – with Roscommon, who eventually won the Series. It was my first time visiting Boston and Hartford and I was delighted to meet a number of people from North Kerry, including the Barry family from the Six Crosses who knew my parents. Whenever I played in New York subsequently, they always travelled from Boston to support me.

On our return from the US visit we beat Offaly in the semi-final of the U21 championship in Tralee. We went on to defeat Mayo in the All-Ireland U21 final in Ennis in September 1973. It was a great achievement because we had no collective training session as a team that year, not even for the All-Ireland. It was a case of turning up and performing on the day. Mayo were well on top until the last ten minutes of the game. It was a significant win for me because it brought me my first All-Ireland medal and more so because my father was present to enjoy the occasion (he passed away before I won my next All-Ireland in 1975). John Barry, in his report on the U21 final in *The Kerryman*, wrote:

Kerry U21 All-Ireland champions, 1973.
Front row left to right: Paudie O'Mahoney, Batt O'Shea, John Coffey, Christy O'Connell, E. Nagle, Mickey Ned O'Sullivan (Capt.), Mike O'Shea, John Egan, Niall Brosnan, myself.
Back row left to right: Tim Kennelly, Martin Ferris, Mikey Sheehy, Barry Harmon, Páidí Ó Sé, Ger Power, Ger O'Keeffe, Paudie Lynch, John Long, Ger Coffey, Kevin O'Donoghue.

This was a victory that gladdened the heart of every Kerry man present, primarily because of the manner in which it was achieved. Twenty minutes from the end Kerry trailed by six points (0-9 to 0-3) and in the kind of game that had developed, this looked an unassailable lead. We only took the lead in the 52nd minute when Mikey Sheehy punched home a goal. When Mayo found the initiative slipping from them they were unable to do anything about it, as has happened the county's team more than once in the past.

Kerry finished off the year with victories in the National League over Roscommon, Wicklow, Longford and Offaly, while losing to the All-Ireland champions, Cork, by one point. Overall, 1973 was a good year for me personally; despite the defeat in the Munster final, I won an U21 All-Ireland and a National League medal and established myself on the Kerry panel.

1974

I SUFFERED a serious setback early in 1974 when I badly damaged a joint in my big toe in a clash with Brian Mullins while playing indoor soccer at NCPE. It cost me my place on the Kerry team for the remainder of the league and championship. I was a sub on the Kerry team that beat Roscommon in the replay of the 1974 National League final. In May, by way of preparation for the championship, Kerry played Sligo in a challenge game in Killorglin and I was selected at centre half-back. The Kerry selectors were looking for a centre-back at the time and were trying out different players. The game didn't really work out too well for me as I picked up an eye injury early on and I required a number of stitches afterwards. It was Mick O'Dwyer's last game for the county, having worn the Kerry jersey for 18 years. That fact, which lent a lot of significance to the occasion, was somehow not recognised on the day.

ONE of the saddest moments of my life occurred the following morning when I was informed that my father had died. He had undergone a bowel operation and appeared to be making a good recovery. I had spent time with him over that weekend at Tralee General Hospital and he was in reasonably good spirits. However, on my return to NCPE the following morning, I got word that he had died. In the end it was a blood clot that caused his death. It came as a major shock to me. An energetic man up to then, I had expected him to live to ripe old age like so many of his contemporaries.

My father was a larger than life figure and very popular locally. It took me some time to get over his death. Being a fanatic about Gaelic football and politics, he undoubtedly would have enjoyed the victories in store for me in both fields in the years ahead. Sadly, it wasn't to be. However, I cherish his words of advice and wisdom even to this day.

ALTHOUGH I was flying in training and had recovered fully from my injuries, I was not selected on the Kerry team for the Munster final against Cork. Kerry were hammered in that game, so maybe I was better off on the sideline. Prior to that game I had the honour of playing with Mick O'Connell, who had returned to inter-county football after an absence of two years, in a challenge game against Meath to mark the opening of a new playing pitch and community centre at Seneschalstown. I can still recall the vociferous reception he received from appreciative Meath supporters when he came on the field and every time he fielded the ball. The Munster final marked the last occasion that Mick O'Connell played for Kerry. He came on late in the game and was continuously jeered by the Cork supporters whenever he touched the ball. Another group of them behind our dugout were shouting, 'Why don't ye bring on Dwyer as ye are at it!' It was not an appropriate send-off for an icon of Gaelic football.

It was the end, too, of an era for a number of great Kerry stalwarts, including Derry Crowley, Paudie and Eamonn O'Donoghue, Seamus Fitzgerald and Donie O'Sullivan. The selectors, under the guidance of the chairman of the County Board, Ger McKenna, decided to do a major clean-out and introduce some new blood for the first National League game against Offaly in October. Ger played a vital role in the re-shaping of the Kerry senior team for the league campaign, starting with the Offaly match. He was present at the selectors' meeting in early October 1974 with Mick O'Dwyer, Johnny Walsh, Murt Kelly and Donie Sheehan when a decision was made to reshape the Kerry team, playing John O'Keeffe at full-back and introducing Tim Kennelly at centre-back and Ogie Moran in the forwards.

Ger was both admired and respected by the younger players especially; he was excellent company on social occasions and a great storyteller. He was the voice in the dressing room during the team-building phase before Micko took over. He was an able orator and his choice of words was always appropriate to the occasion, as in the league game against Offaly in Tullamore in 1974 when he addressed each player individually, outlining what he wanted from them. He started with goalkeeper Paudie O'Mahoney, saying: 'Paudie O'Mahoney – you have strong vocal cords, use them today – we want to hear you from the sideline issuing instructions to your defence.' Offaly, however, beat us by 0-8 to 0-7.

The next league game was against the All-Ireland champions, Dublin, in Killarney. That was the first time I marked John McCarthy and it was the start of a great rivalry as well as a friendship. Between championship, league, and challenge games, I must have marked him on at least ten occasions over

Paudie O'Mahoney, myself and Dublin's John McCarthy in the 1975 All-Ireland final.

the next seven years. Despite the fact that we were both very competitive and highly motivated players, we never had any altercation on the playing pitch. John was the fastest man on the Dublin team and none of his team-mates could match him for fitness and speed in training.

We drew with Dublin on that occasion and confirmed what a number of us on the Kerry panel thought – that we were as good as they were and definitely had the potential to beat them if we met them in an All-Ireland final. I remember being at the All-Ireland that September 1974 with John O'Keeffe and Ger Power. After the game, and despite all the excitement and hype about the Dublin victory over Galway, we agreed that we were confident we could beat them if we got our act together.

The next league game was against Cork and I remember being in Dublin on teaching practice. On the morning of the game, as I was getting the train from Heuston Station with John O'Keeffe and Ger Power, we discovered that the game was called off because President Erskine Childers had died suddenly. The game took place two weeks later on 9 December 1974.

I renewed my rivalry with Jimmy Barry-Murphy and kept him scoreless for the duration of what was probably my best game ever on him. John Barry in *The Kerryman* reported:

> Jim Deenihan is another Kerry player who deserves top marks for the manner in which he policed Jimmy Barry-Murphy, recognised – and rightly so – as the most dangerous corner-forward in the game. Deenihan never gave an inch at any stage and it speaks for itself that Barry-Murphy failed to raise a single flag. The Finuge man even had the cheek to go on a solo run in the first half with Barry-Murphy right with him challenging for possession.

We beat Cork on that occasion, winning the game by 1-12 to 1-6. Certainly we were sending out the right signals for 1975. Dick Spring, later to become a TD, Minister for Foreign Affairs and Tánaiste, was brought on as a sub in that game and performed very well. Dick would have been very much in contention for a place on the 1975 panel but for professional and rugby commitments.

I decided to spend some time at home with my mother in the summer of '74 following my father's death. During that spell I played hurling with nearby Lixnaw and, on one occasion, had the pleasure of marking Dick Spring who was playing with Crotta O'Neills – another stronghold of hurling – in a North Kerry/West Limerick tournament. At one stage in the game a melée erupted involving everyone on both teams with the exception of Dick and myself. We decided to sit out the brawl and engaged instead in a political discussion about the possibility of peace in the North.

1974 WILL always be remembered for the emergence of Dublin as a major force in Gaelic football for the rest of the decade. Despite the fact that St. Vincent's was one of the best Gaelic football clubs in the country (losing the 1973 All-Ireland club final to Nemo Rangers after a replay) this was not reflected in the county's performance. This may have been due to poor organisation and to a lack of interest on the part of the county senior team. When Kevin Heffernan took over the management of the Dublin team in September 1973 he ushered in a new era for the game. He introduced a whole new approach to the training and preparation of the team. Over the winter of 1973/74 he had Dublin do indoor training in a school hall in Finglas. The players were introduced to circuit training and plyometrics – using motor tyres for stepping and bouncing. Come spring, the training transferred to Parnell Park and was equally gruelling.

Apparently he got ideas from the former St. Vincent's and Dublin stalwart, Mickey Whelan, on how to develop the team's speed and endurance. Mickey was studying for a Master's degree in sports science in the US at the time. (Mickey was a selector of the Dublin team that won the All-Ireland senior football final in 2011 and played an important role in the physical preparation of the team).

Heffernan was laying the foundation for future success. I had even observed a more positive attitude towards Dublin football on the part of Brian Mullins and Fran Ryder, my fellow students at NCPE. I remember watching Dublin play Wexford in the first round of the Leinster Championship which was a curtain-raiser for the Kerry/Roscommon league final in May 1974. I was impressed by their performance and remarked to some fellow players that Dublin seemed to be on the way back.

As they progressed through the championship that year, they attracted an increasing following that swelled to a sea of blue by the time they reached the All-Ireland final against Galway. The media were suddenly captivated by this new phenomenon that was capturing the imagination of Dubliners and GAA followers everywhere.

While Heffernan, affectionately known as 'Heffo', was the tactician, Tony Hanahoe soon established himself as a formidable team leader on the field and an able spokesman off it. He was articulate and polished and enhanced the image of the GAA in media circles. He popularised the game and broadened its appeal in parts of Dublin hitherto associated with rugby. As a centre-forward he was innovative and a great creator of space from which his team-mates benefited. By taking the centre half-back out of position, he created a corridor for players like Mullins and Brogan to solo through and wreak havoc on opposing defences.

Dublin had now set the scene in terms of tactics and fitness. They had raised the bar for others to match and had become the team to beat.

1975

WE played Meath in the league quarter-final early in 1975 and were beaten by 11 points to 6 in a hotly contested match in Croke Park. The defeat by Meath put huge question marks over the future of this young and emerging Kerry team. Peadar O'Brien summed up the Kerry defeat in the *Irish Press* as follows:

> Kerry's troubles began at midfield and spread like a plague throughout the field. Meath tore down the centre of their defence as if it were non-existent and only for the brilliance of John O'Keeffe and, more especially, Jim Deenihan, Kerry would have been engulfed long before they were.

I marked Matt Kerrigan who was a tremendously strong player for most of the game. Later in the game I marked another Meath stalwart – Cormac Rowe. Years later, at the agriculture show in Virginia, Co. Cavan, he reminded me of a comment I made to him when he scored a point towards the end of the game from about 40 yards out under the Hogan Stand. I made every effort to block his kick, but the ball sailed over the bar. When I got off the ground I said to him, 'That must have been one of the best points ever scored in Croke Park'. I wasn't trying to flatter him; it was truly a phenomenal score. Nowadays, his marker would have rewarded him with a dig.

Before the Meath match the chairman of the County Board, Ger McKenna, made an inspired decision when he drove to Waterville to ask Mick O'Dwyer to become trainer of the Kerry senior team. This ushered in a whole new era for Kerry football. Micko wasn't too worried about the outcome of the Meath match. His focus was on the championship and our first championship game under his managership was against Tipperary in Clonmel. I asked to be left on the bench as I was doing my final exams the following morning in NCPE. However, with 15 minutes to go, the game was finely balanced. One of the Tipperary forwards, Liam Myles, who later became an inspector in the Department of Agriculture and whom I got to know well when I was Minister of State in that department, was creating problems for the Kerry defence.

O'Dwyer called me and said: 'To hell with the exam, get out there and steady the ship, or there'll be no Munster final.' I went on and, fortunately for me, the game swung in Kerry's favour and we emerged easy winners in the end.

The switching of John Egan to centre-forward by the selectors midway through the second half was the decisive factor. Babs Keating, one of the greatest dual players ever in the GAA, was playing with Tipp that day and he tormented our defence all through that match.

The way was now clear for the Munster final clash with Cork. The team was taking shape and O'Dwyer was still only beginning to assert his authority and win the confidence of the players and the Kerry public.

I remember having to travel down from Limerick to Killarney to train the following week after the Tipperary game. I had arranged for a lift from Dr. Dan Kavanagh, who was doing an internship in the Regional Hospital in Limerick and who was also on the panel. I went out to the Regional Hospital on Tuesday evening to discover that Dan had work commitments and couldn't get away. I called a County Board official to see if I could get a taxi to Killarney. However, he advised me that a taxi would be too expensive and instead to call the late Mike Moran, who was a well-known Kerry supporter in Limerick, to see if he would oblige. Mike wasn't available so I had to hitch a lift.

By the time I arrived in Killarney my team-mates had completed their usual two lap warm-up. Because I was late Micko had me do four laps even though I explained to him that I had to hitch a lift. 'That's no excuse,' he said, 'you should have been here on time.' He made his point and I left it at that. From then on, Michael Kennedy, a Kerryman who lectured in geography at NCPE at the time, drove me each evening to training in Killarney until I finished in Limerick that July.

Three weeks before the Munster final I picked up a worrying injury during a game between Finuge and Listowel in the first round of the Intermediate County Championship. The games between Finuge and Listowel are always very competitive and this one was no different. Ironically, it was one of our defenders who took me out of the game and badly damaged my knee ligaments in the process. But for the advice and treatment of Maeve Leask, a physiotherapist in Tralee, I doubt if I would have recovered in time for the Munster final.

Although I was still limping slightly, I convinced the selectors the Sunday before the match that I was fit to play; I wanted so much to play against Cork after the defeats of '73 and '74. There was a big build-up to the game, with Cork clear favourites and going for an historic three Munster final victories

The Kerry team that won the Munster final in 1975.
Front row left to right: G. O'Keeffe, J. Bunyan, J. Egan, M. O'Sullivan, P. Ó Sé, M. Sheehy, G. Power, B. Lynch.
Back row left to right: P. O'Mahoney, P. Lynch, P. McCarthy, P. Spillane, T. Kennelly, J. O'Keeffe, myself, Leo Griffin.

in a row over Kerry. Very few, if any, of the sports commentators gave us a chance of winning. O'Dwyer used this lack of confidence in us very effectively; after all, at that stage, most of us had won an All-Ireland U21 medal and two National Leagues and had been very successful in college football. He really convinced us that we were much better than the sports media made us out to be and that we should go out and show them how good we were.

Our defence was probably the youngest ever to represent Kerry; the oldest member was John O'Keeffe, who was 24. Ger O'Keeffe, John O'Keeffe and myself in the Kerry full-back line were faced with the challenge of marking Declan Barron, Ray Cummins and Jimmy Barry-Murphy – arguably one of the most lethal full-forward lines ever to play Gaelic football. Cork got off to a great start and Dinny Allen scored two points. However, a Cork defender deflected a harmless lob by Pat Spillane into his own net and this set us on the road to an easy victory with a score of 1-14 to 0-8.

99

An incident during the 1975 Munster final against Cork, left to right: Myself, John O'Keeffe, Jimmy Barry-Murphy.

I was again marking Jimmy Barry-Murphy and kept him scoreless for the second game in succession. He gave me the slip once during the game and I was forced to trip him to prevent a certain goal. Fortunately for me and for Kerry, Paudie O'Mahoney saved the resultant penalty, which was a crucial factor in the outcome of the game.

The victory was greeted with jubilation throughout Kerry. There was a sense of relief as people had feared that Cork, given the talent they had, would dominate Munster football for some time to come. Kerry had now regained its supremacy and it would be 1983 before Cork beat us again in a Munster final.

After the Munster final victory, with a settled team at his disposal and the scent of an All-Ireland victory in his nostrils, Micko really got down to hard, well-organised training.

We had an easy victory over Sligo in a semi-final notable for a penalty save by Paudie O'Mahoney early on in the match. The Sligo team received a thunderous reception from their supporters as both teams marched behind the Artane Boys Band before the throw-in. I can still remember the frenzied atmosphere during the parade. Unfortunately for the Sligo fans their team didn't perform on the day; the fact that Sligo celebrated too much after winning their first Connaught title since 1928 in the weeks before the match did not help their chances against a very hungry and ambitious Kerry team, now growing in confidence with every training session.

Dublin came through the Leinster Championship, beating Meath narrowly in the final. They beat Tyrone in the semi-final and so the way was now clear for the first All-Ireland clash between Kerry and Dublin since 1955. Dublin, as reigning All-Ireland champions, were firm favourites to win the game. However, whether it was due to our youthful exuberance or whatever, we were very confident that we could beat them and approached the game in an upbeat mood.

In a pre-match interview with Donal Carroll, a well-known sports reporter with the *Irish Independent* at the time, I said that I thought that Kerry would win because 'we were more natural footballers than Dublin'. Con Houlihan picked up on the comment after the 1976 All-Ireland final, which we lost, and reminded me in an article in the *Evening Press* that 'you should never cast aspersions on the alligator's mother before you cross the river'.

By the 1975 All-Ireland, the Dublin team had captured the imagination, not only of the Dublin sporting public, but also of the rest of the country, so there was huge interest in the final. On All-Ireland final day, for whatever reason, most counties were supporting Kerry. GAA supporters everywhere were impressed with the style of football this new Kerry team was playing.

Micko left no stone unturned with his preparation. He moulded us painstakingly as a team. A great spirit and understanding developed among the panel of players, especially in training and on the field of play. Mickey Ned O'Sullivan was an inspiring captain and led by example. Before the match he gave us a stirring pep talk and we went out onto Croke Park on fire, possibly as the youngest team ever to play in an All-Ireland final. An early goal from John Egan, when a Dublin defender spilled the ball in front of goal, set us on course to victory. The fact that Mickey Ned was knocked unconscious at an early stage in the game and had to be stretchered off the field made us more determined. Eventually we ran out comfortable winners.

The 1975 All-Ireland winning Kerry team.
Front row left to right: D. Moran, P. Ó Sé, M. Sheehy, myself, M. O'Sullivan (Capt.), P. McCarthy, G. O'Keeffe, Leo Griffin (team attendent).
Back row left to right: P. Lynch, P. O'Mahoney, P. Spillane, T. Kennelly, J. O'Keeffe, J. Egan, B. Lynch, G. Power.

The highlight of the 1975 championship campaign for me was the fact that I succeeded in keeping my immediate opponent scoreless in all games. It was also a very rewarding campaign for the Kerry defence collectively. John Barry, in his report on the match in *The Kerryman* on Friday, 3 October 1975, summed up the defensive performance as follows:

> Take the Kerry backs. They were so good last Sunday that goalkeeper Paudie O'Mahoney could nearly have stayed at home and Kerry would still have won. As I recall, he was really tested only once in the whole game and he handled the situation with his usual brilliance. Facts speak for themselves, they say. And the facts are that O'Mahoney and the Kerry backs haven't given away a single goal in the entire championship campaign. There could be no greater tribute paid to them than to say that.

My sister Patricia and myself on the train to Dublin for the 1975 All-Ireland final.

John Joe Brosnan, reporting in the same football final special, was equally complimentary:

> They were the youngest side ever to wear the green and gold jerseys in an All-Ireland final and their speed, their boundless enthusiasm and their football prowess induced the belief that they will be a powerful force in the championship for years to come. Above all things, it was their speed that proved the decisive factor in forging Sunday's comprehensive victory. This was especially true in the battle between the Dublin forwards and the Kerry backs. Usually we associate a nimble turn of foot with forwards and visualise backs in a more static role – but on Sunday the Kerry backs were the fastest defensive sextet we have seen in Croke Park – and their ability to outrun the opposing forwards was a major factor in spiking Dublin's guns.

103

The 1975 full-back line, left to right: Ger O'Keeffe, John O'Keeffe and myself.

In retrospect, I think that the Kerry defence never got the recognition that it deserved, especially the full-back line; collectively we were the fastest line on our team from 1975 to '81. In the first 25 minutes of the 1978 All-Ireland we withstood wave after wave of Dublin attacks and ensured that Dublin hadn't built up an unassailable lead before John Egan's goal. In the 1980 and '81 All-Ireland finals the full-back line held firm when we were not performing in other sectors of the field. The philosophy of our full-back line during those years was to win All-Irelands for Kerry and, if required, to sacrifice one's own individual performance for the overall good of the team.

The team and everyone associated with it were elated with the success – the first All-Ireland win since 1970 and by a team with an exciting future ahead of them. We got a tremendous reception when we returned to Killarney and the celebrations continued for months afterwards. For those of us living in Kerry, we were on the go almost every Friday and Saturday night for months, visiting villages and towns all over the county and beyond with the cup. We were elevated to the position of superstars overnight in the eyes of the sporting public and we revelled in our new-found stardom.

The fact that we were all single made us even more attractive at social occasions. John B. Keane wrote a very humorous article for the *Evening Herald* on our bachelor status which was titled 'The Kerry uncatchables. And it's just as difficult for Damsels as the Dubs':

> Dan Paddy Andy O'Sullivan, the great Lyreacrompane matchmaker, would have been greatly attracted to the present Kerry football team. Every man of this resolute squad is as fine a specimen of homo sapiens as ever laced a football boot. They are all fit as fiddles, sound in mind and limb, each one happier than the next and most important of all, from a matchmaking point of view, there isn't a married man in the lot. Dan Paddy Andy would have no problem with the placing of this Kerry team in his heyday and how could he go wrong with every one a household word, 'the idols of the ladies' as the song says, 'and the envy of the men'.

John B. got it right; we did attract a lot of attention.

1976

WE played Cork in a National League play-off on 7 March. Con Houlihan's report in the *Evening Press* the following Monday evening was rather insightful into how the team had gone off the boil from the previous September.

> This league play-off was far from being the great explosive clash of general forecast – yet it was a satisfactory game in that Cork's win was so comprehensive that no excuses could explain away the All-Ireland champions' downfall.
>
> Indeed one hesitates to call them champions any longer: since that day in Croke Park last September when they were like Midases, turning everything into Kerry gold, they have not given a convincing display. And when a

champion is so clearly beaten, even when his crown is not at stake, there must be doubts about the validity of his title.

Last autumn Kerry were generally acclaimed as the likeliest lads of all time: in retrospect that view seems hasty – it ignored the significance of 'on the day'.

A new star emerged on the Cork team in that game – Tom Creedon. He became a permanent fixture on the Cork team up to his tragic death in a car accident while moving house in 1983. He was an outstanding athlete and was unfortunate to have come up against that great Kerry team, otherwise he would definitely have won a few All-Ireland Senior Championship medals. His passing was not only a great loss to his family but to the GAA itself. He was one of the finest individuals that I came across during my playing years with Kerry.

We went on a memorable visit to the US cities of New York, San Francisco and Los Angeles in May 1976 as All-Ireland champions and played an All Star selection in each city. As it was the team's first trip away as All-Ireland champions, we really let our hair down and enjoyed three weeks of revelry. We were treated like kings in New York and San Francisco by the Kerry diaspora who went out of their way to look after us, as they continued to do on subsequent visits.

On the San Francisco trip with Pat Spillane and John Egan.

1976 was the first of the five All Star trips as All-Ireland champions I made to the USA in the 1970s and early 1980s. Broadway always fascinated me and during visits to New York I went to several shows, including *Evita, Cats, 42nd Street* and *Chicago*. When in Los Angeles I always visited Universal Studios and I developed an appreciation of film making. On one such visit Alfred Hitchcock was being honoured in the studio and I got to have a brief chat with him. I mentioned that his film, *The Birds*, had similarities to a short story entitled *The Crows of Mephistopheles* by Kerry writer George Fitzmaurice.

At that time there was a fitness revolution in California resulting in the opening of fitness studios and the 'jogging craze' sweeping the state. During my stay, I made it my business to visit some of these studios where I picked up the most recent information on new fitness techniques, including tapes on aerobic dance by Jane Fonda and Kate Smith. I also acquired the latest publications on running by Jim Fixx, Joe Henderson and Dr. George Sheehan. These proved an invaluable asset for my keep-fit classes.

At that time the teams stayed with families in San Francisco and Los Angeles. For that 1976 and subsequent trips to San Francisco, I always stayed with the McHale family. The late Kathleen McHale was McElligott from Lixnaw so, in a sense, it was a home away from home.

We came home from the US a tired team having revelled in the celebrations and the welcome we had received there. We had an easy victory over Waterford in the first round of the Munster Championship and faced Cork once again in the Munster final in the newly opened Pairc Uí Chaoimh. On this occasion we were the hot favourites. However, Cork had prepared well for the game, and really put it up to us and we were lucky to get a draw.

Once again I was marking Jimmy Barry-Murphy. He scored one point from play, which I felt was a good performance on my part because the Cork midfielders were very much in control and were feeding him a very accurate ball. Kerry won the replay after extra time. I was again marking Jimmy Barry-Murphy and doing a fairly good containing job on him until Paudie O'Mahoney mis-kicked a kick-out, putting the ball directly into the path of Jimmy Barry who pounced on it and stuck it in the net.

I was raging with Paudie and lost my concentration, with the result that Jimmy Barry again got possession from the subsequent kick-out and scored a further point, bringing his total to 1-3 – the most he ever scored off me in any game. He was at his peak at that time as a footballer and arguably the best corner-forward in the country.

The game was decided by a disputed goal for Kerry by Seán Walsh and a disallowed goal for Cork by Declan Barron. Brian Murphy, Cork's corner-back, was adjudged to have stepped behind the line when stopping a shot

(Courtesy of Kerry's Eye, www.kerryseye.com)

After Jimmy Barry-Murphy scored the goal in the 1976 Munster final replay.

from Walsh, and Barron was adjudged to have been in the square when flicking a ball to the net at the other end. In the dying seconds of normal time, John Moloney blew for full-time, denying Mikey Sheehy the point he had just scored. The game went to extra time and we won easily in the end. Jimmy Barry played in the half-forward line in the period of extra time. Relieved of the responsibility of marking him, I enjoyed that period of the game best.

There is no doubt but that Cork deserved to beat us in the 1976 final. With a little luck on their side, they would certainly have been a force to reckon with for the rest of the '70s. They had the ability to win a few All-Irelands and, had the back door system been in place then, they would have benefited hugely from it.

After our narrow escape against Cork, we got down to serious training for the All-Ireland semi-final against Derry. They had a very successful Ulster

Clearing a ball under pressure from Jimmy Barry-Murphy.

Championship campaign and went into the game with a fair degree of confidence. However, in what was probably our best game in the 1976 championship, we had a comprehensive win over the Ulster champions by 5-14 to 1-10 and were now clear favourites to win the All-Ireland as Dublin struggled against Galway in the other semi-final.

In the run-up to the match there was an obvious air of indifference and over-confidence at our training sessions in Killarney, and this permeated throughout the county. Supporters were under the impression that it was just a case of going up to collect the cup. This rubbed off on the team and no matter how hard Micko tried to get our heads right, he couldn't get through to us; at that stage we needed a psychologist more than a trainer. A big contingent of the team, myself included, attended the Festival of Kerry and celebrated in the festival club a few weeks before the game. The team were

Contesting a ball with
Jimmy Barry-Murphy
in the 1976 final.

(Courtesy of The Kerryman, www.kerryman.ie)

Presentation of jerseys for the 1976 All-Ireland final. Left to right: Mick O'Dwyer, John O'Keeffe (Capt.), Mick Moran, John Egan, myself, Paddy Moran, Murt Galvin, Andy Molyneaux.

special guests of the Tralee Race Company on the Wednesday of the races. The craic was so good that someone was appointed to contact Micko and ask him to cancel the training session, which he agreed to do. It was probably the only time he ever proved to be a soft touch and he lived to regret it.

Apart from the lethargy, the team also had injury problems going into the game. I went out for a kick-around before the customary final trial match, which always took place on the Sunday before the All-Ireland. I was practising fielding the ball over my head when the individual I was jumping against caught me by the shoulders when I was at the height of my leap and I came down awkwardly and badly tore the ligaments in my right ankle. I went immediately into the dressing room to pour cold water on the ankle – we didn't have ice packs in those days – but it swelled up in a matter of minutes despite the cold water and elevation treatment.

Ger O'Keeffe also suffered a similar ankle injury in training that week and these injuries probably cost us the match. Both Ger and I always played well against Dublin and we were well able to match forwards like John McCarthy and Bobby Doyle for pace. Both of us went on the field hobbling that day and, strictly speaking, shouldn't have played, regardless of how confident we were of beating Dublin.

I remember getting my ankle strapped before the game by Dr. Con Murphy, the Cork minor team doctor (the Cork minors were playing in the All-Ireland final that day). Con worked in the General Hospital in Tralee for a number of years in the '70s and struck up a very good friendship with many of the Kerry team. He remarked that I was crazy to be playing and that I wouldn't last ten minutes. He was right: my ankle went after a few minutes and I spent the match in pain trying to contain Bobby Doyle. While I managed to keep him scoreless (the only Dublin forward not to score that day), there was so much more that I could have done had I the full use of my foot. Luckily for me, Bobby carried a strained hamstring into the game and that curtailed his movements to some extent.

Kevin Heffernan had left no stone unturned in his preparation of the Dublin team for the 1976 All-Ireland. His training regime was even tougher than it had been in 1974 and he had his team in peak shape, both mentally and physically, for the match. He had strengthened his team from the previous year and brought in players like Tommy Drumm, Kevin Moran and Pat O'Neill – a whole new half-back line. In an interview before the game, Brian Mullins summed up the attitude of the Dublin team: 'We know what we have to do to win.' He was proven right. In the very first minute, Kevin Moran cut right through the Kerry defence and blasted the ball just outside the goalpost. It was a harbinger of things to come: Dublin meant business. They tore us apart and emerged easy winners. We were brought down to earth with a bang and our dressing room after the game – save for the panel of players, Micko and a few officials – was a desolate place.

The difference between winning and losing was painfully obvious. Our media followers were all in the Dublin dressing room: we were also-rans. I remember Kevin Heffernan coming into our dressing room and declaring proudly that he 'had been waiting for this moment since 1955'. Back in 1955, Kevin played

The 1976 defeated Kerry team.
Front row left to right: Ogie Moran, Ger O'Keeffe, Páidí Ó Sé, John O'Keeffe, Brendan Lynch, Mickey Ned O'Sullivan, John Egan.
Back row left to right: Pat Spillane, myself, Mikey Sheehy, Tim Kennelly, Paudie O'Mahoney, Paudie Lynch, Pat McCarthy, Ger Power.

on the Dublin team which was defeated by Kerry in an historic All-Ireland final. In that game, Kerry, who were very much the underdogs, were captained by my father-in-law, the late John Dowling. Kevin didn't mind rubbing it in, which, from a Dublin standpoint, was understandable.

For the record, there is one incident from that game that I would like to clarify which has been reported inaccurately on a number of occasions on sports programmes. In the first half I had a clash of heads with Tony Hanahoe, resulting in Tony's eyebrow being split open, while mine just swelled up. I stayed on my feet, half-dazed, no doubt influenced by my father's advice from years previously, while Tony went to ground and got treatment for his injury. The Dublin dugout started remonstrating with the referee that I had struck him with my elbow, which was not the case. In the commentary box, the late Micheál Ó Hehir gave a similar impression. Although it was an accidental clash

113

Bernard Brogan and myself in the 1979 Dublin v Kerry All-Ireland final with Jack O'Shea, Vincent O'Connor and David Hickey looking on.

of heads the referee took my name. In all fairness to Micheál Ó Hehir, he apologised to me during a commentary on a subsequent league match.

Although very disappointed and annoyed at my inability to play to my full potential due to my injury, I was genuinely pleased for Bernard Brogan, who played midfield for Dublin that day. I had met Bernard the previous October when he was working in Tarbert ESB station as an engineer and I was teaching at Tarbert Comprehensive School. We met at a training session with Listowel Rugby Club in the town park and went for a drink afterwards. For the next two years of his stay in Tarbert we trained together whenever possible and spent many evenings running over the sand dunes in Ballybunion where the Cashen Golf Course is now.

We also did interval resistance training on the very steep hill at the back of the school. I remember John O'Keeffe coming into the gym in Tarbert on one occasion as I was putting Bernard though a circuit training session.

He couldn't believe his eyes and exclaimed that I could be building Bernard up to beat Kerry in the All-Ireland final and might live to regret it yet: his words were prophetic.

Bernard went on to win two All-Irelands with Dublin, in 1976 and 1977, scoring a spectacular match-clinching goal in the 1977 semi-final in the dying minutes of the game. Ironically, he also beat Johnno to win the Irish Superstar Competition in 1979 and went on to represent Ireland in the World Superstar Competition, winning the 100 metres and beating some of the top sportspeople in the world in the process. Even more important for Bernard, I introduced him to his future wife, Marie Keane Stack, at the Finuge Carnival during Easter 1976. He certainly never regretted meeting Marie, a special lady. Although I was disappointed that Kerry lost the final to Dublin in 2011, I was delighted that their sons, Alan, Bernard and Paul, won All-Ireland medals in this match.

After the 1976 All-Ireland final, we soon discovered how fickle public opinion can be. That night, in the Grand Hotel in Malahide, following our defeat, a few of the players were verbally abused by disgruntled Kerry supporters while Pat Spillane had a pint of beer poured over his head.

We did receive a reasonable reception in Killarney on our return home, but it was a different feeling to 1975. When we retired to the bar in Fitzgerald Stadium after the reception, John O'Keeffe and I had a long discussion with a young Jack O'Shea over the course of the evening. Both Johnno and I had watched Jacko the previous year in the parade before the 1975 All-Ireland minor final and were astounded by his coolness and his confidence. There he was marching after the Artane Boys Band, waving to the Kerry supporters and enjoying the whole occasion. Kerry won that minor final and Jacko emerged as an up-and-coming hero.

However, he subsequently enjoyed the social scene that was very much part of South Kerry life at that time. On his own admission afterwards, we convinced him to give up the drink that night. He played his first senior match for Kerry against Meath in Navan that October in the National League and went on to become one of the greatest midfielders who ever played for Kerry, winning seven All-Ireland Senior Championship medals.

1977

WE qualified for the final of the National League against Dublin in April 1977 and beat them in a closely contested match, 1-8 to 1-6. However, the team did not get too excited about this victory as Dublin were without Brian Mullins and would clearly be a different proposition with him on the team in the championship. Ironically, that victory may have unwittingly contributed to our All-Ireland semi-final defeat that August by Dublin. Having defeated Dublin in the first round of the league and again in the final, we felt convinced that we had regained the initiative and that our defeat in the 1976 All-Ireland was an unfortunate misadventure arising from a combination of injuries and over-confidence.

In the run-up to the '77 semi-final we had easy victories over Tipperary and Cork in the Munster Championship. Because I felt that I played poorly in the 1976 Munster final matches against Cork, I prepared diligently for the Munster final in 1977 and was moving very well in training. The evening before the match, however, I came down with a flu. I found it difficult to get out of bed the next morning and could hardly walk. My mother gave me hot drinks and porridge and I set out for Killarney in a daze.

The 1977 National League winning team.
Front left to right: M. Sheehy, myself, G. O'Keeffe, P. Ó Sé, J. O'Keeffe, G. Power, J. Egan, B. Walsh.
Back left to right: D. Moran, P. Lynch, P. Spillane, C. Nelligan, T. Kennelly, S. Walsh, J. O'Shea.

Seán O'Shea (Cork), Paudie O'Mahoney and myself in the 1977 Munster final.

In the first five minutes of the game, Seán O'Shea, whom I had marked in the U21 final in 1973, scored two points off me from play. I was about to head for the sideline and ask Mick O'Dwyer to take me off when, fortunately in my case, the Cork midfielders decided to play the ball to Jimmy Barry-Murphy at full-forward and to Dinny Allen in the other corner. This took the pressure off me and gave me time to come to terms with my condition. Con Houlihan, writing in the *Evening Press* the Monday after the match, said that during the first five minutes I was 'like a cowboy who had lost his lasso'. I survived and Kerry had an easy victory in the end. The stage was now set for another showdown with Dublin.

Three weeks before the Dublin match, the County Board decided to play the quarter-finals of the County Championship. Feale Rangers were pitted against Kenmare and the game was played at the Austin Stack Park in Tralee. I was playing midfield for Rangers on Pat Spillane. Before the game I had a bet with Tim Kennelly that I would keep Spillane scoreless, which I did, scoring 1-2 in the process for Feale Rangers.

Midway during the second half, while contesting a high ball near the sideline, I was hit in the back by one of my own players. Friendly fire was always a risk when playing with the Rangers players who were so committed and fearless there was no holding back when they were contesting a ball. Because I was enjoying keeping Pat Spillane scoreless, I foolishly stayed on the pitch until the end of the match. I went for an x-ray afterwards and discovered I had partially dislocated my collarbone. I was unable to lift my left hand over my head up to the day of the Dublin-Kerry game. Thanks to the treatment I received from the team masseur, Owen McCrohan, I managed to play.

The injury definitely hindered my performance and I basically pulled on most balls that came my way rather than catching them, aware that if I were hit my shoulder would not hold up. With six minutes to go we were two points up and looked to be coasting to victory. However, a defensive error put the ball in the path of Tony Hanahoe who passed it to David Hickey, who stuck it in the net. To compound our troubles, within minutes Bernard Brogan soloed through our defence unopposed to score a classic goal. The match was effectively over at that stage.

It was a galling defeat for Kerry and especially for Mick O'Dwyer. Questions were being asked about his judgment; many commentators felt, with some justification, that individuals were played out of position. For example, the best midfielders in training were Pat McCarthy and John Long, yet, Jack O'Shea and Páidí Ó Sé were selected there. Ogie Moran was posted to wing-back rather than centre-forward, his favourite position.

The game will go down in the history books as one of the greatest games ever. It was truly gripping and played at a fast tempo with the lead changing several times. Both teams, however, made a considerable number of incomplete passes, resulting in a lot of loose balls. The manner in which Dublin won, coming from behind, made it a great sporting spectacle that would be long-relished and recounted by their fans.

Shortly after the All-Ireland semi-final, Feale Rangers played Austin Stacks in the county semi-final. Stacks, who were reigning county champions and All-Ireland club champions, were powered by players like John, Ger and Anthony O'Keeffe, Ger Power, Mikey Sheehy, John L. McElligott, and Cork star Dinny Long. Feale Rangers won after a very hard-fought contest. Again I was playing at centre-field and performed well there. However, my hard luck with injuries continued. Before the end of the game, I was pulling on a ball on the ground when a Stacks player put his boot over it. I made contact with his steel studs, aggravating the same toe joint which I had damaged in January1974 while at college in Limerick.

As a result of this injury I was unable to train for the County Championship final against Shannon Rangers which took place three weeks later. Dr. Paddy O'Shea froze my toe joint before the game and I played in persistent pain for the sixty minutes. Although we were favourites to win the final, Shannon Rangers proved too clever for us. With players of the calibre of Paudie and Eamonn O'Donoghue, Jackie and Barry Walsh, Ogie Moran and the emerging Bomber Liston, they outclassed us and, in the end, won comfortably by four points. Their tactics paid off. In the first half, while playing against a gale-force wind, they held possession. We just couldn't adapt to their tactics. After losing this match I thought that I would never win a County Senior Championship medal. Happily, I didn't have long to wait as we came back and won it in 1978.

After the defeat in the All-Ireland semi-final and the county final I was fairly down. I had serious foot and collarbone problems and worse was to come: I remember walking on the beach in Ballybunion one evening that autumn with Pat Spillane who taught PE in the vocational school in Listowel for a short period in October 1977. After the walk we decided to drop in for a drink to the Castle Hotel where someone brought an article by Tom O'Riordan in the *Evening Herald* to my attention. The article read as follows:

> The Kerry selectors have dropped a bombshell in the selection of the county senior football team to play Offaly in the National League in Tralee on Sunday. Sensationally dropped is Pat Spillane, one of their current Carrolls All Stars and reckoned by many to be one of the best forwards in the country... dropped also are defenders Jim Deenihan and Ger Power, the latter a Carrolls All Star wing-back for the past two years... Neither Power nor Deenihan have been named among the substitutes.

119

We received no warning and no phone call, and there was no explanation afterwards; surely this was not the way to treat players and it reflected poorly on the County Board and the team management at that time. I was told indirectly that I was getting too many injuries and that I was becoming paranoid about them. Despite feeling disappointed, I took it on the chin, kept my counsel and went about getting my injuries right. I was determined to show those who had me written off that I still had an inter-county career ahead of me.

THE 1977/78 league campaign was a disaster for Kerry. After winning the first game against Offaly, Kerry lost their next three to Dublin, Cork, and Galway without much of a fight. A draw in the last game of the National League, against Kildare, helped Kerry to narrowly avoid relegation. By the end of 1977, the knives were really out for the selectors and even for Mick O'Dwyer. The headlines in the *Evening Press* on Thursday, 24 November stated in bold print, 'Many Problems in the Kingdom: Kerry Face Revolution'. The article, written by John O'Shea, stated that a revolution in Kerry football was very much a possibility following the spectacular outburst the previous evening by Dr. Jim Brosnan, former County Board chairman, when he stated that Kerry football 'is in a shambles'.

Jim Brosnan said that everyone connected with Kerry football had lost confidence in the present set-up and that players were being blamed for the defeat by Dublin in the All-Ireland semi-final when the ones at fault were not the players, but the selectors. He went on to say that, after the match, the players were the ones who suffered – not the selectors. Joe Keohane, in the same article, said he wanted to endorse everything that Brosnan said and added: 'There is an urgent need in Kerry for a change of policy with regard to administration and team training, but more importantly, I want to see a will to win, which has been glaringly lacking in recent games, return to the Kerry team. We have become lethargic, listless and indifferent. We are poised to suffer the greatest indignity ever to our football pride.'

Mick O'Connell also gave his support to Brosnan's sentiments: 'The people at the top should be there with a deep knowledge of Gaelic football. That is not the case with the present set-up. They must be men of conviction,' he said. Ger O'Keeffe, captain of the team, admitted that 'people within the county seem to think something is wrong. I cannot deny that there is a problem'. Another player, who preferred not to be named, was quoted by John O'Shea as saying: 'The players are sick to death of the situation. They have apparently lost interest in whether we win or lose a game. We are tired of the chopping and changing that has been going on.'

During all this turmoil, I remained totally focused on getting my body right and rid of injury. Mick O'Dwyer and Ger McKenna survived at the January county GAA convention and, by the end of September 1978, the county was celebrating another All-Ireland victory. I went to see a specialist in Croom Hospital about my collarbone injury and he recommended an operation which would include wiring of the joint but I decided against it. Another specialist suggested injecting my toe joint with Cortisone, but I decided against this too as I was never in favour of Cortisone injections. Instead, I went on a very good weight training programme and, by Christmas, I was on the mend. I worked out a few times a day with the students during their physical education period in the school and I also started training with the Tralee Rugby Club two evenings a week.

I was selected to play in the centre for the Tralee firsts against the Exiles in the annual St. Stephen's Day match. Moss Keane and Donal Spring, both Irish internationals at the time, played on the Exiles team. Tralee won and I went on to play a number of matches for the club over the next five weeks or so. Barry McGann, an ex-Irish international, played at fly-half for a number of these games; it was a great experience to play outside him and I learned a lot about three quarter play from him. The training was tough and consisted of maybe 10 to 14 sprints the length of the rugby pitch on a very sodden surface, with a short rest in between the sprints, along with other heavy exercises.

Tralee had lost the final of the Munster Junior Cup the previous two seasons and hopes were high that this might be their year. Ger O'Keeffe also got involved and was playing on the wing. I was scoring on a regular basis and was looking forward to the first round of the Junior Cup. However, the Thursday evening before the game, one of the selectors called me aside to inform me that, regardless of how well I was playing, they could not select me before their own regulars, but I was welcome to travel as a non-playing reserve. I was taken aback but not too disappointed.

When I arrived home, there was a letter in the post inviting me to play in a trial match for the Munster team for the upcoming Railway Cup in Killarney. Had I been selected on the Tralee junior team, I would have elected to play for them rather than in the Munster trial.

When I arrived in Fitzgerald Stadium, the County GAA convention was in progress in the pavilion. Because of the rugby training and the weights programme, and the fact I was now injury-free, I was in superb shape compared to the others, and I made sure to send a clear message to Mick O'Dwyer and his selectors that I was not past tense. I rarely soloed out of defence as a corner-back, but I got great satisfaction from doing a few solo runs in front of the pavilion that day, especially for the benefit of one of the selectors on the sideline who had dropped me from the panel. The same man had just lost the vote to remain on as a selector at the convention. I recall that after the trial game he came over to me and said, 'It's great to see you back in action and in such good form'. I thanked him for giving me the rest and we have remained great friends ever since.

1978

AFTER the trial match in Killarney I was selected on the Munster team to play in the Railway Cup semi-final against Leinster, which we won. We went on to beat Ulster by 4-12 to 0-19 in the final after extra time in a replay on 6 April in what was rated one of the greatest Railway Cup finals of all time. Shortly after this game I was asked to rejoin the Kerry panel. I was selected on the Kerry team to play Dublin in a fund raising match for Sr. Consilio in Gaelic Park, New York, on Sunday, 14 May. At this point there were huge question marks hanging over the Kerry team. We had been lucky to avoid relegation in the league and the general view was that we just could not match Dublin's physical game. While the Dubs lived it up in New York the two nights before the match, we took it easy. For us there was much more at stake: we were in New York to beat Dublin, not to enjoy ourselves socially.

On the day of the game conditions were dreadful and we played the match in torrential rainfall. It was a tough physical encounter, with Bomber Liston establishing his physical presence up front. In the end we emerged easy winners by 2-11 to 1-3 in front of a very partisan crowd who cheered every time a Kerry player handled the ball.

I didn't emerge from the game intact as Pat O'Neill, the Dublin half-back, broke my nose. Before the game Micko gave instructions that no player should get a clear pathway to goal, like Bernard Brogan got in 1977 and Kevin Moran in 1976. Pat was soloing up the field unmarked so I left my immediate opponent, John McCarthy, to tackle him, dispossessing him in the process and clearing the ball up the field to resounding applause from the crowd. Annoyed at being dispossessed, he turned around and hit me from the side, shattering my nose. I didn't see the punch coming, otherwise I would have protected myself. In any case, the referee was on hand and sent O'Neill off immediately. John McCarthy, my immediate opponent, confirmed that my nose looked broken or, as he said, 'It's in shite', so I made straight for the dressing room.

I understand that someone sent for Pat O'Neill to have a look at my nose but he declined. It would not have been easy for him. As there was no doctor or any medical person around, I was lucky that my sister, Annette, and her husband, Mick, who were living in New York at the time, were at the game and were able to take me to Mosholu Parkway Hospital, where my broken nose was straightened.

That night I had arranged to meet Fran Ryder in Rosie O'Grady's Bar in downtown Manhattan. Pat O'Neill happened to be there too and, during the course of the night, he passed a message to me through Fran that he was very sorry for striking me and that it was a case of mistaken identity; as visibility was bad, he had mistaken me for Páidí Ó Sé. My nose healed in a matter of weeks and I just forgot about the incident. I can't recall Pat making any further sorties into the Kerry half during our future encounters. We never again crossed swords on the field of play and whenever we met off the field I always enjoyed his company.

The victory over Dublin was a huge psychological boost. We now knew that we could match them when it came to a physical contest and that in Eoin

Liston we had a leader up front who could mix it physically if required and also create scoring opportunities and space for the other forwards.

Bomber became the chief architect in the Kerry revival and if I were asked who would be the first player that I would pick on my team, I'd plump for him. He was absolutely unselfish, very skilful and naturally strong. Of all the players I ever marked, he was the most difficult. The first time I played against him was in the North Kerry League in Ballybunion in May 1977 at midfield. I immediately felt his immense strength in the air and witnessed his intelligent distribution of the ball. I remarked to some Finuge players after the game that young Liston had a bright future.

I also brought him to the attention of Mick O'Dwyer; apparently I was not the only one. I remember calling to his father's pub to bring him to Tralee for Kerry training for the first time in the summer of 1977. I had to go up to his room to force him to go. It subsequently transpired that I was marking him that evening in training and we didn't spare each other. He hadn't sufficient time to impress the selectors before the All-Ireland semi-final in 1977; I am convinced he would have made the difference that day. Later in the year, when Kerry played Dublin in the league, he scored two goals and gave Seán Doherty, the Dublin full-back, a bit of a roasting.

It was obvious that Bomber was going to be our driving force for the championship and our trump card against Dublin if we met them in the All-Ireland final. He had become a formidable player and, for a number of years afterwards, he was almost impossible to mark by one defender alone. He usually drew a number of defenders, releasing unmarked forwards. Spillane, Sheehy, Egan, Moran and Power revelled in their new-found space and freedom: all that any of them needed was a yard or two and they were almost unstoppable.

On our return from New York we went on a programme of very strenuous training for the Munster Championship, much harder than for any previous Munster final. We knew that nothing less than an All-Ireland victory would appease the Kerry supporters. Losing to Dublin in 1976 and '77 had put serious question marks over certain individuals and over all the team in general. Our credibility as footballers was at stake. Dublin were heading for a record-equalling three-in-a-row and we were very much regarded by the sports commentators and public in general as the second best team in the country. We were determined to change this perception.

However, we had to win three games to get the opportunity to knock them off their pedestal. The first round was against Waterford and we emerged easy winners, 4-27 to 2-8, with Pat Spillane scoring 2-6 and Mikey Sheehy 2-4 from play. Although we won by 25 points the headline in *The Kerryman* report of the game read, 'Midfield dilemma remains and now doubts about the defence'. The reporter in question singled me out for special mention as having a poor game which put extra pressure on me going into the Munster final. Micko always advised us not to read the papers until the championship was over; foolishly, I did so on that occasion.

At the commencement of the 1978 championship season it was generally perceived that Kerry were on the slide, having just avoided relegation from Division 1 in the National League. As a result, many Cork players and supporters thought that 1978 would be their year, and with some justification. We trained for the Munster final as if it were an All-Ireland and the build-up was intense.

Before the game started there was an explosive atmosphere both in the dressing room and on the pitch. I was clearly more fired up for that particular match than for any for other one that I can remember. The drive to Cork that morning was not the best preparation. The taxi organised by the County Board to collect me was overcrowded and I had to share the passenger seat with another individual for the 70-mile trip. Since then I have advised players to travel to Cork the evening before a Munster final.

Our forwards, led by Eoin Liston, just tore the Cork defence apart in the first half. Cork did get two goals in the second half but we emerged easy winners in the end, 3-14 to 3-7. I was marking Jimmy Barry-Murphy for the last time in a Munster final or in any competitive game. Though he played in the 1979 and 1980 Munster finals, the National League in 1978 and 1979, and the National League final in 1980 against Kerry, I was not marking him in those games. So the Munster final of 1978 was not the end of his Gaelic football career because of exchanges between us in that match as has been implied by some commentators.

During the first half of the game there were some robust exchanges between Jimmy Barry-Murphy and myself which were, in my opinion, parsed and analysed excessively and unfairly in the following years. Whatever happened

Myself and Jimmy Barry-Murphy compete for possession.

on the field of play that day was trivial when compared to incidents before and since on GAA pitches. Both Jimmy Barry-Murphy and I shook hands after the match, walked off the field together and had a drink afterwards in the Imperial Hotel in the company of his wife. I was always an admirer of his footballing ability and got immense satisfaction seeing him outclass other defenders. I marked him on eight occasions at senior level and for periods of two U21 championship matches in 1972 and 1973. He was certainly one of the greatest corner-forwards of his time and, in my opinion, right up there with Mikey Sheehy, John Egan, Matt Connor and, more recently, Colm Cooper.

Despite the close attention which I gave him in the 1978 Munster final, he still managed to latch onto a ball which was dropped by a Kerry defender in the square and slide it into the net in the final minutes of the game. The first thing that Micko said to me after the match in the dressing room was, 'How did you let him score that goal?' If Cork had taken their scores, it would have been much closer but it just wasn't their day, despite a tremendous second half display by Declan Barron at midfield.

WE were now on our way to Croke Park to play Roscommon in the semi-final. Very few gave Roscommon any chance of beating us. However, because of the rivalry which probably emerged from the Cardinal Cushing Games in 1973 and subsequent league matches in the years leading up to the semi-final, the Kerry players did not take Roscommon for granted. They had some excellent footballers, notably the late Dermot Earley, one of the greatest midfielders in Ireland at that time. The difference between the teams on the day was the ability of our forwards to take their scores and capitalise on mistakes made by Roscommon defenders. The surface being very slippery, it was difficult to stay on your feet. However, we adapted to the conditions better than they did.

My outstanding memory of that match was of the midfield display by Jack O'Shea and a spectacular goal by Pat Spillane when he pulled on a rolling ball and slammed it into the net. Although we won the game, which was played in torrential rainfall, by 12 points, we did not impress the sports journalists, some of whom raised question marks about our capacity to beat Dublin in

Being tackled by Tony McManus in the 1978 semi-final against Roscommon.

the All-Ireland final. One headline read, 'Back to work – Kerry – Big Improvement Needed for Final'.

We were back in the All-Ireland final again, having been written off 12 months previously. The stage was now set for the showdown of the decade between Kerry and Dublin, provided that Dublin beat Down in the other semi-final the following weekend, which they did. The build-up to the match was intense. Dublin were favourites and were going for their third All-Ireland in a row. The game really caught the imagination of the Dublin public and the city became a sea of blue in the weeks leading up to the game. Previous Dublin teams had achieved three in a row on three occasions; 1897–1899, 1906–1908 and 1921–1923. The headline in the *Sunday Independent* on 24 September, the day of the match, read, 'NO.21 FOR DUBLIN – Immortality is one step away'. Tom O'Riordan, the writer of the article, went on to say:

> These have been heady days for Dublin football fans and the mighty men of the modern game are but one step away from near immortality. To achieve the treble on the same occasion as the county would celebrate their 21st All-Ireland final triumph at the expense of a county already legendary would surely be something akin to Ireland beating Wales at Cardiff Arms Park to win the Triple Crown.

Obviously we had every intention of spoiling their party and Micko's experience really came into play in the lead-up to this match. We were in superb physical and mental shape. We were shielded very skilfully from the media to whom very few interviews were given. In any case, the media focus was very much on Dublin and their bid to become the team of the '70s and arguably the greatest team ever in the history of the GAA.

Our preparations were going according to plan up to the Sunday before the final. We had even analysed videos of the 1976 and 1977 matches against Dublin – something Micko never did previously.

However, disaster almost struck the Sunday before the All-Ireland. In order to get us warmed up before the traditional A v B trial game, Micko decided to have us do a few sprints in pairs across the pitch. Both John O'Keeffe and Seán Walsh were pitted against each other for the sprint. They pulled up halfways across the pitch with muscle strains, Johnno with a groin strain and Seánie

Ogie Moran leads the team in the pre-match parade.

with a thigh muscle one. Fortunately, both managed to play the following Sunday and, despite their injuries, they made major contributions. Johnno got an injection before the match but it didn't really work and he played under considerable pain. The injury certainly created problems for him down the road and may have contributed to cutting his playing career short.

The Saturday before the final we travelled to Dublin by train and stayed in the Grand Hotel in Malahide. We went for our usual stroll on the beach that evening after eating. When it came to Micko addressing us, he was brief and to the point. He more or less said that if we lost this final he would be gone and the future would be uncertain for the team, which he was confident could still become the greatest team ever. The players clearly got the message. I was really looking forward to the game as I had carried injuries into the 1976 final and the 1977 semi-final games. I was in peak condition that day, with no niggling injuries and, mentally, I was a much more mature player.

130

DUBLIN totally dominated the first 25 minutes of the game. The full-back line of Mick Spillane, John O'Keeffe and myself were under continuous pressure from wave after wave of attack. Although our forwards showed a few flashes of skill and promise, they were not stringing moves together and Eoin Liston even wanted to come off, as he had a back pain. Dublin led by six points to one at one stage and looked to be coasting to victory. Even the full-back line wanted to be part of the action and Robbie Kelleher, one of the pillars of their defence line, came forward and had a shot for a point which, luckily for us, went wide.

At this stage Dublin looked like they were only out for a stroll and this would be an easy All-Ireland for them. But the course of the match was about to change dramatically. Bobby Doyle got possession but was called up for over-carrying. Mick Spillane took a quick free to Eoin Liston; he passed the ball to Jack O'Shea who, in turn, passed to Pat Spillane, who set up the unmarked John Egan for a one-on-one with Paddy Cullen. Egan didn't miss an opportunity like that and put the ball into the net over Paddy's raised hands. So, having been very much on the back foot for 25 minutes, we were now just two points behind Dublin. Points by Jack O'Shea and John Egan saw us draw level. The whole dynamic of the game had changed in the space of four minutes.

Then, within a matter of seconds, two further incidents occurred which would decide the eventual result. Kevin Moran pulled up sharply with a hamstring injury while he was chasing back a ball in defence and Mikey Sheehy chipped Paddy Cullen for one of the most talked about and spectacular goals ever seen in Croke Park. Referee Seamus Aldridge gave a free to Kerry following a minor incident between Ger Power and Cullen. There was a previous incident shortly before this when Paddy Cullen brushed into Ger Power and the referee obviously didn't see it.

However, the crowd, with the exception of the Dublin supporters, started booing Paddy Cullen. Obviously, the referee was influenced by the crowd's reaction. Minutes later Paddy and Ger had a further brush, resulting in the crowd booing again and the referee awarding a free to Kerry. While Paddy was remonstrating with the referee, Mikey placed the ball down and chipped it into the corner of the net over Paddy's head. The score was allowed and we were ahead. Another player would have played safe and settled for a point, but not Mikey, who was always prepared to play on his instincts. It was a moment of pure genius and opportunism that will be forever part of GAA history. It broke the heart of Dublin.

(Courtesy of Kerry's Eye, www.kerryseye.com)

My father-in-law, John Dowling, selling football boots in his shop in Tralee in 1959.

The second half was very much Eoin Liston's show; he scored three goals and two points, the first goal coming 90 seconds after the re-start of the second half. He confirmed that day, especially in the second half, that he had the potential to become the greatest full-forward that the game ever produced. He had skill, vision and raw physical strength and, more importantly, he was a team player and totally unselfish. In my opinion he did become the greatest full-forward ever in Gaelic football, even greater than his close friend and my late father-in-law, John Dowling, or Kieran Donaghy. Why he was not selected on the GAA team of the century I just don't know.

Eventually, we ran out winners by 5-11 to 0-9, a 17-point margin and a record for an All-Ireland final. Dublin managed to score only two points in the second half, both from frees. It was a great achievement by the Kerry back line to hold Dublin to nine points after being under so much pressure for 25 minutes.

The Kerry public was ecstatic with the victory and gave us a tremendous reception when we returned with the cup. The stage was now set for one of the greatest periods in Kerry's football history. This victory over Dublin was the confidence booster that we needed. I recall sports journalist Tom O'Riordan asking me on the parade bus in Killarney what the difference was between this celebration and the one after winning in 1975. I responded that we were now more mature and would not be carried away by the euphoria, and that we would not be caught again by Dublin or, for that matter, anybody else, for a number of years in an All-Ireland final.

In the Grand Hotel, Malahide, after winning the 1978 All-Ireland.
Front row left to right: Andy Molyneaux, myself, Ogie Moran, Leo Griffin, Murt Galvin.
Back row left to right: Frank King, Charlie Nelligan, Tommy Bridgeman, Jack O'Shea.

The loss of the 1978 All-Ireland was a devastating blow for Dublin. It was best summed up by Jim O'Sullivan in his match report in the *Cork Examiner* on Monday, 25 September:

> One has only to ponder on what Dublin lost in defeat – the three-in-a-row and perhaps confirmation as a super team of the seventies – to really appreciate just how much a magnificent Kerry gained with their historic victory in yesterday's All-Ireland senior football final at Croke Park. It was the end of an era, maybe, but just as possible the beginning of a new one, heralded by a devastating display of football splendour from the new champions. The myth of Dublin's invincibility was shattered once and for all and in such a manner as to mirror the fanatical determination of the Kerry players to make victory possible, and the enormous contribution of trainer-coach Mick O'Dwyer which enabled them to achieve it.

Jim O'Sullivan was right; it did herald a new era for Kerry football and led to a history-equalling four-in-a-row All-Ireland championship success.

After the All-Ireland finals of 1975 and 1976 and the semi-final of 1977, we played Dublin in the early stages of the National League. Dublin won in Croke Park in 1975 and 1977 and we won in Tralee in 1976. For Dublin, the 1978 league match was seen as a crunch game. It was played in an acrimonious spirit; in the first half I was struck by a Dublin forward after fielding a high ball and I lost two teeth as a result. I should have come off but, foolishly, insisted on staying on. Johnny Geraghty, who was goalkeeper in the great Galway three-in-a-row team, was the referee on the day and he immediately put the Dublin forward off.

Years later I met him on holidays in the Canaries and when I asked him if he was still refereeing inter-county games, he replied that he never got a match after the putting off incident in the Dublin v Kerry league game in 1978. He had forgotten that I was the injured party but I was able to show him the plate with the two false teeth as confirmation of the injury. The injury initially led to a lot of discomfort, especially in cold weather. I had to go for two operations afterwards, in July of 1980 and October of 1982, to get my teeth and upper cheekbone right. Thanks to Cork dental surgeon Liam Murphy, who is married to Listowel girl, Gráinne Keane Stack, the operations were successful.

After the Dublin match we played Kildare and Laois in the National League in Tralee. We were very much on top of our game at this stage and we beat Kildare by 7-8 to 0-7. Kildare had some outstanding footballers in their team at that time, including All Star goalkeeper for 1978, Ollie Crinnigan. In the next league game of 1978, we beat Laois by 6-11 to no score, despite the very wet conditions. It was a remarkable achievement by our defence to hold Laois scoreless for 60 minutes, considering that they had players of the calibre of Robbie Millar, Eamonn Whelan, John Costelloe, and Tom Prendergast. We defeated Galway in the final league match of 1978 in Killarney.

So ended 1978, which was a very rewarding year for me in my football career. I had won back my place on the Kerry team, contributed to an historic All-Ireland final victory over Dublin, and won the County Championship for the first time in the history of Feale Rangers, beating the champions, Shannon Rangers, in the semi-final and Mid Kerry in the final.

I was now part of a Kerry team that was at its peak, both mentally and physically, and one that was not going to get carried away by its success as had happened in 1975.

1979

WE faced 1979 with considerable confidence. As usual, we did no collective training for the National League and Roscommon beat us in the semi-final by a point. This was their third victory over Kerry in six months; they had beaten us in the Ceann Áras Tournament in Dr. Hyde Park in Roscommon the previous October and they also beat Kerry in the All-Ireland U21 final on the same day. After that league defeat we got down to serious training and we sent out a clear warning to the country that we were in great physical shape and highly motivated with a runaway victory over Galway in the Dr. Paddy Mahon/Denis Moran Tournament game at the Clahane club grounds in Limerick in June. We won the game by 21 points (5-16 to 1-7) when our forwards just ripped the Galway defence apart.

Following the match against Galway, we played Clare in the first round of the Munster Championship in Miltown Malbay in what became known as the 'Miltown Malbay Massacre'. We beat Clare by 9-21 to 1-9. This was vintage Kerry forward play; Pat Spillane scored 3-1, Ger Power 2-3 and Eoin Liston 2-2. There was no let-up right up to the final whistle. Our forwards just kept piling on the scores and trying different moves. I remember when a Kerry defender dropped the ball late in the game to present a Clare forward with an easy goal, he was rounded on by the other defenders.

The question is often asked, 'Why give such a hiding to Clare?' It didn't matter who it was, the forwards just enjoyed hitting as many scores as possible and stringing moves together. The extraordinary thing about the Clare performance that day was the fact that they scored more than any other team against us in the 1979 campaign. I remember listening to a Clare mentor on Des Cahill's sports programme a few years ago and he mentioned that Seánie Moloney gave me a roasting in that match. Seánie did get four points but I was not marking him at any stage during the game; I was marking Paddy O'Shea that day and then his replacement, Anthony Moloney.

135

Myself and David Hickey in the 1979 All-Ireland football final.

(Courtesy of The Kerryman, www.kerryman.ie)

In the Munster final in Killarney we beat Cork easily by 2-14 to 2-4. I was marking Christy Kearney on that occasion. Jimmy Barry-Murphy played in the other corner and scored a spectacular goal, as well as setting up the other Cork goal for Dinny Allen. Cork missed two penalties, one put over the bar by John Courtney and the other one saved by Charlie Nelligan from Dinny Allen. Ger Power was Kerry's Man of the Match, scoring 2-4 from play.

The semi-final against Monaghan was described by *The Kerryman* as a 'Kerry Blitzkrieg'. Kerry emerged easy winners – 5-15 to 0-7 – and, again, the Kerry forwards ran rings around the Monaghan defence and could have scored another five goals but for the very fine goalkeeping of Paddy Lindon.

We were now in another All-Ireland final against Dublin and we approached the game with a high degree of confidence. The game, though not great, will enter the history books for a number of reasons. It was the 25th All-Ireland final victory for Kerry, now established as the team of the '70s, and Mikey Sheehy equalled the existing record of Jimmy Keaveney for the highest individual score in an All-Ireland final, with two goals and six points. The game will also be remembered for the spectacular catch by Seán Walsh over Brian Mullins. It was more like an Australian Rules mark. Seán had a tremendous leap from a standing position and he could also hold himself momentarily in the air, which gave him a great advantage over opponents.

It was also a special day for Feale Rangers as Tim Kennelly brought the Sam Maguire Cup back to Listowel for the first time. I would also consider it to be my best All-Ireland final. I was on the ball more often and, for the fourth All-Ireland in a row, kept my immediate opponent scoreless. 1979 was the pinnacle of that Kerry team's achievements. No team could live with us in that year's championship; we had perfected our game and had brought to it a new level of skill, understanding and team cohesion.

1979 was the last year I played against that great Dublin team in championship football. Offaly took over in Leinster from 1980 to 1982. In all, I played against Dublin in five championship matches, including four All-Ireland finals and a semi-final, winning three and losing two. I also played against them in seven National League games and in at least six challenge matches.

Arising from these numerous encounters, players from both teams got to know one another very well, resulting in many cases in enduring friendships.

During this period, I must have marked John McCarthy on at least ten occasions. We became great friends and often chatted with each other before and during matches.

Despite their intense clashes on the pitch, the late Tim Kennelly and Tony Hanahoe developed a lasting friendship. When the Listowel Emmets organised a special tribute to Tim in 2003, Tony pulled out of a commitment to attend the Breeders' Cup in the US to join Tim as his special guest that night. When Tim passed away in December 2005, Tony, Jimmy Keaveney and a number of their team-mates attended his funeral in Listowel.

Since the time Bernard Brogan worked in Tarbert in 1976 we have remained close friends. I also meet up occasionally with former college-mate Brian Mullins and with Tony Hanahoe. Jimmy Keaveney continues to make his annual visit to the Listowel Races.

I always enjoy meeting various members of that distinguished team. They were a tremendous group of players who did much to revive interest in Gaelic football in Dublin and throughout the country.

1980

WHEN Feale Rangers won the County Championship in 1978, Tim Kennelly and I had tossed for captaincy of the Kerry team for 1979. He won the toss and so we agreed he would be captain for the championship and I for the league. My stint as captain was less successful as we lost to Cork in the final of the league by a point in May of 1980. Not having played particularly well, I was really pushing myself in training the following Tuesday evening in Killarney when I pulled my thigh muscle (*rectus femoris*) which kept me out of the game for a number of weeks. Regrettably, I made the mistake of coming back to training too soon.

During my first training session after the injury, Micko asked me to take Tim Kennelly on my back across the field, which I did comfortably. When he asked how the injury felt, I responded positively whereupon he instructed me to carry Tim back again. The muscle couldn't take the pressure and I did some serious damage to it. I worked very hard on the injury for a number of weeks and got excellent treatment from Claire Edwards, who worked as a physiotherapist in the Hotel Europe in Killarney at the time. It came right

The defeated Kerry team in the 1980 league final.
Front row left to right: D. Moran, S. Walsh, P. Ó Sé, myself, P. Lynch, T. Doyle, J. Egan.
Back row left to right: J. O'Shea, P. Spillane, P. O'Mahoney, E. Liston, J. O'Keeffe, T. Kennelly, G. Power, M. Spillane.

the Sunday before the Munster final but it was too late and I was not selected for the match against Cork.

Kerry got a bye that year into the Munster final, which they won rather easily by 3-13 to 0-12. Although I had made a full recovery by the All-Ireland semi-final against Offaly and was playing very well in training, I was not selected on the starting 15. When the team was announced, I was contacted by John Barry, sports reporter with *The Kerryman*, for a comment. I was quoted by him as saying 'It doesn't matter how I feel because nobody cares – there is just no sympathy in Kerry football'. I suppose that's what makes Kerry football; tough decisions have to be made by selectors at times and the team management is prepared to make them.

For the semi-final against Offaly I was resigned to spending the game on the bench. I was settling down for a relaxing 70 minutes in the dugout when Seán Walsh became concussed minutes after the start, following a clash with Seán Lowry. Crucially for me, Micko immediately sprung me from the bench and, overruling another selector's preference, handed me the slip of paper for the referee. In what turned out to be a high-scoring game, Kerry won by 4-15 to Offaly's 4-10. Matt Connor scored 2-9 and Gerry O'Carroll 2-1 for Offaly.

Although I played reasonably well on Johnnie Mooney in that game, I wasn't sure that I would be retained on the team for the final against Roscommon. The final trial did not work out too well for me: before it started I said to John Egan, whom I was marking, that I really needed a good game if I were to impress the selectors. He just smiled at me. However, he proceeded to make life very difficult for me and scored 1-3, which he had never done previously in any trial match or training session. I left Killarney that Sunday evening thinking that I had no chance of making the team.

Feale Rangers were playing a challenge game in Tarbert so I went to see it. I felt utterly dejected and was looking for an excuse to drown my sorrows after the game. My gloom, however, was quickly dispelled when I got home and received confirmation from John O'Keeffe that I was selected on the team for the final. I remember when I went into John B. Keane's pub later, the whole bar erupted. It was as if we had won the final. The selectors replaced Ger O'Keeffe and Mick Spillane with Paudie Lynch and myself. It was a courageous decision but tough on the two lads, although Ger would get back on when Eoin Liston had to cry off due to appendicitis. Mick Spillane was a tremendous corner-back and certainly had reason to feel peeved having done an excellent marking job on Jimmy Barry-Murphy in the Munster final that year.

1980 was another milestone in my football career. Having been dropped for the Munster final and not been selected on the team to play Offaly in the semi-final, I thought that my inter-county career had come to an end but, thanks to Micko and his selectors, I got the green light to play in the final against Roscommon.

The selectors were vindicated, as both Paudie and I acquitted ourselves very well, being ideally suited to the physical game that Roscommon decided to play. The loss, however, of Eoin Liston and the early departure of Ger Power upset our forward play. At this stage, the entire team depended very much on Bomber and without him we were seriously struggling up front.

At the Grand Hotel, Malahide, on the morning of the 1980 All-Ireland final. Left to right: Frank King, Páidí Ó Sé, Ger Power, myself, Mick O'Dwyer, Johnny Mulvihill, Paudie Lynch, Ogie Moran, John O'Keeffe.

Roscommon went into the game with a lot of confidence; they had beaten Kerry on three occasions in 1978/79 – in the Ceann Áras Tournament, the All-Ireland U21 Championship in 1978, and the National League semi-final in 1979. These victories boosted Roscommon's morale going into the All-Ireland final in 1980. They had trained twice daily for three weeks before the match and had great leaders in Dermot Earley and Pat Lindsey, as well as a very capable manager in Tom Heneghan. Their goalkeeper, Gay Sheerin, was one of the best in the country at the time. They had an excellent full-back line in Harry Keegan, Pat Lindsay and Gerry Connellan. Keegan and Lindsey were traditional style defenders, while Connellan was very fast and skilful.

Their half-back line was equally as effective, with Gerry Fitzmaurice, Tom Donnellan (with whom I went to college for four years and who was an excellent footballer) and Danny Murray. They conceded very little due to the tight marking of their disciplined defence and, coupled by the absence of Eoin Liston, we registered a lower score (1-9) than in any of our All-Ireland final victories.

Roscommon got a dream start and had the ball in the Kerry net after only 35 seconds. Dermot Earley intercepted a Kerry free and sent a good ball to the full-forward, Tony McManus, who slipped it to an unmarked John O'Connor, who duly palmed the ball past Charlie Nelligan. They followed this score with a Seamus Hayden point in the third minute and a John O'Gara point from fifty yards in the 11th minute. We had yet to score; points by Mikey Sheehy and Ger Power kept us in the game but the defining moment came in the 20th minute. Tom Donnellan kicked a free straight into the hands of Tommy Doyle who passed it to Pat Spillane, who went on one of his penetrating solo runs through the middle. He drew Mikey Sheehy's marker and slipped the ball to an unmarked Sheehy in front of goal. Mikey did not waste these opportunities and flicked the ball to the net: we were level and back in the game.

At half time the score stood at 1-3 each. The second half was dour and tight-marking. Roscommon missed several scoring chances, including a 21 yard and 35 yard free, while Charlie Nelligan made a great save from John O'Connor, and Páidí Ó Sé made a similar save from Aidan Dooley when goals were certainly on. In the end, we considered ourselves lucky to win by just three points, 1-9 to 1-6. The swirling wind and the heavy underfoot conditions certainly didn't help our style of play and were not conducive to free-flowing football. The loss of Eoin Liston was a hammer-blow for Kerry as he would have won more possession and created more scoring opportunities for his fellow forwards.

After the game, Roscommon's alleged strong-arm tactics came in for a lot of criticism. Regardless of the tactics they used that day, they were a very good side and deserved to win an All-Ireland. Hard and physical though that game may have been, I didn't witness any dangerous tackles or off the ball incidents. Presumably, some of our forwards came in for close attention from the Roscommon backs but, basically, no different to what they'd receive had they been playing Cork or Dublin. Roscommon obviously went out to rattle Kerry. They were programmed to play a tight-marking game and to limit the space available to the Kerry forwards; as a result, they weren't able to capitalise on their bright start. We were there for the taking but Roscommon missed some easy scoring opportunities. Strictly speaking, this should have been their day and, somehow, they haven't played in an All-Ireland senior football final since.

Myself and Seán Walsh going in to tackle Dermot Earley of Roscommon.

Shadowing Eamon MacManus of Roscommon in the 1980 All-Ireland final.

143

The following Sunday, Feale Rangers beat Austin Stacks in the county senior final and, as the county champions in Kerry nominate the captain for the following year's championship, I was automatically captain for 1981. Fortunately, I was at an age when it meant a lot to me and I was very conscious of the responsibilities that went with it, especially when the team was going for four All-Irelands in a row.

After the 1980 All-Ireland, we embarked on another National League campaign. One game that stands out in my mind from that campaign was the game played at Davitt Park in Lurgan on 16 November against Armagh. It was at the height of the H-Block protest and feelings were very strong amongst the nationalist community in Northern Ireland, especially in Armagh. We were advised that a show of solidarity with the hunger strikers would take place on the pitch before the ball was thrown in. There was a chilling silence as people with black flags paraded around the field, then the referee commenced the game and Armagh emerged winners after a hard-fought match.

1981

MICKO began 1981 with a get-together in Ballybunion in early January. We had a training session and then a team meeting in the Cliff House Hotel in Ballybunion. The idea of going on a holiday to the Canaries at the end of the year was suggested. However, I recommended that we should consider doing a tour of Australia and repeat what the Kerry team had done in 1970 and the Meath team in 1967. I had always been interested in Australian Rules football and I felt that our team had the fitness levels, the physical strength and the skill to adapt to the game if given the opportunity.

Micko and others agreed and the stage was set. Páidí Ó Sé suggested that we invite Tommy McCarthy to be chairman of the fundraising committee. Tommy proved to be a brilliant choice and he came up with a few simple but effective money-spinning ideas, including the production of a special portrait of the team and a Mayor of Kerry competition. Micko suggested that we would play a series of challenge matches in Ulster in order to avail of the strong exchange rate between sterling and the punt. A players committee was set up to organise the tour but there was reluctance, for some reason, to involve the officers of the Kerry County Board. Tom McCarthy was appointed chairman, Ogie Moran and I became joint secretaries, while Seán Walsh and Liam Higgins were joint treasurers.

The two weekends in Ulster were rather demanding; we played six matches in all, starting on Friday evening and finishing with a midday match on Sunday. We played Monaghan, Down, Antrim, Tyrone, Donegal and Louth. In the Tyrone match in Carrig Mhór, I had the experience of marking Mickey Harte who was a very nifty attacker and very quick. We were given a great reception in Carrig Mhór where there was a carnival atmosphere, with the village pubs staying open into the small hours.

We were very well-received everywhere we played and, overall, it was a worthwhile exercise. Apart from the gate receipts which we received for the Australian visit, the matches gave Micko a chance to give players a run out. The fact that we were going to Australia was a great motivating factor for the team and we felt we had to go as All-Ireland champions. The trip was the constant topic of conversation running through our training sessions that summer, especially during our post-training meals at the Park Place Hotel in Killarney. Most of the players felt that the trip should be a reward for winning the four-in-a-row rather than the three-in-a-row we had achieved the previous year.

GALWAY beat us in the semi-final of the National League in Ennis in April. I missed the match as I was in New York at that time. We played Offaly in a challenge game to mark the opening of the Listowel sportsfield in May. Although we won rather easily, Offaly showed a lot of flair and confidence and some of their new players, like Pádraig Dunne, were impressive. We destroyed Clare by 4-17 to 0-6 points in the first round of the Munster Championship on 28 June. It was simply a mis-match, despite the fact that Clare had some really good footballers on their team at that time.

On 19 July in Killarney we beat Cork by 1-11 to 0-3 in the Munster final. Cork, despite having forwards like Dinny Allen and Declan Barron on their team, could only manage one point from play. Although it was a poor game, played in sweltering heat and a strong breeze, the fact that our defence held the Cork forward line to just one point from play and conceded so few frees, said a lot for our defensive strategy. Plainly speaking, it wasn't so much about Cork not being able to score as a demonstration of Kerry's highly developed system of collective, defensive play that other teams found very difficult to break down.

Two things come to mind from that game; one being the confusion with the hand pass. There was total misunderstanding when referee Paddy Collins called up players from both sides for the improper use of it. It's extraordinary that similar confusion would again surface at the start of the 2010 championship. You'd expect that, by then, the correct striking action employed in a hand pass would have been resolved. The other vivid memory I have is of an incident in which Billy Morgan and Eoin Liston clashed while competing for a 50/50 ball. Billy was concussed and suffered a broken collar bone. He was a courageous goalkeeper and fearless when it came to competing for possession around the square. Bomber was in full flight when he collided with a totally committed goalkeeper as they arrived at the ball simultaneously. Thankfully, Billy made a full recovery.

The All-Ireland semi-final in 1981 against Mayo was one of the best displays of football that we gave in the four-in-a-row campaign. In the first half, Mayo were more than a match for us and we did well to lead by 2-7 to 1-6 at half time. Willie Joe Padden gave one of the finest exhibitions of high fielding that I have ever witnessed in Croke Park. In the second half, Mayo failed to score while our forwards scored 12 points. Eoin Liston gave one of his greatest displays ever in Croke Park in the second half and set up most of the scores. The final score was Kerry 2-19, Mayo 1-6.

If I were to recommend a video to demonstrate effective team play and attacking football, I would choose the second half of that match. From a Kerry perspective, it had everything. The headline in the Mitchell Cogley corner in the *Irish Independent* on the following Tuesday was 'Kerry Were Just Sheer Perfection'. Mitchell went on to write:

> The pessimists say such a one-sided result must be bad for the game, a massive discouragement to all challengers; the alternative view, to which I subscribe, is that the type of game played by Kerry on Sunday sets standards to which everybody should aim in the search for sheer perfection and surely that was what this Kerry team attained on Sunday. There just wasn't a single

player on the team who was less than brilliant in his individual chores and when this is combined into the highest degree of team work all through the field, the net result is quite simply an unbeatable combination.

Mayo endeavoured all through to play constructive football and it was certainly no disgrace to find themselves outclassed in this respect by what must rate as one of the greatest teams the game has known. At one level, the Kerry team on Sunday reminded me of the great Down team of 1960–1961, only twice as fast, and at another level, I saw the positional play and expert handling of the celebrated Harlem Globetrotters basketball squad and a Welsh rugby team with their tails up and running everything. It was all quite irresistible, and an absolute treat to watch. This was perfection.

These are comments, not by a Kerryman, but by a respected and unbiased journalist, and they just about sum up the level of excellence we had attained as a team since our defeat of Dublin in 1978.

Offaly defeated a highly fancied Down team in the other semi-final by 0-12 to 0-6. We were hoping that Down would win because it would have given us an added incentive as Kerry had never beaten Down in an All-Ireland final. (In fact, Kerry have never beaten Down in championship football, losing to them in the 1960 and 1968 All-Ireland finals, in the 1990 All-Ireland semi-final, and the 2010 All-Ireland quarter-final).

Following Offaly's victory, the stage was set for a re-match of the 1980 All-Ireland semi-final which had produced such a high-scoring and exciting game. Offaly had every reason to feel confident coming into the match; they had matured from the previous year and obviously learned from that experience. Furthermore, they had added players of the calibre of Liam O'Connor, Pádraig Dunne, Mick Fitzgerald, Brendan Lowry, and Charlie Conroy to their team, giving them more strength and balance.

Their manager, Eugene McGee, knew absolutely everything that was to be known about the Kerry team. He had shared a flat with John O'Keeffe and Ger Power in Dublin in the early '70s and Kerry players like Ogie Moran, Jackie and Barry Walsh were on his UCD winning teams. The managers of other counties knew our strengths but McGee knew more about our weaknesses than anyone else.

Myself and referee Paddy Collins with Offaly captain, Richie Connor, taking the toss before the match.

Our preparation for the 1981 final against Offaly was excellent and Tim Kennelly, who had not played in the Munster Championship or started in the All-Ireland semi-final, was back to his best and in the starting line-up. However, we did suffer one major setback which could have cost us the four-in-a-row. On the Sunday after the Mayo match, Pat Spillane damaged his knee in an Intermediate County Championship match while playing for Templenoe against Kenmare. In the pre-All-Ireland trial match in Killarney he suffered further damage to the injured knee. As a result, he was not included in the starting line-up on All-Ireland day, having undergone a fitness test on the morning of the match.

Mikey Sheehy also suffered an injury three weeks before the All-Ireland final in a County Championship game with his club, Austin Stacks. As a result he was unable to take part in most of the training programme leading up to

148

Leading the parade before the 1981 All-Ireland final.
From front to back: myself, Charlie Nelligan, John O'Keeffe, Paudie Lynch, Páidí Ó Sé, Tim Kennelly, Mick Spillane,
Jack O'Shea, Seán Walsh, Ger Power, Tommy Doyle, Mike Sheehy, Eoin Liston, John Egan.
(Missing from the photo is Ogie Moran who was receiving pre-match physio.)

the match and had to get two pain-killing injections before the game and a further one at half time in order to stay on the field.

Spillane was certainly a loss to the overall team cohesion and the forwards had to adjust to playing without him in a competitive match situation. Tommy Doyle, who replaced him at very short notice, had a very good game, scoring an important point in the first half. In the course of his pre-match talk on the beach in Malahide the evening before the game, Micko, as far as I can recall, presented us with two scenarios: we had an opportunity to equal the historic achievement of the great Kerry team of 1929–32 or we would travel to Australia as the team who lost the All-Ireland. If he harboured any fears that the absence of Spillane left us vulnerable, he didn't show it, and exuded no less confidence going into the game than he always did.

Luckily for us, Offaly had injury problems too. Tomás Connor, their outstanding player against Down in the semi-final, had a knee injury, and their star forward, Johnny Mooney, was unable to play because of a shoulder injury. He was one of the most difficult opponents I marked at that time. A very good fielder of the ball and very skilful, he would prove his worth in the All-Ireland in 1982.

On the day of the match there was a gusty, swirling wind in Croke Park and because of heavy rainfall before the start of the game underfoot conditions were very poor. After five minutes Offaly were two points up while it took ten minutes for us to get our first score – a point by Ogie Moran. Shortly before half time, Brendan Lowry, whom I was marking, scored a point. A fellow Kerry defender called for the ball so I hesitated; Lowry won it and duly put it over the bar. This was the only point I conceded in six All-Ireland finals, an achievement I take some pride in as a recognised tight man-marker. At half time the score stood at five points apiece.

We had the wind to our backs in the second half and shortly after the resumption Gerry Carroll hit the crossbar. Although I was not his marker, I saw the impending danger. I got a hand in on Gerry as he was about to kick the ball and I just may have put him off sufficiently to ensure that he didn't hit the target; a goal at that stage could have made life very difficult for us. After this close call, we scored four points without reply from Offaly, which put us into a fairly comfortable lead heading into the final quarter.

There was always a danger that Matt Connor or Gerry Carroll would hit us for a few goals like they did the previous year, but our defence held firm and focused. In the closing stages, I got possession of a ball that was put in over the top by Liam Currans and appeared to be going wide. Micko always warned us that the ball is never dead until the referee blows the whistle.

Although I was facing the end line, I spotted Tim Kennelly over my shoulder and delivered a 30 yard pass to him which he kicked up field to Tommy Doyle. Doyle passed it to John Egan who played a one two with Eoin Liston and then punted the ball to Mikey Sheehy; Sheehy then hand passed it to Jack O'Shea who hit an unstoppable shot into the roof of the net for the only goal of the game. As Micheál Ó Hehir said in his commentary during the course of the passing movement, 'They are really rolling now'.

Me clearing the ball to Tim Kennelly under pressure from Brendan Lowry.

I was now trying to remember my acceptance speech which I had rehearsed over the previous week after having acquired some good Irish phraseology from my old Irish teacher, Johnny O'Flaherty, and good coaching from Bryan McMahon who met me on the street one day before the match and insisted that I go into his house to discuss what I was going to say. 'Remember,' he said, 'that you are speaking to Kerry people all over the world next Sunday and don't forget to remind them that the team will be going to the USA and the Southern Cross in a few weeks.'

I can still remember the early part of my speech:

Is stairúil an ócáid í seo, mar is í seo an chéad uair ón mbliain 1932 i leith a bhuaigh contae ar bith Craobh na h-Éireann ceithre bhliain as a chéile. Na Ciarraígh a dhein an uair deireanach é agus is mór an onóir domsa go

After receiving the Sam Maguire Cup,
with Garret FitzGerald in the background.

(Courtesy of The Kerryman, www.kerryman.ie)

(Courtesy of Kerry's Eye, www.kerryseye.com)

Myself and Mick O'Dwyer leading the parade in Killarney with the Sam Maguire Cup.

pearsanta agus bród nach beag a bheith im chaptaen ar fhoireann eile ón ríocht a bhfuil an gaisce stáirúil céanna bainte amach acu arís anseo inniu. Ní haon rud beag é sin. Táim fíor bhuíoch de gach éinne a chabhraigh liom imbliana, go mór mhór ár bhfoireann bainistíochta, Bord Peile Chiarraí agus sibhse, lucht tacaíochta Chiarraí. Go raibh míle maith agaibh go leir.

Our homecoming to Kerry with the four-in-a-row in the bag was memorable. Despite the negative publicity about the standard of play in the match, thousands turned up in Killarney to welcome us. Dick Hogan, writing for *The Irish Times*, described the homecoming as follows:

Written clearly on every face was elation, joy and a very full sense of pride. If the men, women and children who travelled to Killarney had read in yesterday's newspapers the outpourings about poor football it did not put

Addressing supporters in front of the Ashe Memorial Hall in Denny Street, Tralee.

them off one bit. After all, Mick O'Dwyer is not on record as having told his charges to entertain the crowds with flowing and stylish play, all he had asked them to do was to win the four-in-a-row and now they'd done it. Last night, that was enough for the thousands who lined the Killarney streets. During the long nights to come there will be plenty of time for argument as to which performance of the four-in-a-row was best. No doubt, one point will remain outside the realm of dispute – that this Kerry team is the greatest of all time, perhaps, even the greatest ever Gaelic football team.

Bringing back the Sam Maguire Cup to Finuge Cross was memorable for me. As a youngster this had been my Croke Park, where I played with my friends in the late 1950s and early 1960s (there were very few cars on the roads then), re-enacting many a Kerry footballing victory there. Apart from a large presence from among my team-mates, accompanied by Mick O'Dwyer, I was

Boyhood friends: Myself, Timmy O'Sullivan, Liam Hayes, John Buckley and John Lyons (in the background) celebrating the arrival of the Sam Maguire in Finuge.

Seán Lowry touching the Sam Maguire Cup with Tom Sullivan (RIP) smiling in the background.

At Balloonagh school in Tralee with the cup.

delighted that Seán and Brendan Lowry, as well as Gerry Carroll, showed up. Despite losing, they were magnanimous enough to come all the way to Finuge to join in the celebrations. Seán made a very humorous speech ending with very prophetic words as he eyed the Sam Maguire, 'It will be in Offaly next year'. For their gesture in coming to Finuge I didn't begrudge Offaly beating us in the All-Ireland of 1982.

It was really special for the young and old of the village having the Sam Maguire at the crossroads and it would be talked about for a long time afterwards. Hopefully, some future member of a Finuge team will repeat the feat. Paul Galvin came very close in 2008, when Kerry lost by two points to Tyrone in the All-Ireland final. He still has a few years left in his inter-county career and may get an opportunity again.

157

WITH the All-Ireland in the bag, the focus was now on the Australian tour. As captain, I was very much involved in the organisation of the trip. There was an issue about taking two players on the tour – Pat Sheehan and Tom Spillane – who were brought into the squad during the summer. When I insisted that they be part of the travelling party I had the full support of Micko and they were included. It would have been most unfair otherwise, considering their contribution. Thanks to the fundraising initiatives of Tom McCarthy and Micko, each player received £1,800 in pocket money for the trip and all flights and hotels were paid for. We were presented with blazers and slacks by Denis Moran's of Limerick and Tralee; the players couldn't have asked for more.

The tour departure date was 9 October 1981. As our take-off at Shannon was delayed due to high winds, most of the team went to Dirty Nelly's pub in Bunratty to pass the time. When we eventually set off for New York, the touring party was in high spirits. We played a game against Galway in New York on our way to Australia but, because of the celebrations in Shannon and later when we arrived in New York, they hammered us. We then set off for Australia via San Francisco and Hawaii and arrived in Melbourne on 15 October. We were greeted by a few Kerry supporters at the airport, prompting someone to say that our arrival was the best kept secret in Melbourne. One person in particular whom I remember being there was Sr. Brendan Molyneaux from Woodford, Listowel, who had been in Australia for over 50 years at that stage and who only passed away a few years ago. She was an aunt of the County Board secretary, Andy Molyneaux, who had died suddenly that summer of a heart attack and who, no doubt, would otherwise have been with us on that trip. Her sister was married to my uncle, Tom, making for a family connection.

As captain of the team I had to take prompt action when we booked into our first hotel in Melbourne. There was a lot of maintenance work going on there, and tradesmen were even carrying out repairs in a few of the rooms. I raised the matter with the late Joe Walsh, the tour organiser, and without further ado he booked us into the Old Melbourne, one of the finest hotels in Melbourne. Thanks to Joe's quick response, everyone was happy with the new arrangements, making our stay in the city a truly memorable one.

At a fundraising event in Castleisland before the Australian tour. Front row left to right: Billy Browne, Norma Browne, myself, Ogie Moran. Middle row left to right: Mick O'Dwyer, Tom McCarthy, Páidí Ó Sé. Back row left to right: Tom Spillane, Ger Lynch, Pat Spillane, Bernard O'Sullivan.

While we were there we played a local Irish selection in an exhibition game. A large number of Irish people turned up at Keys Borough, the GAA grounds outside the city, and that evening became a great social occasion. We also went to a local Australian Rules club for a coaching session in Aussie Rules. The coaches there were most impressed with our handling and kicking of the Australian Rules ball.

From Melbourne we flew to Adelaide where we played a South Australian Aussie Rules selection in Gaelic football, under lights, at the Norwood Oval, using the round ball in the first half and the oval in the second. The Australians were coached by Daryl Hicks, a well-known Aussie Rules coach at that time. We won the game easily enough and adapted very well to the oval ball in the second half. I was marking John 'The Rat' Platten who figured

Left to right: Pat Spillane, Bernard O'Sullivan, Páidí Ó Sé and myself at Shannon Airport on our return from the tour.

very prominently afterwards in the Compromise Rules series. In 2003, Platten was inducted into the Australian Football Hall of Fame for his contribution to Australian football.

The spectators enjoyed the game, and their positive response afterwards convinced me that there was scope for a compromise game between both codes. Hicks was very impressed with our level of fitness and skill and was of the opinion that a number of our team could make the transition to Aussie Rules in a very short period of time. While in Adelaide, most of the team went to the Barossa Valley where they enjoyed a visit to the vineyards – a truly worthwhile experience.

Our next port of call was Perth where we played a Western Australian Aussie Rules selection, again in Gaelic football, at the Subiaco Oval, which we won rather easily in hot and humid conditions. Again we showed that we could match the Australians for fitness. From Perth we travelled across Australia to Sydney where we played a local Irish selection in Gaelic football. In Sydney I met that great Kerryman, Kerry Murphy from Knocknagoshel, to whom I gave one of my All-Ireland winning jerseys, which he wore proudly in many St Patrick's Day parades afterwards.

After a most enjoyable tour of Australia we left Sydney for Hawaii where we spent five days at the Waikiki Beach Hotel and had a wonderful time. For those of us who had some previous experience of surfing it was exhilarating. We enjoyed five days of sunshine and water sports, with memorable parties every night; during the day we had great sessions in the Davy Jones Locker Bar on the beach. Most of the travelling party regretted leaving Hawaii which everyone just loved. We then stopped off in San Francisco for a few days and played a local selection there before flying home.

Tired and weary though we were when we arrived back in Shannon on 10 November, we were all agreed that it had been the trip of a lifetime. Everywhere we went in Australia and the US we were very well received by the Irish diaspora, especially by Kerry people. It was a great honour to have captained Kerry to win four-in-a-row, but it was also a special privilege to be the team's spokesman on such a memorable tour.

THERE have been times since when I have felt that, from a football perspective, the tour was a lost opportunity. We should have played the Australians under their own rules for some part of the two matches in Adelaide and Perth. The Australian coaches and Aussie Rules players were very impressed with our skill and fitness levels and suggested that we could adapt very easily. Nonetheless, it's possible that the interest generated from our trip Down Under in some way influenced president Paddy Buggy and general secretary Liam Mulvihill to renew links with the Australian Football League.

When I returned to Ireland I did a few interviews on RTÉ television and with the *Irish Independent*, urging the GAA to look at the possibility of forging closer links with the AFL. I had originally developed an interest in Aussie Rules following a game Kerry played against an Australian football touring team in Páirc Uí Chaoimh in late October 1978. In that game, which we won by 3-9 to 0-16, the Australians demonstrated their magnificent fielding and hand passing skills. The report of the game by John Joe Brosnan in the 3 November edition of *The Kerryman* was most complimentary of the Australians' performance:

> The game provided some lessons that provoked plenty of discussion afterwards. The magnificent fielding of the Australians highlighted the fact that this wonderful art has been all but lost in Gaelic football due to the emphasis in recent years on the passing game rather than on the high kick forward. The ability of the visitors to punch the ball at lightning speed emphasised how unnecessary the 'throw' is in our Gaelic game. It has greatly damaged the game as a spectacle and indeed there is a rising public clamour for its discontinuation. The Australians were just about the fittest bunch of men I have ever seen on a playing field, and their speed and expert positioning was a delight to behold.

In the summer of 1982 Paddy Buggy set up a committee under the chairmanship of Gerry Fagan of Armagh to draw up a report on the feasibility of establishing competitive links on an international level with the AFL. He invited me to join the committee that included Pat O'Neill (Meath), Frank Murphy (Cork), Dan Hanley (Dublin), and referee John Moloney (Tipperary).

When the late John Moloney and I were drawing up the Compromise Rules for our report, we recommended the full Australian tackle because the Gaelic tackle is so hard to define and, as we predicted, would lead to a lot of confusion for the Aussie Rules players. Initially, the use of the Gaelic tackle almost scuppered the series and could have led to serious injury.

We also included the Aussie Rules mark if you fielded a ball cleanly. However, the Irish players did not realise that you had to retreat from the spot where you landed on the ground to take your free kick. This led to a lot of unnecessary argy-bargy with the Aussie Rules players, as they stood on the spot of the mark and some of the Irish attempted to kick from on or beyond the mark. Having completed our report, we were never again consulted, which was regrettable. We should have been asked to explain the

Compromise Rules to both sides, and this may have prevented some of the confusion that existed in the early years of the series.

Over the years since 1984 the series has produced some exciting games and great individual performances. However, I feel that the full potential of the Compromise Rules was never realised and it seems that the future of the series is uncertain. This is reflected in the difficulty in finding players who want to play after their football season has finished. It appears that, as both the AFL and GAA competitions become more and more professional and the demands on the players become greater, fewer seem to want to play in the International Series.

It would also seem that playing in the International Series is not as prestigious as was previously the case. AFL players get six weeks off after their season and those who are selected to participate in the Series find that their preparation for the following season is put back significantly. Some AFL clubs, apparently, don't encourage their top players to make themselves available for the Series in case it would interrupt their 'building phase' for the coming season. The same pressure would seem to be on some of the top Gaelic players from the leading counties. Clearly, over the years, not all of our leading GAA players were committed to the Series.

I think, at this stage, the main question that needs to be addressed is what status the Series should hold for both codes. Should it be just exhibition football or something more important and competitive? Should winning be the main consideration, or should skill and athleticism be encouraged by rewarding players for the most spectacular mark or score?

Both codes have influenced each other and have developed along the same lines since the Compromise Rules were introduced. Both are much more concerned with maintaining possession and getting numbers behind the ball. Even the Australians are not using the long ball to the same extent anymore. Both games are now characterised by quick hand movements to running players, who can then deliver an accurate pass into the attacking zone to a team-mate. A predominant feature of both codes now is for players to keep possession and not kick the ball forward until an opportunity presents itself.

With the speed of both games increasing significantly over the past 10 years, the use of the interchange in AFL has become very much part of their game. I read a statistic recently in an Australian Rules magazine that in 2003 there was an average of 22 interchanges per match; this has now increased to 116 per game. It is probably only a matter of time before this type of rotation will come into Gaelic football. I also notice that in AFL games, spare footballs are kept behind the goals, as they are in GAA matches, in order to keep the game moving.

It appears to me that the Australian game has been more influenced by the International Series than Gaelic football, judging by the way their game has evolved. The Series has influenced both codes and also has given the opportunity to many GAA players to play for their country, which I know Northern Ireland players, in particular, value. Having been involved in drawing up the initial Compromise Rules with John Moloney, which have not changed to any great extent since, I still retain a special interest in the Series and, if it continues, would be delighted to be involved with it in some way in the future.

WHEN we returned from Australia in November 1981, we had little time to recover and had to play a National League game against Dublin the following Sunday, which we won. In the next league game, against Mayo in Crossmolina, I was selected in goals as neither Charlie Nelligan nor Paudie O'Mahoney was available. Some commentators expressed surprise at my selection at the time. However, they were obviously not aware of the fact that I had played in goals for my club, Finuge, on a number of occasions in 1969 and 1970. I conceded no goal that day but, in truth, I didn't get a whole lot to do. I also played in goals for Kerry for a short period in the 1978 All-Ireland final when Charlie Nelligan was sent off with my direct opponent, John McCarthy, until I was replaced by Paudie O'Mahoney. I must be one of the few Kerry goalkeepers who never conceded a goal.

1982

HAVING defeated Armagh in April 1982 by 3-14 to 1-5, we reached the final of the National League against Cork. The first match ended in a draw in Killarney, 11 points all, and we won the replay in Cork rather easily by 1-9 to 0-5. The National League final against Cork was to be my last major competitive game for Kerry.

*Accepting the National
League Trophy, 23 May 1982,
in a Cork jersey!*

(Courtesy of the Irish Examiner, www.irishexaminer.ie)

The following Sunday, 31 May, Kerry played Mayo in a tournament game to mark the opening of Lixnaw sportsfield and dressing rooms. I played at full-back and felt in superb shape.

On the following Tuesday evening in Killarney, Micko called us all together in the centre of the field before training commenced. He reminded us that we were now preparing for the championship and for a record five-in-a-row, starting with the match against Clare the following Sunday. His advice was to give it everything in training from that evening onwards. We went through speed work and ball drills and then we had Micko's favourite practice, backs v forwards, which was played in the usual competitive spirit. As the session was drawing to a close, Micko called for one last attack. However, play broke down and the ball was cleared.

Micko always liked to end training on a score and, unfortunately for me, he called for one more attack. The ball was played in the direction of John Egan and myself; I got a hand to the ball and it fell to the ground. I went to pull on it but somehow got entangled with John Egan and we both fell. My right foot remained rooted to the ground and, having taken the full impact of both our body weights, it just snapped.

I can still recall the horrific sound of my bones breaking, which could be heard all over the pitch and even on the stand. When I was taken off the field my ankle was twisted a full 180 degrees. I can still recall the ambulance trip to Cork – the pain was excruciating and every bump on the road accentuated it. I was shocked to discover that my leg was broken in three places and that my ankle ligaments were ruptured. I was operated on the following morning by consultant Freddie Moore (RIP) who did an excellent job.

It was certainly a defining moment in my life. I was giving serious consideration to doing a post-graduate course in sports science at Berkeley College in California either that September or September 1983. I had met with Sr. Nuala Costello from Abbeydorney during my visit to San Francisco in November 1981. She was studying for a Master's degree in Berkeley at the time and suggested that I should consider doing a post-graduate course there. I visited the admissions office and got the necessary application form. I had a number of conversations over the phone with the admissions office in the early part of 1982 and was seriously contemplating taking up the challenge that

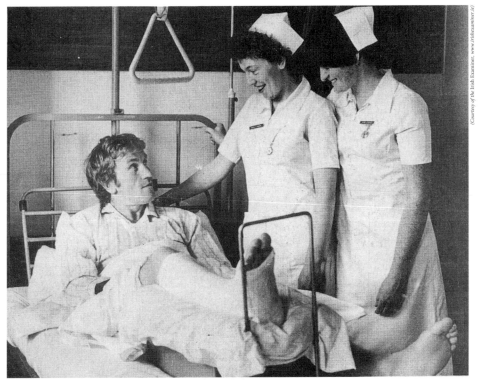

With nurses Eithne Molloy and Anita Mangan in hospital after my injury.

September after the All-Ireland final. Following the accident, I abandoned any ideas of going to Berkeley that September, and obviously my entry into politics that November put paid to any further ambition I had of pursuing that course.

I found it very difficult to deal with the obvious implications of this injury as I felt I was at my peak both mentally and physically at that time. Having been an integral part of the team since 1975 and captaining Kerry to win a record-equalling four-in-a-row, I wanted very much to be part of the team that was aiming to win an historic five-in-a-row, which had never been previously achieved.

While my initial reaction was one of depression, I found some solace and inspiration in a book I had been given by the great Pittsburgh Steelers player, Rocky Bleier (*Fighting Back: The Rocky Bleier Story*), following an interview

I did with him in Pittsburgh in 1980 during the Feale Rangers' visit there. He had been badly injured while in Vietnam and was told he would never walk again. By sheer persistence and determination, he not only walked again but was an integral part of the Pittsburgh Steelers team that dominated the Super Bowl for a number of years. I applied the message of Rocky's book so that I wouldn't have to reproach myself at a future date with 'what if'. I devised and followed a regime of training, commencing most mornings at 6am on Ballybunion Beach and continuing with weight training in Jimmy Mahony's gym in Tralee and the Europe Hotel in Killarney. By September, I had made a miraculous recovery. However, although I was running freely, there was no way I could play in an All-Ireland final.

The defeat by Offaly, which deprived us of the five-in-a-row, was devastating. However, the team accepted their defeat with dignity and just walked off the field with their heads understandably down after the final whistle. There were no remonstrations about the nudge on Tommy Doyle by Seamus Darby or the decision to award Seán Lowry a very soft free prior to Darby's goal. Seán was dispossessed fairly in my opinion, by Tim Kennelly, but the referee thought otherwise. Matt Connor duly pointed the free which put just two points between the teams, leaving Kerry very vulnerable in the event of Offaly scoring a late goal, which they did.

Apart from the nudge, which was brilliantly executed and well disguised by Seamus Darby, his strike for goal was one of the most clinical pieces of finishing ever in Croke Park. It will go down as one of the most, if not *the* most, historic goals ever scored in Gaelic football. It deprived Kerry of making sporting history, which that team undoubtedly deserved. It ensured,

(Courtesy of Kerry's Eye, www.kerryseye.com)

On crutches in the dugout at the Munster final replay in August 1982.

Consoling Mick O'Dwyer after losing the five-in-a-row to Offaly in 1982.

however, that a gallant Offaly side won an All-Ireland and that one of the greatest players ever to play Gaelic football, Matt Connor, won an All-Ireland senior medal.

There was a chilling silence and a numbing sense of disbelief in the dressing room afterwards. Micko was philosophical as usual, and thanked the team for the immense pleasure and entertainment that they provided for so many people since 1975 and told us that we should be proud of ourselves as footballers and the contribution that we had made to Gaelic football and sport in this country.

Whether my absence cost Kerry the five-in-a-row is now academic. There is no doubt that it unsettled the Kerry defence to some extent. Having been a fixture there since 1975, I had, over the years, developed an understanding bordering on the telepathic with my fellow defenders, especially with full-back John O'Keeffe and goalkeeper Charlie Nelligan. Had I been marking Brendan Lowry he may not have scored those three points. Suffice now that it's history.

Myself, Charlie Nelligan and John O'Keeffe.

Frank King, myself and Claire Edwards walking off the field after the match.

Eugene McGee was very magnanimous in victory and he delivered a very appropriate few words when he came to our dressing room afterwards and recognised that the All-Ireland meant even more to them because they had beaten Kerry, especially being the year that it was. The chairman of the County Board, the late Frank King, when asked by an RTÉ reporter after the game for his reaction, remarked that the result was 'good for the game'. The response of our team to defeat brought to mind the words of Garry McMahon in his celebrated song, 'Dúchas': 'And when we lose, there is no excuse, we just pick up our bags and go.'

Knowing Eugene, he spared no effort after the 1981 set-back to defeat Kerry in the 1982 All-Ireland final. Apart from the very strict training regime that he put the panel through, he also organised a training camp for the team in Torremelinos in May. Most importantly, he persuaded Johnny Mooney to return from San Francisco, where he had emigrated, and Seamus Darby to come out of retirement. Both of these players played crucial roles in Offaly's victory in the 1982 All-Ireland final.

The Offaly full-forward line for the All-Ireland final of Johnny Mooney, Matt Connor and Brendan Lowry doesn't come any better. Magee played a two man full-forward line, with Matt Connor drawing John O'Keeffe out-field, allowing Mooney and Lowry ample space which they exploited effectively for Lowry to score three points and Mooney one.

I am convinced that no other manager in the country could have master-minded Kerry's defeat to the extent that Eugene Magee did. For the first three months of 1982 the Offaly team did intensive interval training on the punishing slopes of Croughan Hill, under the guidance of a former college mate of mine in Strawberry Hill, Tom Donoghue.

Apparently, this was a major contributory factor in building the mental strength and stamina of the panel. Croughan Hill became to the Offaly panel what the taxing 'wire to wire' sprints were to the Kerry players during training. Magee just lived and breathed football for the six years leading up to the 1982 final: his single-mindedness paid off.

1983

I WENT back to Tarbert Comprehensive determined to get my broken leg right for the 1983 championship. I was making good progress until my life took a radically new direction when I was asked to run as a candidate for Fine Gael in the November 1982 election. Having lost the general election by just 144 votes and also lost the Senate election by a small margin, I was nominated to the Senate by Dr. Garret FitzGerald and took my seat there on 23 February 1983.

In April '83 I rejoined the Kerry panel for the Munster Championship preparation and was going okay in training. However, I found it increasingly difficult, as the training intensified and the season progressed, to focus on politics, teach and try to regain the level of fitness and speed required for championship football. I had to drive to Dublin every week for the Senate sitting. I also had to cope with a huge constituency workload while trying to maintain the high level of commitment that I always gave to teaching. It was to prove impossible.

I played my last game for Kerry in a tournament to mark the re-opening of Tarbert sportsfield against Galway in May 1983. I was marking Mike Brennan who is now managing director of *The Kerryman* newspaper in Tralee. I played reasonably well and Micko told me afterwards that he was happy with the rate of my recovery and that he was confident I would feature on the team later in the year as we advanced through the championship. I was named as a substitute on the Kerry team to play Cork in the Munster final in July. Kerry looked like they were going to win the game until a last minute goal by Tadhg Murphy; it was similar to the Darby goal the previous September. That game brought the curtain down on my inter-county career.

Although I played well for Feale Rangers in the County Championship campaign in 1983 – we lost the final in a replay to Killarney – it would have taken a tremendous effort for me to achieve the level of fitness necessary for the 1984 championship. In any case, there were some young blades needed on the team. Micko did invite me to participate in the training sessions at the beginning of 1984 but I was realistic and accepted that I no longer had the capacity or energy to regain the level of speed and fitness required for top level inter-county football.

Myself and Mick O'Dwyer at my last training session with the Kerry team on 12 July 1983.

Mike Brennan, MD, Kerryman Ltd. – the last opponent I marked in inter-county football.

I had already taken leave from teaching, having found that the commitment that I was giving to politics was energy-sapping and a major physical and psychological challenge. The more I established myself politically, the more constituency work I generated, so I decided to call it a day. Thus ended my inter-county career: I just bowed out quietly, without any fanfare or media hype.

PEOPLE often ask me about the personal sacrifice that the four-in-a-row team made, considering that we received no payment or adequate expenses. Most of the players in that team were certainly out of pocket due to the amount of time they devoted to training and travelling to matches. Generally, players pooled cars to attend training sessions. Those who made their cars available received very modest travelling expenses. Players who would otherwise have been free over the summer months had to forego the opportunity to play in the UK or the USA for very attractive money. While still a student in Strawberry Hill in June 1972, I was offered a sum of £200, a job and free accommodation if I would transfer from Finuge to the Kingdom club in London; this was never an option due to my commitment to my club and county.

Players further missed out on the social life enjoyed by most of their contemporaries. Foreign holidays were out of the question for team members during the championship, and even the pleasures of seasonal dancing and traditional revelry associated with summer in places like Ballybunion, had to be foregone. Undoubtedly, the demands on relationships, especially on married players, could be taxing, with wives and girlfriends certainly losing out.

We tried to mix our social life with training in 1976 and it cost us dearly. We quickly learned that success in sport at that level came with a Spartan price tag. Besides, in instances where players went on a binge, word invariably got back to Micko who promptly took corrective action. In fairness, the only voice raised in those years advocating a better deal for players was O'Dwyer's. He put his head above the parapet in 1981 when he struck a very good deal with Adidas to secure funding for our Australian tour. We were given £10,000

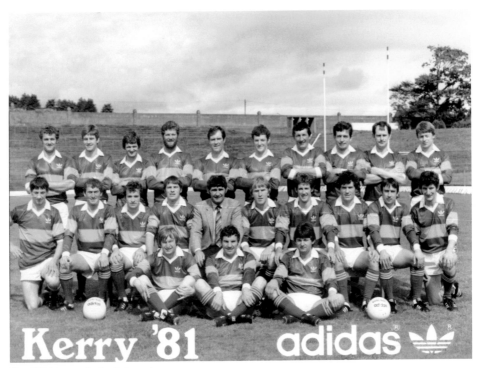

The 1981 Kerry senior football panel.
Front row left to right: Barry Walsh, John Egan, Diarmuid O'Donoghue.
Second row left to right: Pat Sheehan, Ger O'Keeffe, Mikey Sheehy, Páidí Ó Sé, Mick O'Dwyer, myself, Mick Spillane,
Ger Power, Ogie Moran, Bernard O'Sullivan.
Back row left to right: Jack O'Shea, Tom Spillane, Paudie Lynch, Eoin Liston, John O'Keeffe, Charlie Nelligan,
Tim Kennelly, Paudie O'Mahoney, Ger O'Driscoll, Seán Walsh.

for our team photograph with their logo. Adidas also supplied us with football boots and gear over those years.

Things have certainly changed for the better with the founding of the Gaelic Players Association in 1999 and its agreement with the GAA in 2009 for enhanced player welfare. It set about putting in place a programme to assist players with their careers during and after their playing days. This involved a wide range of services in the areas of career development, education support, life skills, health and wellbeing, and benevolent support. All county players can avail of an enhanced injury scheme while critical health checks, such as cardiac screening, are now in place for all squads.

175

Travelling expenses have also improved and are set at 50 cent a mile and county players further benefit from a government funding scheme, in operation since 2008. For some years now, I have been publicly advocating that county players should receive a percentage of gate receipts from championship matches, while never subscribing to the idea of a semi or full-time professional game. Obviously, the team that would progress furthest in the championship would benefit most. So far this suggestion has not been taken up by the GAA authorities.

County Championship Football
with Feale Rangers

1972–1985

THE NAME 'FEALE RANGERS' first appeared in the Kerry County Championship in 1956 and included all the clubs of the North Kerry Football Board. In 1963 the board put forward two clubs in the County Championship: Shannon Rangers and St. Vincent's. In this new arrangement Finuge played with Shannon Rangers, winning the County Championship in 1965. In 1971 the clubs under the North Kerry Board's jurisdiction were realigned and Listowel, Finuge, Duagh, Moyvane, and St. Senan's became Feale Rangers, while Ballylongford, Beale, Ballydonoghue, Tarbert, and Ballyduff became Shannon Rangers. Shannon Rangers won the Kerry County Championship in 1942, 1945 and 1965; Feale Rangers had yet to win a Kerry Senior Championship.

I played my first game for Feale Rangers on 27 August 1972 against Shannon Rangers in the quarter-final of the County Championship which was played in Ballylongford. Shannon Rangers won that match 1-16 to 2-6. In 1973 we reached the semi-final and lost to Na hAghasaigh (West Kerry) by 1-11 to 1-8. I was playing full-back that day and was marking the late Liam Higgins, who was full-forward on the Kerry senior team that won the All-Ireland finals in 1969 and 1970.

IN 1974, after a narrow victory over Mid Kerry in the first round of the championship, we played reigning champions Austin Stacks in the quarter-final in Moyvane. Feale Rangers came of age that day and won by 0-12 to 1-6. The headline in *The Kerryman* read 'Stacks Lose in Muddy Moyvane'. Stacks were a dominant force in Kerry County Championship and club football in the 1970s and early '80s. They won County Championships in 1973, '75, '76 and '79, as well as an All-Ireland Club Championship in 1976. They were

177

powered by county players like John O'Keeffe, Mikey Sheehy, Ger and Anthony O'Keeffe, Ger Power, Dinny Long, John L. McElligott, along with a very strong panel of players. I have very fond memories of the 'Muddy Moyvane' match; I was playing centre-field and had the pleasure of marking four different opponents including John O'Keeffe, during the course of the game. It was probably my best game ever for Feale Rangers.

Feale Rangers had some epic contests, marked by intense rivalry, with Austin Stacks over the '70s and early '80s. Although a number of us played together for the county, our camaraderie was put aside when we played against each other in the County Championship. The spoils were almost equally shared: we beat Stacks in 1974, 1977 and 1980, and they beat us in 1979 and 1981.

After our victory over Stacks, we had high hopes of winning the County Championship. However, we lost to Kenmare in the semi-final by just two points, 2-6 to 0-10. The Kenmare half-backs, Mick Spillane (who was only 17 years old at the time) and Mickey Murphy scored both Kenmare goals. Kenmare were powered on the day by Mickey Ned O'Sullivan and Pat Spillane. They went on to win the County Championship and Mickey Ned became captain of Kerry for 1975.

We were knocked out in the first round in 1975 by Kerins O'Rahillys, with Dick Spring as their player/manager. Later in 1975 I was captain of the Feale Rangers team when they won their first major trophy, the Kerryman Shield, beating Mid Kerry in the final.

IN 1976 we were again knocked out in the quarter-finals by Kenmare, following a replay. Significantly, before that game, Tarbert opted to leave Shannon Rangers for Feale Rangers because of some difference. Tarbert contributed enormously to Feale Rangers for a number of years afterwards, providing key players like Johnny and Mike Wren, Patsy 'Skin' O'Connell, Tommy Bridgeman, Gerald O'Sullivan, and many others in our championship successes of 1978 and 1980.

IN 1977 Feale Rangers were joined by Ballydonoghue who provided the Bunyan brothers – Johnny and Robert – along with Nix Riordan. Feale Rangers were not renowned for their forwards until the arrival of the Bunyans who played a key role in the 1978 success. They were excellent players and gave us vital fire power up front. Johnny was full-forward on the Kerry team that won the Munster final in 1975 and was unlucky not to have been on the starting fifteen for the final against Dublin, while Robert captained the Kerry minor team that won the All-Ireland that year.

With the addition of Tarbert and Ballydonoghue, Feale Rangers were now a force to be reckoned with. Under the direction of my old school coach, Johnny O'Flaherty, we approached 1977 with high hopes. Johnny took firm control of the training and preparation of the team; he laid down the law as set out in this letter which he sent to the entire panel:

Dear

I have just come from the first training session which I arranged for the Feale Rangers team. Only four players turned up, Jimmy Deenihan, Tim Kennelly, Pat Flaherty and John Wren. If this is an indication of the interest of the Feale Rangers, then I think you can abandon any hope of winning the County Championship.

The greatest problem facing the Feale Rangers team is that they are *not* a team, they are a group of players from different clubs who come together on the day of the match and who expect to play as a team. This is just not good enough. If there is to be any serious effort made to win the County Championship, then I must be given the opportunity of blending the players into a team. The only way I can do this is at training sessions where I can explain to players what I want and get them to practise what I suggest. Failing that, the whole thing is a waste of time. We have arranged another session for next Thursday night and I hope that it will be better attended. We are also trying to arrange local, mid-week challenge games to give every player on the panel the opportunity of impressing the selectors and winning their places on the team.

I must make my own position clear to you. I was asked to train this team. I took it on because I felt (a) that the players were there to win a County Championship and (b) that I could help them to achieve this ambition.

However, unless I get the full co-operation of the players, I will not continue as trainer. I don't mind spending my time training the team but I refuse to waste it, idling in the sportsfield, wondering if the players will turn up. So, it is up to the players individually, and as a group, to decide what kind of Feale Rangers team they want, a disorganised bunch of individuals or a united team capable of playing well together. If you want a united team, then you must be prepared to give to the Feale Rangers the same loyalty and commitment that you give your own club. If you are not prepared to do this, then, in my opinion the whole exercise is a waste of time, and, as I said earlier, I do not intend on wasting my own time. The decision is yours!

This letter set the tone for the period that Johnny spent with Feale Rangers as trainer. He won the respect of the panel of players and we did everything that was asked of us under his stewardship.

We hammered Kenmare in the quarter-finals by 6-8 to 1-6. I was playing at centre-field in the semi-final where we faced the reigning All-Ireland Club and County champions, Austin Stacks, on 9 October. We beat them in a closely contested game by 0-10 to 1-6.

We now approached the final with a degree of confidence against our neighbours, Shannon Rangers, who drew their players, notably, Paudie and Eamonn O'Donoghue, Jackie and Barry Walsh, Ogie Moran, and Eoin Liston, from Beale and Ballylongford. I went into the match with a badly bruised big toe joint and had to get it frozen before the game. I played in extreme pain for the duration of the game. We played with a gale-force wind in the first half; Shannon Rangers just held possession whenever they had the ball. Masters of the seven-a-side game, winning All-Irelands in 1973, 1974 and 1977, they used seven-a-side tactics with devastating effect.

Shannon Rangers went in at half time leading by five points to three. Despite a gallant effort in the second half against a gale-force wind, we failed in the end by four points, 0-10 to 0-6. Following this defeat, it was felt in North Kerry that Feale Rangers would never win a County Championship. Some even felt we were jinxed, while others believed we just hadn't the wherewithal to win the County Championship. 1978 was to change all of this.

IN the quarter-finals in 1978, we destroyed South Kerry, 5-15 to 2-9. John Egan, Jack O'Shea and Ger O'Driscoll were all on the South Kerry team. Johnny O'Flaherty decided to pull our full-forward out-field and it worked a treat. We just pumped the ball into the open space in front of the goal, where our forwards took full advantage, and tore the South Kerry defence apart.

The semi-final was a re-match of the 1977 final against Shannon Rangers. I was again playing at midfield and was marking Eoin Liston for most of the game. Eoin was now the new idol of Kerry football after his devastating performance in the All-Ireland final against Dublin, having scored three goals. The final result rested on how Feale Rangers would cope with him on the day. I decided to have an ongoing conversation with him for most of the match and it worked to some extent. We won by just one point in a high quality match, by 1-11 to 1-10.

In the final on 20 November we beat Mid Kerry by 0-8 to 0-3 to win the first County Championship for Feale Rangers and make our own piece of history. Winning the championship meant that Feale Rangers could now nominate

The 1978 Feale Rangers team that won the County Championship.
Front row left to right: Patsy O'Connell, Paddy Mulvihill, Pat Flaherty, Johnny Wrenn (Capt.), Johnny Bunyan, Eamonn Fitzmaurice, myself, Robert Bunyan, Seamus O'Donovan, Mike McGuire.
Back row left to right: John O'Flaherty Timmy O'Sullivan, Johnny Mulvihill, Tommy Bridgeman, John Kennelly, Tim Kennelly, Gerald Leahy, Paddy Hannon, Sean Walsh, Gerald O'Sullivan, Mike Mulvihill, Mick O'Brien.
The selectors were Ciaran Rohan, Patrick Kelly, Eric Browne, Pat Joe McEnery and Dan McAuliffe.

the captain of the Kerry team for 1979. It went to a toss between Tim Kennelly and myself; Tim won and proved to be a worthy captain of Kerry that year. On the day, he'd had a thundering game at centre half-back, as had Johnny Mulvihill at centre-field. I played at midfield for all the games in the 1978 championship. Johnny O'Flaherty played me in the role of a defensive midfielder, advising me to go forward only occasionally from deep positions. The tactic worked and Mid Kerry, with forwards like Brendan Lynch, Neilie O'Sullivan and John Coffey, could only score three points in the final. When they had possession in the scoring zone, I usually made it two defenders against one attacker and we closed them down totally with this simple tactic.

There were great scenes of joy and jubilation after the match: Feale Rangers had brought the Bishop Moynihan Cup to Moyvane and Listowel for the first time. We succeeded where great footballers before us had failed. It was a special feeling.

IN the 1979 quarter-final we defeated Kenmare in Moyvane. I played at full-back to mark Pat Spillane and managed to keep him scoreless yet again. We were decisively beaten in the semi-final by Austin Stacks by 2-9 to 2-2.

FOR me, 1980 was the highlight of my playing career with Feale Rangers. We repeated the success of 1978 and won the County Championship again, beating Austin Stacks by 1-10 to 1-7 in the final. Being the trainer of the team gave me additional satisfaction.

Two weeks before the final I asked the late Connie Riordan to referee the backs v. forwards session and call the sprints. As Connie had been present as a spectator at most of our training sessions that summer, he was very familiar with the type of training I was doing with the team. He played a crucial motivational role in the dressing room before the match as well as during the two weeks leading up to it. He had great oratorical skills and certainly made a difference with the mental preparation of the team. Connie continued to train Feale Rangers for a number of years afterwards, losing out narrowly in three County Championship finals.

Feale Rangers County Championship winning team, 1980.
Front row left to right: Donal Mulvihill, Tim Kennelly, Robert Bunyan, Johnny Wren, Mike Wren, Tom O'Connell, myself.
Back row left to right: Con Riordan, Sean Walsh, Patsy O'Connell, John Kennelly, Nix Riordan, Paddy Hannon,
Gerard O'Sullivan, Johnny Mulvihill, Tommy Bridgeman.

In the final, Stacks led by 1-4 to 0-1 after 30 minutes. It looked like the game was over, but we held our heads and Johnny Mulvihill scored a vital goal before half time which put us back into the game. Johnny played an inspirational part in that victory and was deservedly Man of the Match. Mikey Sheehy was the key man in the Stacks team and their leading scorer. I was convinced that if he were contained to some extent, it would greatly help our chances, so I decided beforehand that wherever Mikey played, I would take the responsibility of marking him. When he lined out at full-forward, as expected, I took up the full-back position. In the second half, Mikey switched to centre-forward and I duly followed him.

I considered it to be one of my greatest achievements ever in Gaelic football to have kept Mikey scoreless that day, especially with midfielders like John O'Keeffe and Dinny Long feeding him quality balls. There was also the honour of captaining the Kerry team at stake in our quest for the four-in-a-row and the result of this game would decide whether it would be Mikey or me.

The 1980 county final will be remembered also for the bravery of Tim Kennelly who was marking Ger Power that day. He had dislocated his shoulder early in the game but his insistence on staying on the field and finishing the match would have an inspirational effect on the team. It was typical of his determination, his steely character and his concern for his team. It took him months to recover from the injury.

Kerryman sport journalist John Barry wrote this report on the game:

> Feale Rangers took the title because of greater all-round cohesion, power and flair down the middle and, above all else, because they refused to bow the knee in the face of the tremendous pummeling they had to withstand, especially in the opening thirty minutes...Full-forward Mikey Sheehy was having a mighty tough time of it trying to escape from the attentions of full-back Jimmy Deenihan: in the second half the Austin Stacks wizard moved to the '40. But he was promptly followed there by Deenihan with Kennelly dropping back behind. The move proved to be a right one as far as the winners were concerned, for Sheehy was seldom given the kind of scope and space in which he likes to manoeuvre. And with Sheehy being held by Deenihan, much of the sting was taken out of the Stacks attack.

WINNING the County Championship meant that I was now captain of the Kerry team for the 1981–82 season. This was a singular honour and I felt that I had to give something back to the lads for making this possible for me, so I organised a trip to the US, including stops in New York and Pittsburgh. Our main organisers were John Kerry O'Donnell and Eamonn Fuller in New York and Tom O'Donoghue in Pittsburgh. Tom requested that we bring the Sam Maguire Cup with us as he was anxious to have it photographed with the Super Bowl trophy, won that year by the Pittsburgh Steelers, and the World Series baseball trophy, won the previous year by the Pittsburgh Pirates (these teams shared the Riverside Stadium).

I felt that it was too much of a responsibility and was against bringing it, but when Tom persisted I agreed because he was such a genuine GAA and Kerry supporter. Piloted by Ciaran Rohan, Joe Halpin, Pat Joe McEnery, Paudie Hanrahan and the late John Normoyle, we did extensive fundraising for the trip to the US over the winter of 1980–81. As a result, each player got a free trip, including flight, accommodation and gear.

We left Shannon in high spirits for New York on Wednesday, 15 April 1981 and were met at Kennedy Airport by the late Eamonn Fuller, a North Kerry man, who arranged a memorable reception for the touring party at his bar. We stayed right in the heart of Manhattan in the Abbey-Victoria Hotel next door to Rosie O'Grady's Bar which was owned by Mick Carthy from county Leitrim, who had been a committed supporter of the GAA in New York for the previous 40 years or more.

A huge welcoming banquet, attended by over 500 people, was organised that Saturday evening for the visiting party at Gaelic Park in the Bronx. The organisers insisted we bring the Sam Maguire Cup to the function so that those in attendance could be photographed with it. It turned out to be a great evening, with John Normoyle stealing the show with his rousing repertoire of songs.

Afterwards, a number of us decided to go to Flanagan's Bar in Manhattan, a popular haunt of the Kerry team at that time. Kerry musician, Seán Fleming, used to perform there, so we were always made feel very welcome. The late Brendan O'Donnell agreed to my request that I leave the cup in the safe at Gaelic Park as we had a game there against Ardboe from Tyrone the following day, and the cup could be put on display for those attending.

The next morning, I got a call at 6am in the hotel informing me that John Normoyle and Joe Mulvihill were in hospital following a car accident which happened while they were on their way from the function, and that I should go there immediately. Having been delayed at the hospital for hours, I barely got to Gaelic Park in time for the match. It was a bruiser of a game as the Ardboe lads took it very seriously. I played at centre-forward and was marked by Patsy Forbes, one of the toughest defenders I've ever played on. Ardboe won the game comfortably.

After the match I went into the bar in Gaelic Park to collect the cup only to be told by the caretaker that it had been taken from the safe by someone unknown to him that morning. The following day, before leaving for Pittsburgh, I called to the park again to see if the cup had been returned. It wasn't there and we had to leave without it.

When we arrived at the Riverside Stadium in Pittsburgh there were a number of TV stations and sports journalists waiting to capture this unique photo opportunity.

Donal Musgrave wrote in the *Cork Examiner*:

> Both cups were on the sideboard of the Riverside Stadium in Pittsburgh yesterday afternoon – there was a gap between them for the Sam Maguire and a lot of red Kerry faces.

Tom O'Donoghue was most embarrassed and in the same article he was quoted as saying: 'Personally, I'm very upset about the cup because I asked Feale Rangers to bring it to America so it could be pictured beside the Super Bowl and World Series Cups, both of which are here in Pittsburgh.' By now the news of the missing cup was making the headlines in the Irish national newspapers and on the RTÉ News. The Blarney Stone Restaurant in Pittsburgh, which Tom O'Donoghue owned, was bombarded with telephone calls from reporters. Luckily for me it was before the days of the mobile phone and I was not always contactable. John Kerry O'Donnell, in New York, was quoted extensively in the *Cork Examiner*. When asked about the disappearance of the cup, he replied:

> 'It was taken out of the park and that was the last we saw of it. The cops are looking for it all over the place. Everybody's looking for it.'

Asked if he had any idea where it might be, he replied:

> 'That's a hell of a question to ask me. Sure if I knew where it was wouldn't I be there? To tell you the truth, I'm going sour with all these press calls from Ireland. But the *Cork Examiner* has been kind to me and you can ask me any questions you want.'

He was asked if he had any idea who had taken the cup.

'I have an idea who he is all right but we'll have to wait and see. If it is who I think it is, I saw him ten years ago in a dressing room when a player was injured. This guy came in and said, "I got him". Well, now he has the Sam Maguire Cup too. A guy just phoned here and said he had the cup. He was from Roscommon and wanted to give the cup to the people of Roscommon because he thinks they were cheated out of last year's All-Ireland.

'Whether that's true or a hoax we don't know yet. But there's no cup and nobody knows where he is either. We are very worried about it and so are the Feale Rangers team. A big press conference has been arranged for Pittsburgh tomorrow and the cup is supposed to be there. I was invited to go along, but how can I without the cup? At the moment the team is scattered around New York. They'll be leaving for Pittsburgh tonight. They'll have to leave, cup or no cup. They'll have to go.'

In a final comment he observed:

'It would be all right if it was lost in a field. But New York City is a hell of a big field. Nothing is safe here anymore. They come through the roof and take everything. Not even the birds are safe but they're getting wise and flying away from Gaelic Park these days. I sure hope they find the cup, and soon.'

Donal Musgrave, in a follow-up article the next day, wrote:

The FBI is investigating the mystery of the Sam Maguire Cup in New York where the GAA's premier trophy has been missing since Sunday. Last night Kerry football team captain Jimmy Deenihan told the *Examiner* from Pittsburgh: 'We haven't recovered the cup. We don't know where it is. We presume it is in New York with Mr. John Kerry O'Donnell.' But in New York Mr. O'Donnell was adamant that the cup was missing, is still missing, and is not being held in a safe at his office. He has accused a Roscommon supporter of stealing the cup for the people of Roscommon because they lost the All-Ireland football final last year to Kerry.

The Sam Maguire story took a bizarre turn yesterday when another prominent GAA man in New York, Mr. Terry Connaughton of Roscommon, accused Mr. O'Donnell of hiding the cup as a personal publicity stunt. Last month, Mr. O'Donnell was eliminated after the first count of the GAA presidential election in Killarney and Mr. Connaughton claimed he was now hiding the Sam Maguire as a reprisal against the GAA. The real situation, said Mr. Connaughton, is that the cup was never stolen at all. 'It's still in O'Donnell's office. If it is missing we all know where it is. There's no doubt in the world that he has the cup.'

Mr. O'Donnell's response to this charge was phrased in the colourful New York language of writer Damon Runyon.

'You couldn't expect anything else from that skunk,' he told me over the transatlantic phone link. 'I certainly deny that and you can quote me. It was missing, it is still missing and the theft is being investigated by cops from the 50th precinct. The only thing to do with Connaughton is ignore him.'

I returned to New York on the Wednesday and went directly to Gaelic Park where I met John Kerry as he was putting out a barrel of rubbish from the bar. He advised me that I should get back home to Kerry on the next flight and be rested for the National League semi-final the following Sunday against Galway in Ennis. I responded by saying that I would not leave New York without the cup, no matter how long it took me to get it.

By now Tom O'Donoghue had made contact through his many political connections with the FBI and I was directed to meet Detective Bill Novotney of the 50th precinct. I called to his office at a particularly bad time as he had two murder investigations on his hands. 'What do you expect me to do,' he said, 'drop everything and go looking for a football trophy?' On my way out the woman at the reception sensed that I was under pressure and advised me that Detective Novotney always went to the diner across the street when he finished work and that I should wait there for him.

I took her advice and waited for a considerable time until he eventually came. I excused myself and reminded him again who I was and my problem with the cup. When I showed him some of the paper cuttings from Ireland about the missing cup and explained to him that the Sam Maguire was a national emblem, he began to take me seriously.

I have no doubt that his intervention helped recover the cup and I understand that a major police blitz to recover it was planned for Gaelic Park that Sunday. I called to the park at about 1.30pm on Sunday and, shortly afterwards, I was advised by the caretaker that the cup would be available there on the following morning. I passed this information on to Detective Novotney and he didn't proceed with his investigation.

When I called to Gaelic Park the following morning at 11am, the Sam Maguire was in the bar wrapped in a black plastic refuse bag. I was very relieved to have it back as I would have been blamed had the cup not been recovered. Both the Feale Rangers officers and I had been mindful of the huge responsibility of bringing it with us on the tour and we believed that it could not have been placed it in safer keeping than the secure safe in Gaelic Park which, over the years, had held millions of dollars. When Feale Rangers visited New York in 2008 we made a presentation to Detective Bill Novotney in appreciation of his support back in April 1981.

While I was in New York looking for the cup, I stayed with Mickey and Phil Moynihan who lived close to Gaelic Park at that time. I will always be indebted to them for their support during those difficult days. The late Brendan O'Donnell, son of John Kerry O'Donnell, was also very helpful. On my way home on the Monday evening I was on the same Aer Lingus flight as the Ardboe team. Patsy Forbes very generously organised a whip-round among the touring party for the fund for those who had

The Moynihan family and myself with the just-recovered Sam Maguire. Left to right: Phil, Timmy (in the cup), Johnny and Mike Moynihan.

Myself and Patsy Forbes in August 2011 at a tribute to Jim McCartan in Newry, Co. Down.

been injured in the car crash on the previous Sunday. I have remained friends with him ever since and we have regular contact. He is still a fanatic on fitness and continues to work in his very successful furniture business in Ardboe.

IN 1980 I had my last County Championship win as a player. Austin Stacks beat us in the quarter-final by just two points in 1981. Unfortunately, a number of the team went to Puck Fair after training on Monday and did not return until Thursday on the eve of the match. Understandably, this did not help our chances.

In 1982 we lost to South Kerry in the final by just two points, 0-7 to 0-5. I couldn't play in that game as my leg had not properly healed; had I been available, I would surely have been worth a couple of points to the team.

In 1983 we lost the final after a replay to Killarney. In 1984 the departure of Listowel from Feale Rangers weakened our panel considerably. We reached the semi-final against West Kerry, but we refused to play on the date that was fixed as one of our clubs, St. Senan's, was playing the North Kerry League final the previous evening. The County Board took a firm line on our stance and threw us out of the competition; a decision that I felt was very harsh.

We reached the final again in 1985, losing to West Kerry, 0-11 to 1-5. In previous games that year I had adopted a roving role as full-forward. Unfortunately, for the final I was instructed to stay in front of the goal for the entire match but got a negligible supply of ball. It was probably the most ineffective game I ever had for Feale Rangers. Before the match I had decided to retire from County Championship football, irrespective of the result. I had given 14 years to Feale Rangers and felt that I had to make way for younger players, although I would have liked to have gone out on a winning note and with a better performance.

My years playing with Feale Rangers form some of the fondest memories I have from my entire Gaelic football career. We were one of the top teams in the County Championship from 1977 to 1985, contesting seven county finals that included one replay and two wins. During that period I played with some exceptional club players. I also played against my colleagues on the Kerry team who were the greatest players in Ireland at that time.

I had a major input into the team as trainer and selector at different times and got to play top class football in my favourite positions at centre-field and centre-forward. I also played at full-back, centre-back and full-forward for the club in County Championship finals. It gave me the opportunity to mark players of the calibre of Paudie Lynch, Eoin Liston, John O'Keeffe, Jack O'Shea, Mikey Sheehy, Pat Spillane, and John Egan in different games and in different positions. County Championship football provided me with freedom of expression; I was able to play to my full potential – as a midfielder, defender and attacker – and not to be restricted by the discipline of corner-back play for Kerry or by the very physical nature of North Kerry football with Finuge.

Feale Rangers is a collection of clubs rather than a geographical entity. However, during the period that I was playing with them, we built up a unique spirit and pride in the jersey. In County Championship football we established a reputation for being physical and very competitive. After my playing career ended, I continued my involvement with the club as manager of the senior team from 1991–1993 and 2000–01, and as a selector from 1998–99. We came very close to making an impact on a number of occasions, losing the County Championship final to a Seamus Moynihan-inspired East Kerry in 1999.

I managed the Feale Rangers minor team that won the County Championship in 1983 and was a selector on the team that won the County U21 Championship in 1998. The 1983 minor team was one of the best teams I ever trained or coached. We simply destroyed a very good Kenmare team in the final. Our team included Philip Danaher, who later played international rugby for Ireland. In the semi-final of that competition we beat St. Kieran's when Mick Galwey, later to become an international rugby star with Ireland and a Munster stalwart, was at midfield for the team.

In 2007, when Feale Rangers won the County Championship after a lapse of 27 years, I was overcome with joy and organised a trip to New York and Boston for them as a reward for restoring the club's esteem and pride in its football. Feale Rangers won the County U16 Championship in 2010 so the future looks positive for the club.

The Greatest Football Team
of All Time

IF I WERE ASKED to name my greatest football team of all time, I would select the Kerry four-in-a-row team of 1981 because, at that stage, it had reached a level of perfection and understanding that, in my opinion, was unrivalled before or since. However, as this would be a very subjective opinion I decided to ask Eugene McGee, the architect of Kerry's defeat in their quest for the five-in-a-row and someone who knew more about individual Kerry players than any other manager in the country, to give his views on the four-in-a-row team.

The following analysis by McGee sums up the qualities of that team:

Putting a great football team into an historical perspective is usually fraught with difficulty because it can be very hard to compare football players individually, and also the team they were part of, with similar groups of previous generations. But in the case of the Kerry four-in-a-row team of the nineteen seventies and eighties, it was a much more clear-cut matter than usual.

There were so many things about that Kerry team which made it different from previous great teams in the county who had also achieved greatness through winning two, three or, on one previous occasion, four All-Irelands in succession. The most obvious distinguishing item was the style of play employed under the tutelage of the great Mick O'Dwyer as manager in those years. For over 70 years since they won their first All-Ireland in 1903 Kerry football was synonymous with the style known and revered all over Ireland as 'catch and kick'.

Many great players were past masters at each of those two primary skills of Gaelic football and I would mention as examples just two from what is a very long list indeed: we had Mick O'Connell as one of the greatest high catchers and Tadhgie Lyne as a brilliant kicker of scores from play. The Kerry football gospel was preached for over 70 years by people like Dick Fitzgerald and Dr. Eamonn O'Sullivan with the odd intervention from Antrim in the forties with the hand pass, Dublin in the fifties with interchange of positions and, of course, Down in 1960/61 who were the first team to change the style and actually win All-Irelands in the process.

But then came a revolution in Gaelic football from Kerry itself with a new running game, hand passing, hand pass scores and great emphasis on athletic fitness. Suddenly speed of movement became the driving force in football and possibly the fact there were half a dozen graduates in physical education on the Kerry panel was a factor. People like John O'Keeffe, Ogie Moran, Jimmy Deenihan, Mickey Ned O'Sullivan, Mike and Pat Spillane for instance.

So if we try to place that Kerry team in the context of the previous 70 odd years it is easy to see that Kerry traditional football had been rocked to its foundations – and lots of Kerry people were not too happy and feared for the future. But people had faith in Mick O'Dwyer to do the right thing for Kerry because he had been one of the county's greatest ever players. Then, when a crowd of young Kerry lads came to Croke Park in 1975 and beat the then All-Ireland champions, Dublin, in the final, a lot of old fears were dispelled.

As always, winning an All-Ireland absolves the participants from all criticism. With Dublin under Kevin Heffernan employing much the same style as the new-look Kerry, the Irish public were watching a revolution taking place in front of their eyes for several more years. But it was only when Eoin Liston arrived on the scene for 1978 that Kerry really blossomed into the super team they were about to become. He restored some traditional values so beloved of GAA followers. He was a huge man, threw his weight around, distributed the ball to his fellow forwards with great results and, of course, could score goals himself to set the fans alight, such as when he scored three past Paddy Cullen in the 1978 final against Dublin.

So we can say that the most notable attribute of the four-in-a-row team was that they deviated from the previous Kerry football style to an enormous extent but still achieved almost unprecedented success. In reality, that team turned out to be the forbearers of a revolution in Gaelic football in terms of fitness, playing style and modernisation that changed the game forever.

The four-in-a-row captains and Monsignor Liam Brosnan. Left to right: Ogie Moran, Tim Kennelly, Monsignor Brosnan, Ger Power and myself.

Nearly all the innovations in tactics and preparation since 1980 can be traced back to the influence on the game of football by what those Kerry teams did. Traditional lines on the field such as the 3-3-2-3-3 soon disappeared and gradually evolved from that stereotyped line-up to the 'organised chaotic' structures we have today where backs play in the forwards and forwards in the backs with consummate ease. Remember how often we used to see Pat Spillane collecting the ball in the Kerry backline all those years ago?

Therefore, that Kerry team can be seen as apostles for change and you can judge for yourself whether that change of approach in the 1980s was a blessing or a curse in subsequent years! For many years afterwards, I met older Kerry GAA followers who still have mixed views on the partial abandonment by Kerry of their traditional catch and kick style, although those two primary skills are still a key component of modern Kerry teams.

We can state with some conviction that the Kerry four-in-a-row team broke many moulds and not just on the playing fields. They were the first county team to dabble in commercial sponsorship, something which had been regarded like the plague by every GAA official of the day.

In summary, therefore, that great Kerry team which included so many iconic figures whose names reverberate forever through the ranks of the GAA, changed the mindset of traditional Gaelic footballers on the field with their revolutionary style of play, and off the field they were catalysts for the modern independence in inter-county players who, prior to that, had been largely people who, in a GAA dominated by officials, were supposed to be seen but never heard. That Kerry four-in-a-row team was definitely seen with admiration by countless thousands of GAA fans all over Ireland and around the world – but they were also heard like players had never been before that. That is their legacy which is secure for as long as the GAA exists.

I think that it is also appropriate to include extracts from an interview with *Sunday Independent* journalist, Liam Kelly, with Kevin Heffernan on 29 November 1981, when Heffernan gave his opinion on the reasons for the unrivalled success of the four-in-a-row team:

Kerry are successful because of the physical hard work they put into preparation, because they maintain concentration for the full period of a game and because they never spare effort on the field....The success of Mick O'Dwyer and Kerry is to have remained motivated to winning over the last six years, despite the extent of their success. It's a fantastic achievement. How long more is the major question, and looking at Kerry in the All-Ireland I didn't see any signs of staleness about them.

Six months to a year can make an awful lot of difference. A team can lose its edge very quickly after a long time at the top. Should they lose three or four players at once it could completely unbalance the team.

Heffernan was prophetic in his commentary.

The Players that Were Part of
Kerry's Four-in-a-Row Victories

CHARLIE NELLIGAN: Certainly one of the greatest goalkeepers of all time, winning seven All-Ireland medals in goals. He was an outstanding athlete, winning several titles in weight throwing events. He also played in goals with Home Farm soccer team for a period and was picked to play for the Irish amateur international soccer team. He was one of the longest kickers ever of the placed ball and he could vary his kick-out very effectively. He had a strong voice and he continuously marshalled his defence, providing information on unmarked opponents.

Opponents found it very difficult to beat him, irrespective of the angle or level of their shot on goal. He was equally adept at stopping ground balls as he was with aerial shots. Over the years, he developed a great understanding with his full-back line in particular, and was totally courageous when it came to challenging for any ball in the vicinity of his square.

MICK SPILLANE: Perhaps one of the most underrated corner-backs who ever played Gaelic football for Kerry and one of the fastest players on the team. He was an excellent footballer and was totally unselfish as a defender. He was a team player who automatically picked up your opponent if you switched on to his. I found him a pleasure to play with in the full-back line.

PAUDIE LYNCH: Played centre-field on the 1970 minor team. He also played in most positions on the Kerry senior team from 1972 to 1983. He was very skilful and always seemed to have time when he had possession. He was also a very good distributor of the ball and rarely gave it away. Like Mick Spillane, he was totally unselfish and excelled at covering for a team-mate when required.

GER O'KEEFFE: Played wing-back on the 1970 minor team. He was a champion sprinter at college level and had a devastating burst of speed. He was an excellent defender and was a great reader of the game. Again, he was most unselfish when it came to supporting his fellow defenders and was always prepared to pick up unmarked opponents.

He was unlucky to miss out on the 1978 and 1979 All-Ireland finals because of an injury he received playing rugby with Tralee RFC early in 1978. However, he stuck with it and his perseverance paid off when he was selected at wing-back for the 1980 All-Ireland final against Roscommon. Ger has gone on to become a very successful selector with the present Kerry team.

JOHN O'KEEFFE: In my opinion John was the greatest full-back to ever play Gaelic football. He was a tremendous fielder of the ball and could reach to extraordinary heights from a standing position. He was rarely ever out-jumped in front of the Kerry goals. He had explosive speed and developed tremendous strength from years of weight training at Mahony's gym in Mitchel's Crescent in Tralee.

Over the years I developed a great understanding on the field of play with him, having played alongside him in six All-Ireland finals. We usually shared the same room on away matches. As we were both into physical education and fitness we always enjoyed each other's company and developed a great rapport off the field which continues to the present day. Johnno is still affectionately referred to as 'The King' – a richly deserved title.

(Courtesy of The Kerryman, www.kerryman.ie)

With Páidí Ó Sé after the Munster final in 1975.

PÁIDÍ Ó SÉ: Played at wing-back in front of me in all four-in-a-row finals from 1978 to 1981. He was one of the first of the attacking wing-backs and being a great ball-carrier, loved to go forward. He was a very accurate distributor of the ball to the Kerry forwards and rarely wasted a clearance out of defence. We struck up a very good understanding on the right wing. In the four-in-a-row All-Ireland finals, we just conceded one point each to our immediate opponents.

Páidí took over my position where he really displayed his defensive skills at corner-back for the three-in-a-row All-Ireland victories from 1984 to 1986. He later successfully managed Kerry to victory in the 1997 and 2000 All-Ireland finals. The team's achievement in winning the 1997 All-Ireland was of particular importance as Kerry had not won an All-Ireland for 11 years and football in the county was in a depressed state. Páidí's enthusiasm and passion for the game certainly rubbed off on the players and, as manager, he made a significant contribution to the revival of Kerry football at championship level. Since then the county has won six All-Ireland finals.

TIM KENNELLY: Certainly will go down as one of the greatest centre half-backs Kerry ever produced. When Kerry were team-building after the 1974 defeat by Cork in the Munster final, Andy Molyneaux, then secretary of Kerry County Board, recommended Tim for the centre half-back position. Tim took on the challenge and held the position with distinction until his retirement in 1984. He was noted for his natural strength and his footballing ability. The bigger the occasion the better, and he was

Tim Kennelly and myself at a County Championship game.

Man of the Match in both the 1980 and 1981 All-Ireland finals. While he loved going forward he never neglected his defensive duties.

I played with Tim at St. Michael's College, with Listowel Under 16s, with Feale Rangers for 11 years, and with Kerry for eight years. We struck up a great friendship and normally travelled to training sessions together. His untimely death was a shattering blow to his family and to me personally. He had so much to live for and had so much to give to Gaelic football, both to his club and to Feale Rangers. He was one of the pillars of the four-in-a-row team.

JACK O'SHEA: Would certainly rank with Mick O'Connell and Darragh Ó Sé as one of the greatest midfielders that Kerry has ever produced. He played for 16 years until 1992 at top class level, winning seven All-Irelands in the process. Jacko was a great athlete and could cover the pitch from end to end for the duration of a game. He was an indispensable part of the Kerry defensive strategy, as he continuously dropped back behind the Kerry half-back line and acted as a defensive sweeper for years.

He was always available for a pass out of defence, which was essential for the team if they were to hold possession, especially when under pressure. He also provided invaluable support to the forward line and many vital scores that resulted from his deep runs into enemy territory, including his famous goal that clinched the 1981 All-Ireland against Offaly.

SEÁN WALSH: Had a spectacular career with Kerry, starting in 1976 when he played a central role in winning the Munster final, having come on as a substitute at 19 years of age. He went on to win four All-Ireland medals at midfield, partnering Jack O'Shea, and took over from John O'Keeffe at full-back for the three-in-a-row from 1984–1986; he performed in both positions with distinction. Seán was also an underage champion sprinter and, as a result, he had an explosive turn of pace. He was undoubtedly one of the greatest high fielders of the ball ever to play Gaelic football. This is reflected in his spectacular catch over Brian Mullins in the 1979 All-Ireland final.

He had the extraordinary knack of holding himself in the air momentarily when leaping for a high ball. This gave him a decided advantage. Seán was a very unselfish player who always tracked back into our defence after his opponent and never allowed unmarked opposing players to run into scoring positions. In my opinion, he would certainly rank among the greatest midfield players and full-backs ever to play for Kerry.

GER POWER: Ger Power played at wing-back in the 1975 All-Ireland final in front of me. Like Páidí, he was an attacking wing-back, and he loved to go forward with the ball. He had a devastating turn of pace and was very skilful and courageous. In the four-in-a-row campaign he played at wing-forward, where he had started with the Kerry minors in 1970. He was acknowledged

Myself, Ger Power and John O'Keeffe at the North Kerry/West Limerick charity cycle event in April 2011.

as one of the most exciting players of the period and went on to play a critical role in the subsequent three-in-a-row campaigns from 1984–86.

There were very few defenders who could match Ger Power for sheer pace and ball-carrying ability. He was a great distributor of the ball and very much a team player. He was also fearless in the tackle and made a critical turn over in the 1986 All-Ireland final against Tyrone when he dispossessed Plunkett Donaghy to set up a goal for Mikey Sheehy.

OGIE MORAN: The only man ever to win eight All-Ireland senior football medals playing in the one position. Ogie had lightning pace and was very skilful; he was totally unselfish and was an out-and-out team player. As club colleagues and close friends, he had a great understanding on the field of play with Eoin Liston.

He was forever buzzing around the pitch and was always available for passes out of defence and for supporting his fellow forwards. He both scored and set up vital scores during the four-in-a-row campaign. He was an inspiring captain in 1978

With Ogie Moran at a gallery opening in Tralee.

and was very popular among the squad. He could read the game very well and was an expert at anticipating the broken ball.

PAT SPILLANE: Undoubtedly the greatest right-footed kicker of long-distance points. He had tremendous endurance and could run continuously for the full 70 minutes of the game. By coming deep into our defence he was always available for a short clearance, then quickly switching into attack, often leaving his markers flat-footed. He showed great courage and perseverance in recovering from a cruciate ligament injury, which he picked up before the 1981 All-Ireland, to come back and make a critical contribution to Kerry's three-in-a-row from 1984–86.

Of all the Kerry forwards, I liked marking him most in County Championship football. I was very familiar with his style from the time we played together at the NCPE. The fact that he had a weak left foot made it easier to mark him. Pat has gone on to become a very effective panellist and presenter on *The Sunday Game*. Some would say that he is to Gaelic football what Eamonn Dunphy is to soccer and George Hook to rugby.

MIKEY SHEEHY: Was the epitome of skill and coolness. He was our free-taker and rarely missed a scoring opportunity. His chipped goal over Paddy Cullen against Dublin in 1978 is now very much part of the folklore of Gaelic football. No other player in the country would have had the confidence to try it or the skill to execute it. His goal against Roscommon in the 1980 All-Ireland final was also crucial in our victory that day as it put us back into the match.

He struck up a great understanding with Eoin Liston and John Egan in our full-forward line. The only full-back line that could hold them scoreless was our full-back line in 'backs and forwards' in training. Mikey will be remembered as one of the greatest stylists who ever played Gaelic football.

EOIN 'BOMBER' LISTON: In my opinion the greatest full-forward ever to play Gaelic football, winning seven All-Ireland medals. He had height, speed, skill and strength. For a forward he could be very physical when required, as many full-backs discovered. In his prime, during the four-in-a-row, he was simply unmarkable by one opponent alone. He, more than any other player, was the linchpin of the four-in-a-row team. It usually took a few players to stop him, which provided the space for his fellow forwards that they thrived on.

(Courtesy of Brendan Landy, www.landyphoto.com)

Eoin Liston, myself and Ogie Moran launching a charity walk for the Kerry Parents and Friends of the Mentally Handicapped.

Bomber was one of the players who was closest to Mick O'Dwyer. Micko took him under his wing when Bomber started teaching in Waterville Vocational School in September 1978. Over the long winter months for 10 years or so, both of them trained together on the beach, in the local football pitch and in the gym. Over the years, Bomber improved his fitness and speed, but, more importantly, he perfected his kicking with his left foot, making him the complete footballer. He scored many a vital point for Kerry in championship football, especially with the left foot during the three-in-a-row campaign from 1984–1986. He would be my first choice on any team.

JOHN EGAN: Undoubtedly one of the greatest corner-forwards ever to play for Kerry. John scored the vital goals in both the 1975 and 1978 All-Ireland finals. His goal in the 1978 All-Ireland was crucial as we had been totally out-played up to that point. John was very difficult to dispossess and had great balance and control when in possession.

John Egan and myself in 1975.

He was an expert at shielding the ball from his marker. In training between 1975 and 1982 I must have marked him at least 300 times between backs and forwards and trial games. It was the best training and preparation that either of us could have had and there was no quarter given or taken; it was always full-blooded competitive stuff.

GER O'DRISCOLL: Ger was a great utility player and scored a vital goal for Kerry in the 1975 All-Ireland final. He was very skilful and could play in any forward position or at centre-field. He was unlucky that there were such great forwards in Kerry at that time, otherwise he would have got more opportunity to display his skill.

PAUDIE O'MAHONEY: Would rank amongst the greatest goalkeepers that ever played with Kerry. He did not concede a single goal in the 1975 championship campaign, saving two penalties – one against Cork and the other against Sligo; he also saved a penalty in the 1970 All-Ireland minor final against Derry at a critical stage of the match. He had a very long kick-out with the left foot and could vary his kick very effectively. He was very good at communicating with his defenders.

MICKEY NED O'SULLIVAN: Was an inspirational captain of the Kerry minor team in 1970 and the senior team in 1975. Players listened and responded to his pep talks and they respected his honesty and total commitment. He was an exciting ball-carrier and was courageous when he had to take on defenders. He was unfortunate to be taken out of the game in the 1975 All-Ireland final against Dublin but luckily for him, he avoided serious injury.

He would have played a more significant part in the four-in-a-row campaign but for this injury. He went on to be a very successful manager of the Limerick senior football team and is currently in charge, along with John O'Keeffe, of the Kerry minor team.

TOMMY DOYLE: Was a talented, versatile footballer, who played both at half-forward and half-back. He was one of the fittest players on the team and was also able to mix it physically, as he showed in the clash with Brian Mullins in the 1979 All-Ireland final. He had the distinction of captaining Kerry to the three-in-a-row success in 1986.

PAT McCARTHY: Was possibly the most influential player in the 1975 championship campaign. Kerry had a midfield problem for a number of years and he solved it. He had tremendous natural strength and a great leap for a high ball. He would have played more championship games for Kerry had he been based in the county. Due to living in Kildare, he missed out on Micko's intensive training regime.

VINCENT O'CONNOR: Another great utility player. He played in defence and at midfield for the team. He was one of the highest fielders of the ball in the game during the four-in-a-row period. He was unlucky not to have played in more championship games as he was a player of immense ability.

JOHNNY MULVIHILL: Played at midfield in the first round of the Munster Championship in 1978. Were it not for the formidable midfield partnership of Seán Walsh and Jack O'Shea, he would have figured more often on the team. A player of incredible strength, he played with great heart and had a key role in the team's training in Killarney. He epitomised the selfless spirit of Kerry football.

PATIE O'MAHONY: Came on as a sub in the 1978 semi-final against Roscommon. He had tremendous pace and would have figured regularly on most other Kerry teams, before and since. It was extremely difficult to get a place in the forwards during the four-in-a-row era. Additionally, an injury which he picked up while playing soccer didn't help his inter-county career.

BERNARD O'SULLIVAN: From Dingle, he came on as a sub in the Munster semi-final against Clare in 1981. He was an excellent defender and made a major contribution in training and trial matches.

Mick O'Dwyer

The Ultimate Manager

WHEN I WAS GROWING UP in the late 1950s and early 1960s, Micko was one of my boyhood heroes. Sharing the same dressing room with him when I joined the Kerry panel for the 1972 All-Ireland final was exciting for me at the time. In May 1973 I went on to win a National League title with him against Offaly. In the spring and early summer of that year, at the invitation of John Kerry O'Donnell, we made a number of visits to New York together to play with the Kerry club there in the New York Championship.

We were joined by players like Mick O'Connell, Neilie O'Sullivan and Derry Crowley, Mick Breen and Noel Power from Kerry, Brian McEniff and Pádraig McShea from Donegal, Mickey Whelan from Dublin who was studying in the USA at that time, as well as local New York players Mick Moynihan (Rathmore), Jimmy Moloney (Listowel), Jim Foley (Hartford and Keel), Mike Walsh (Ballydonoghue), Pat Ferris (Mid Kerry), Joe O'Driscoll (Camp) and Brendan O'Donnell (RIP) (New York). It was an exciting time for me as I was attending the NCPE in Limerick and I was getting $100 a match, which was a lot of money then for a student (I discovered years later from Micko that he was getting substantially more).

When we arrived in New York, our first port of call was always a golf shop near Macy's in Manhattan where Micko struck up a great friendship with the owner and we could get Ping putters for $15. I started bringing a few back to club members in Ballybunion because they were not available in Ireland at that time. I got to know Micko well during those trips and we developed a good understanding about football as well as a lasting friendship.

When Kerry lost the second Munster final in a row to Cork in 1974 there was genuine concern in the county that Cork would dominate football in Munster for the foreseeable future as they had a relatively young team with a very strong panel from which to pick. Despite the fact that Kerry had a pool of very talented players available in 1975, they needed a motivator and an organiser. Micko provided these qualities when he was appointed manager of the team.

He inherited a panel of players in Kerry who had amassed a considerable level of experience at underage and senior levels: nine were on the minor team that lost to Galway in the 1970 All-Ireland minor final replay, twelve were on the U21 team that won the All-Ireland title on 1973, five on the National League team that beat Offaly in the final the same year, and twelve on the panel that beat Roscommon in the league final replay in 1974. However, only five had won a Munster Senior Championship medal and only three of the panel – John O'Keeffe, Brendan Lynch and Donie O'Sullivan – had an All-Ireland Senior Championship medal. The seeds may have been sown with the minor team of 1970 and the U21 victory in 1973, but it would require a lot of work to get us to the next stage of beating Cork and Dublin.

Perhaps Micko's greatest achievement was winning the three-in-a-row, from 1984 to 1986. After the 1983 defeat by Cork, he had to reshape the team. Gone were John O'Keeffe, Paudie Lynch, Tim Kennelly, Ger O'Keeffe and myself. He drafted in young players like Tom Spillane, Ger Lynch, Ambrose O'Donovan, John Kennedy, Timmy O'Dowd and Willie Maher. By not over-exposing them to a hard, physical regime, he extended the careers of Ger Power, Mikey Sheehy, Pat Spillane, Ogie Moran, Páidí Ó Sé and John Egan in 1984. He converted Seán Walsh from a mid-fielder to a full-back, and Páidí Ó Sé from wing-back to corner-back. Ingeniously, he managed to motivate the veteran players and keep their appetites up to win Munster and All-Ireland finals during those years.

Micko had all the qualities of a great Gaelic football coach, with an in-depth understanding of the game. He played with Kerry for almost 18 years and trained under Dr. Eamonn O'Sullivan, Jackie Lyne and Johnny Culloty. His training methods were very specific to the game and we wasted very little time doing irrelevant exercises and drills. Our training usually consisted of two easy laps of the field to warm-up, ball handling (including give and go), and short sprints with reversing. We all dreaded the wire to wire sprints across the pitch in threes; there was no place to hide and we usually did three or four in quick succession. This was an ideal exercise for developing speed

With Mick O'Dwyer after the All-Ireland final win over Roscommon in 1980.

endurance which was so essential to our team performance, especially in the later stages of the championship. As the season progressed, he would always devote 30 to 40 minutes to backs and forwards, a routine that was always very competitive and played at game intensity.

Micko was certainly a great motivator. His ever-positive attitude and enthusiasm for Gaelic football rubbed off on most of those he trained. It certainly rubbed off on our team and he got the maximum out of us, both individually and collectively. We developed a very high level of speed with and off the ball and, as time went on, we just did things instinctively. As a defender you knew that if you were clearing a ball, Jack O'Shea or Pat Spillane would always be lurking deep in the defence to take a pass. O'Dwyer's training approach made us more independent thinkers and, as a result, we could automatically adjust to our opponents' tactics if required.

From 1975 to 1982 there wasn't a major turnover of players so Micko got to know his charges very well. He knew from a glance if a player was carrying even the slightest excess weight and needed additional training; in such instances he used to bring in the 'heavy gang' – as he referred to them – for pre-season training, as well as using them during the championship period.

He rarely raised his voice during training and refrained from yelling and screaming when players blundered. He kept his tactics very simple and always reminded midfielders and half-backs to let the ball in fast to the forwards and not to be looking at the O'Neill's lettering on the ball. He never advocated dirty play but was always very clear that, when it came to contesting a 50/50 ball, you went in full-blooded to win it. He didn't like 'wheelers' and emphasised that, whenever the ball was available, it must be won, which required going in with everything.

Our training sessions were always well-organised, with Micko invariably in Fitzgerald Stadium an hour in advance. Most of the panel would be on the field warming up and kicking a half hour before the session began. When Micko blew his whistle to commence the session he got total attention until it was completed. When he spoke, either on the field or in the dressing room, everyone listened.

Some would say he had no appreciation of the importance of stretching and warming up properly; he was not alone, as very few county teams did a warm-up back in the 1970s, and this applied also to international rugby and soccer teams. Micko left it up to the individual to do his own warm-up, which some of us, especially the physical education teachers on the panel, did. At one stage there were six PE teachers – John O'Keeffe, Mickey Ned O'Sullivan, Pat and Mick Spillane, Ogie Moran and myself. I have to say that Micko has learned over the years and a well organised warm-up is now a feature of his preparation. Back in 2005, he asked me to do a few defence coaching sessions with Laois and before each session he had a specialist, Gerry Loftus, doing a very thorough warm-up.

Others would criticise him for not varying his training methods, as we basically did the same type of session from 1975 to 1982. Micko believed in using well-tried and well-liked practices. He was a strong believer in routine in his training sessions and his match preparation. This led to less confusion since players required few directions and knew what was expected of them. He was mostly an observer during the training sessions.

As far as I am concerned, there is no one way of coaching. However, I'm convinced that the most important quality needed is enthusiasm. Players respond to someone who is knowledgeable, highly motivated and energetic.

Celebrating Mick O'Dwyer's 70th birthday in Waterville.
Myself, Mick O'Dwyer and Eoin Liston.

(Courtesy of Don MacMonagle, www.macmonagle.com)

O'Dwyer has proven this over 36 years with Kerry, Kildare, Laois and, more recently, with Wicklow.

Micko was ahead of his time in ways regarding nutrition and diet, and he ensured there was a choice of red meat, fish or chicken-based meals after training, which we had in the Park Place Hotel in Killarney. He was also a great believer in the value of milk after training as a means of stimulating rehydration and helping muscle repair and recovery.

In 2007, Ronald Maghan, a professor of sport and exercise nutrition at Loughborough University in England, published research confirming the benefits of milk for rehydration after exercise. Emma Cockburn, a lecturer in sports coaching at Northumbria University, has published further research confirming the benefits of milk in muscle recovery and its effectiveness in preventing exercise-induced muscle damage.

Her findings state that 'milk contains carbohydrates in amounts similar to many commercially available sports drinks, and contains casein and whey protein, and has a naturally high concentration of electrolytes, potentially making it a good sports drink. Practically, it is a supplement that is convenient, inexpensive and accessible and therefore can be used as an intervention for recovery from muscle damaging exercise'. Before and after training, we drank litres of milk on Micko's advice.

Between 1975 and 1986, he managed Kerry to win eight All-Ireland Senior Football Championships, equalling Dr. Eamonn O'Sullivan's record. In addition, he went on to guide Kildare to their first Leinster title since 1956 in 1998, losing narrowly to Galway in the All-Ireland final that year. After Kildare, he managed Laois to their first senior Leinster Championship title since 1946 in 2003. In 2007 he guided Wicklow to victory over Antrim in the Tommy Murphy Cup final in Croke Park. No other manager in the history of the GAA can match this record of achievement.

Micko has had a positive impact on every team he has ever managed. While not replicating his successes with Kerry, he certainly got the best out of those Leinster counties, instilling confidence in them and ensuring that they performed to their full capacity. Since he joined Wicklow, there is a new-found optimism in that county and, for the first time in years, the team feels that it has a chance of winning a Leinster Championship. Now that Micko has completed his term with Wicklow, he has, as was always his intention, returned to coaching at his local club in Waterville. This should be of immense benefit to the club as there is no Gaelic football manager in Ireland with his vast experience and track record.

Mick O'Dwyer is justifiably ranked as one of the greatest managers ever in the history of Gaelic football. To me, he is *the* greatest and he has the track record to prove it.

Training Methods, Injury and Treatment

Then and Now

DURING MY PLAYING YEARS I often met former players who would question the intensity of O'Dwyer's training and would compare his methods to those of the great Dr. Eamonn O'Sullivan, who had a gentler approach to getting his charges fit. Dr. Eamonn believed in collective training which entailed a special training camp where the entire team and substitutes were housed and subjected to a daily 24-hour schedule of alternating exercise, tuition, rest and play. In his book, *The Art and Science of Gaelic Football*, he wrote that 'any part-time method of training can, of its very essence, only lead to fitness of a restricted, partial type and consequently, is an unsatisfactory substitute for the fuller type of training'.

In his book, Dr. Eamonn set out what a typical day's training would be in his camp. He followed this routine with Kerry teams for decades:

Following a night's sleep of seven to eight hours, each player would rise at a scheduled time each morning. After a brief period of stretching and breathing exercises, all players were to take a 15–20 minute walk before eating breakfast, which included porridge, followed by a suitable fry, substituted with fish and eggs on Fridays, with tea and toast. Following breakfast, all players would undergo at least one hour of complete relaxation, preferably reclining and at rest in easy chairs.

At 11am, all players would assemble in a lecture room which was equipped with a blackboard and accessories and which was adjacent to the training ground. Each talk delivered by him was short, rarely more than 15 minutes, and dealt with one or two principles of play. According to Dr. Eamonn, one could achieve better results by restricting the scope of the lecture.

This lecture would be followed immediately by about 50–60 minutes of a practical training session in 'full togs' on the playing pitch. It commenced with a 450–500 yards run at an easy trotting pace. Usually, the principles of play discussed at the lecture were put into practice during the session. Dr. Eamonn encouraged players to work on their weaker foot, not only in his training sessions, but all year round. The routine of a short lecture followed by active training exercises was repeated in the afternoon after a post-lunch period of complete relaxation; the reason for this was to give the body a chance to digest the main meal of the day.

The second period was scheduled for at least 90 minutes, from 2pm to 3.30pm. Likewise, the evening meal at 6pm was followed by complete rest and relaxation until 8pm. From 8pm to 10.30pm, he suggested a variety of recreational activities including walking, concerts, cinema, and other shows; Dr. Eamonn suggested a light supper of milk and biscuits at 10.30pm and everyone to be in bed by 11.30pm. He emphasised that it was 'of supreme importance that each player should have uninterrupted sleep nightly'. He used the above programme successfully for over 30 years with Kerry.

Being a psychiatrist, he also set great store by players' mental preparation. He used to give players little phrases such as 'fear fatal fouling' to remind them of the team's playing strategy.

Dr. Eamonn was an extraordinary man; he trained Kerry teams over a forty-year period, from 1925 to 1965, training eight All-Ireland winning teams. He was possibly the first trainer to apply science to the training of Gaelic football teams and was using plyometric-type training with skipping ropes, strength training, speed work and intensive drills, long before it was fashionable. His emphasis on recovery after training through rest is one of the main planks of modern day, periodised training. He was, undoubtedly, years ahead of his time.

It was not until the late 1990s that the use of the physical trainer in Kerry was introduced when Páidí Ó Sé appointed John O'Keeffe to take over the training responsibilities of the team. His aim was to help the team reach higher levels of fitness than previously considered possible. Johnno's training certainly paid off in the 2000 championship campaign, especially in the All-Ireland semi-final and All-Ireland replays when superior fitness was probably the determining factor in the victories over Armagh and Galway.

PAT FLANAGAN took over from John O'Keeffe and introduced many new innovations in the preparation of the Kerry senior team, the most significant being what is referred to as 'periodisation'. With this method the training year is planned in great detail from the start of the year. There may be some minor alterations but the blueprint is set out, with each phase of the year identified, as well as the training required at each phase. These are usually organised on a macrocycle (year), mesocycle (month) and microcycle (week) scale. This plan is explained to the players early in the season so that they are fully aware of what is expected and the goals to be achieved. The basic phases are conditioning, channelling or specific conditioning, pre-competition, competition, and recovery. The main aim of all of this planning is to ensure that the team arrives at the critical stages of the season in prime condition.

This level of planning has helped the Kerry senior panel to train smart and not waste time on needless forms of training, such as running laps of fields for two to three months. It has also meant a much greater variety of training sessions as the training stimulus and type will change at each phase of the year. For example, circuit training, speed endurance and core exercises might form the bulk of the training in early phases, while speed, ball skills, power weights and team plays will dominate the pre-competition phase. This wide range of sessions makes training much more palatable for all players, especially those who have been training for a number of years. It also assists greatly in avoiding player burnout, as any one particular type of training will not be overused. The number and intensity of modern day Kerry training sessions are very much built around strength and resistance training.

Weight training, circuits and plyometrics are just some of the types of training that are now extensively used and seen to be far more important than running. Weight training programmes are designed early in the season for each player and may involve three to four gym sessions per week. These decrease as the training year progresses, with power weights replacing the muscle building phase of the early season. Plyometric training is aimed at increasing speed and power prior to the competitive phase. At its basic level, this involves hopping and bounding with and without hurdles and requires a high level of conditioning and co-ordination by the players. A major danger of this type of training is that it causes extensive muscle damage and soreness if overused, leading to reduced muscle power.

One of the approaches to match preparation which has undergone great change since our time under Mick O'Dwyer is the emphasis now on warming up and cooling down at the beginning and at the end of games and training sessions. Warm-ups and warm-downs now form the core of every serious team's training regime at any level. Warm-ups have become more and more complicated, with intricate passing drills and small-sided conditioned games.

There was much comment about the warm-up of the Kerry team preceding the 2006 final as it involved a very competitive small-sided game. The players held little back and lashed into it as they had done in training and the lively start of the game focused even more attention on the warm-up. The interesting thing about these warm-ups is that they vary so much from team to team. For example, Real Madrid and the French rugby team warm-up for nearly an hour prior to games, while other teams can complete their warm-up routine in 20 minutes or less.

Warm-downs are even more vital as they start the recovery process for the next game or training session. Muscles are damaged and tight and players are still on a physical high after the game. Through light exercises and stretches, the body and mind are brought down to normal levels and plans for the next session are discussed. This can then be followed by ice baths and/or massage to ease the muscles further.

One place where warming up and warming down exercises are most important and most enjoyable is on warm weather camps. Although camps were extensively used by Kerry in the '40s and '50s, the winter or spring training camp in the sun is a relatively new phenomenon. Armagh's visit to La Manga training centre in early 2002, and their subsequent winning of the All-Ireland, focused attention on the benefits of such camps. Before and during Kerry's trip to Spain in the spring of 2010, a number of callers to Radio Kerry questioned the benefits of 'running around fields in Spain' and suggested that the panel could run around the fields at home. The answer is yes, of course they could, but a camp has little to do with running and more to do with recoveries, focused injury management and controlled diet, making the camp worth almost two months of training at home.

In actual fact, good camps will involve little or no fitness training but rather lots of technical and tactical work. The cumulative effect of the combined sessions will benefit fitness as well as proving essential for learning new plyometric exercises, good running technique, weight training programmes, football drills and game tactics. To achieve this and be able to train three times per day requires detailed planning involving all the management team. However, there is particular pressure on the training specialist to get the balance right; a badly run camp can do damage to team morale and preparation.

Over the years, Pat Flanagan has given much thought to drills with the ball that require and develop speed in all its forms. He has implemented reaction drills, power drills, acceleration drills, deceleration drills and basic speed drills that can all be done with the ball. The players are much happier to be working with the ball and will generally put in far more effort when it is being used, even if it is hard work. This, in turn, usually transfers positively to the game situation.

At present, the preparation of the Kerry team is conducted by a team under manager Jack O'Connor; it includes Alan O'Sullivan who does the physical conditioning, Donie Buckley who is in charge of ball drills, and Joe O'Connor who oversees the gym work.

While there are differences between the training regimes of Dr. Eamonn, Micko and Pat Flanagan, there are also some similarities. While Micko and Pat Flanagan put a lot of emphasis on ball drills that included power drills, acceleration drills, deceleration drills and basic speed drills, Micko worked more on speed endurance than power endurance. He put major emphasis on backs on forwards practices, whereas full-sided and small-sided conditioned games are used more nowadays.

The major difference between Micko's approach and the present Kerry team's approach is with the warm-up and warm-down. We really did neither; two laps of Fitzgerald Stadium would hardly constitute a warm-up nowadays. Our warm-down was a full sprint from the end line at the right hand corner of Fitzgerald Stadium around the goalposts at the town end and straight for the dressing room, with the first in being first on the table for a massage. A proper, well thought-out warm-up and warm-down practice definitely avoids injuries and extends a player's career.

THE fact that our training was very intensive and explosive resulted in a lot of muscle tears, strains and joint injuries. We didn't have the medical back-up that the Kerry team has now, and for years we depended on people like Owen McCrohan and later Claire Edwards, who both gave sterling service to the team and kept many of us on the field of play. They had to attend to a whole panel of players on their own before and after training and matches, and they deserve great credit for their commitment and service to our team.

We also received considerable help from Amy Johnston in Dublin and Dr. Con Murphy in Cork. Although Con was the medical doctor to the Cork team, he often treated people like Ger Power and Mikey Sheehy before Munster finals and, in a magnanimous and unselfish way, helped Kerry beat Cork on many an occasion, as both players always performed well on Munster final day.

Over the years, Dr. Dave Geaney was always available to us for medical advice while physiotherapist Maeve Leask (RIP) was most accommodating to myself, John O'Keeffe and others. Ossie Bennett from Kilkenny was also involved for a brief period and a number of the panel went to Oliver Brown of Tralee for massage therapy. Amy Johnson looked after the Dublin-based players for a number of years and was very helpful to me after I broke my leg. Anita Browne of Listowel gave me very good advice about an Achilles tendon injury that troubled me for a number of years. Of course there were others, of whom I am not aware, who treated individual players outside the Kerry training camp and they too played their part.

To get a greater understanding of the range of injuries suffered by the Kerry footballers of that time, I would like to refer to a study by Dr. John D. Chute, from Tralee, entitled 'A Retrospective Study of Musculoskeletal Injuries among former Elite Gaelic Football Players'. The study was published in March 2007 and was compiled from a survey of 42 Kerry senior players from the 1975–1987 era of Kerry football.

Injury treatment from the late 1970s into the '80s was managed in a very different manner than is the case today. According to Dr. Chute's findings, it is clear that, within this period, these athletes 'pushed their bodies beyond their physical boundaries in order to achieve success on the field'. He also points out that 'sports medicine was very much in its infancy' and the methods of rehabilitation for players were limited at best. Many injuries sustained by players involved 'soft tissue injuries of the lower limb, with ankle injuries being the most common sustained in 66% of players'. Dr. Chute argues that the 'lack of modern day rehabilitation, an absence of pre-habilitation with appropriate gym work, in addition to insufficient periods of rest, may have contributed to their long-term morbidity'.

According to the study of the 42 players, carried out in November 2006, more than three quarters of the athletes, or 33 individuals, experience ongoing symptoms. This includes two players who had recently undergone surgical hip replacements. Within the total 78.5% of players experiencing ongoing physical symptoms of their career injuries, 58% experience symptoms which affect their present recreational activities, 42% are affected on a daily basis, and 29% of those 31 players experience sleeping problems due to their ongoing symptoms. Six players, or 29% of those reporting recurrent symptoms, experience all three of the above mentioned effects on a regular basis.

Dr. Chute's report also includes responses from the players on the subject of the training and injury treatment received during this period from 1975–1987:

> While all the players interviewed felt the study was very worthwhile, twenty players, 47.6%, had no comment at all to make with regards to their time playing with Kerry. A number of players had no regrets and felt they were lucky with injuries and have remained symptom-free. Of the players who did have a comment to make, most felt that there was a distinct lack of a proper and appropriate 'warm-up.' There was a non-existent stretching programme, with an absent 'warm-down' post-training, and inadequate rest between training sessions. Several felt that, as amateur players, in full-time employment, they were exposed to excessively hard training. It was conceded by all that sports medicine was in its infancy at the time and that team preparation, injury treatment and rehabilitation was quite different to that of modern day inter-county Gaelic football player.

The present back-up medical team for the Kerry senior panel is most impressive and is handled by Dr. Michael Finnerty, who holds specialist qualifications in sports and musculoskeletal medicine. He runs the Tralee Back Pain and Sports Injuries Clinic in Tralee. Dr. Dave Geaney is there as a medical adviser. Harry O'Neill is another long-standing member of the backroom medical team. He is a physical therapist who gives massage treatments which target specific muscle groups to get the best possible outcome from the treatment. The medical team also consists of two physiotherapists, John Sugrue and Paudie McQuinn, whose main role is injury prevention and specific injury treatment. The medical team attends all matches and training sessions and they are constantly observing the players for signs that might indicate that a player is about to get an injury recurrence or develop a new injury. Generally the players are stood down from a match or a training session should this occur.

In the case of acute injuries, such as knee cartilage damage, knee ligament damage or torn muscles, the treatment starts immediately with icing which helps reduce swelling and speeds up recovery. Depending on the type of injury, it is important to investigate to determine its extent. Nowadays, if there is a suspected broken bone, the player will be sent for an x-ray. For all other kinds of soft tissue injuries, such as muscle tears, cartilage damage or ligament tears, the investigation of choice is an MRI scan. This scan usually gives a prompt result and, on the basis of the result, decisions can be made which will determine the next stage of treatment, be it surgery or conservative treatment.

Every possible injury has a specific rehabilitation programme, with the medical team combining to put this programme in place and monitor its effectiveness. There are ice baths provided in Fitzgerald Stadium which the players can use after training sessions and which help to reduce injuries and recovery time after hard training sessions. The medical team are constantly looking for ways of preventing chest infections and upper respiratory tract infections. They are constantly striving to have the team in the best physical health possible. A number of times during the year, a nutritionist attends the training sessions to give advice on diet and hydration and, in the past, use has been made of psychologists.

When you compare the medical back-up of the O'Dwyer era with that which is available now, there is just no comparison, which makes the achievement of people like Claire Edwards and Owen McCrohan even more remarkable. They had to look after a full panel of players on their own both for training sessions and matches.

Reflections on
Corner-Back Play

AS I HAD PLAYED most of my underage club football with Finuge and St. Michael's College as a forward or midfielder, when I was selected at corner-back on the Kerry minor team in 1970, I decided to become the type of defender that I didn't like playing against. As a forward, I always preferred being marked by a defender who followed the movement of the ball rather than my movements – in other words, a ball-watcher. I didn't like a marker who stayed tight on me for the duration of the game, more or less breathing down my neck. I always liked to be marked by someone who committed himself for every ball even when he had no hope of winning it.

Corner-back play demands absolute concentration and focus. You cannot afford to be distracted by your immediate opponent or, for that matter, by any other member of the opposing team; you must accept the referee's decisions and never let the spectators get to you. It is also very important to communicate with your fellow defenders and the goalkeeper at all times. We were very fortunate to have two top class goalkeepers on our team in Paudie O'Mahoney and Charlie Nelligan. They were forever relaying information about your immediate opponent if you lost him.

Initially in the Kerry defence, if an unmarked player was coming through with the ball, the full-back line tended to stay with their immediate opponents, allowing Kevin Moran in the first minute of the 1976 All-Ireland final, or Bernard Brogan in the 1977 semi-final, an unimpeded solo run and shot at goal. Moran put the ball just wide but Brogan scored a vital goal. Over time we developed a system whereby the corner-back picked up an unmarked opponent around the 14 yard line. This proved very effective in the 1980 and 1981 All-Ireland finals, where opposing players came through unmarked and were picked up by the full-back line. It also meant that the half-back line and midfielders could be more adventurous and take more chances.

222

Generally, if possible, I played shoulder to shoulder with my opponent on the goal side. I always tried to keep one eye on the ball and the other on the opponent. I adopted, as much as possible, the man-to-man, defence-marking technique used in basketball. Nowadays, backs play a type of zone defence and man-to-man marking is used in a less rigid manner. In defensive play I tried to reverse as much as possible so that I could have a full view of what was happening out the field. I worked very hard on reversing in training, especially when working out on my own.

Mick O'Dwyer always included reversing in our training sessions, and he had us reverse the full width of the pitch or execute a combination of sprinting and reversing. The fact that I could reverse so fast was a major advantage when it came to defending. Besides, I always tried to stay close enough to my opponent to ensure that, if the ball was passed to him, I had a chance of intercepting it or getting a hand to it as he tried to catch it.

I tried to find out as much as possible about my opponent's obvious strengths and weaknesses before a match. For example, if he was able to use one foot better than the other, I could anticipate his likely choice of kicking foot when he had the ball and then try and force him onto his weaker foot. At that time, very few forwards could kick with both feet.

I always felt that my first duty as a corner-back was to defend. There was no point in our forwards chalking up scores if we were conceding them at the other end of the field. Micko always reminded us that, as we had the best forwards in the country, what they needed was a quick ball out of defence rather than a slow build-up with defenders coming forward clogging up their space in the opposition's half of the pitch. He always emphasised building from the full-back line. For him the full-back line was similar to the front row in rugby; it was the foundation on which a team is built.

The regular corner-backs from 1975 to 1982 were Ger O'Keeffe, Mick Spillane, Paudie Lynch and myself. John O'Keeffe was permanently at full-back. All five of us were close markers, unselfish and very good at switching in defence. None of us would leave another defender isolated or stranded, and if one of us had to leave his immediate opponent for any reason, he could be assured that somebody else would cover for him.

As we were all outfield players with our clubs, we were comfortable if we had to pursue our immediate opponents to any part of the pitch. Good defending is a matter of a group of players working for one another. A defender who played in isolation and for himself would not be tolerated in our defence. I am convinced that one of the reasons why that Kerry team won four All-Ireland finals in a row was because of the discipline and unselfishness of our full-back line.

I always emphasised to teams that I coached that there is an individual and collective responsibility in defensive team play and that both are essential in the winning of matches. The game certainly has changed and positional play is not now as rigid as it was in our time. Nowadays it's common to see a corner-back at the end of a scoring movement. However, when corner-backs come forward and the play breaks down, resulting in a turnover, a team can be left very vulnerable in defence, especially if the ball is played quickly downfield, as happened to Kerry in the 2005 All-Ireland final against Tyrone, resulting in Peter Canavan's goal. We were always instructed by Mick O'Dwyer as full-backs to follow our immediate opponent to all parts of the field wherever that took us; however, the full-forward line in those days, with the exception of Bobby Doyle of Dublin, rarely roamed beyond the 50 yard line. Put simply, if your immediate opponent didn't go forward, you didn't either.

Playing corner-back for Kerry was an exercise in concentration and speed. While I can never remember coming off the pitch physically tired after an All-Ireland final, I was certainly mentally drained because of the tension leading up to the match and the total concentration required during the 70 minutes of play. In retrospect, I'm convinced that the long winter nights that I spent playing chess at Willie Joy's in Finuge developed my capacity to concentrate for prolonged periods and to anticipate my opponent's intentions when attacking with the ball.

As a minor I regularly tried to pass the ball to a team-mate, with either hand or foot, when I was clearing the ball out of defence. The practice at that time was to drive the ball as far as possible and hope that a team-mate would win it. I was also able to kick the ball with both feet and punch it with both hands. I was a natural right-footed kicker but through practice I developed my left foot, resulting in rarely being blocked down or whistled for over-carrying.

Me carrying out a left-footed clearance in the 1978 All-Ireland semi-final against Roscommon.

Basically, to be an effective inter-county corner-back, you had to be able to match the fastest forwards in Ireland for speed and acceleration, you had to be a good fielder of the ball and able to use both left and right foot to clear it.

One of the most frustrating aspects of being a defender in Gaelic football is the lack of a clearly defined tackle. In soccer, rugby, Australian Rules and American football, the tackle is clearly defined. In Gaelic football, the tackle is somewhat similar to the method used to dispossess an opponent in basketball whereby you must knock the ball out of a player's hands with minimum contact. Every referee seems to have his own interpretation of what constitutes a legitimate tackle and even among the top referees there is no consistency. As a result, players become frustrated and confused. I feel it's now time for the GAA to initiate a major nationwide coaching programme for referees, coaches and players at all levels on the correct application of the tackle. If executed properly, the tackle can be a very positive feature of the game.

The use of one hand should be emphasised when trying to dispossess a player in possession. More block-downs of foot deliveries using both hands should be encouraged too. Good defending should also be encouraged and rewarded by referees through enforcing the four consecutive steps rule and penalising forwards for overcarrying.

As a defender, I was always careful not to give away unnecessary frees. I tried as much as possible to use just one hand to dispossess an opponent. We had a deliberate policy in the Kerry full-back line of my time not to concede frees and this was reflected in our favour on the scoreboard.

Teaching Years

1975–1983

I STARTED WORK as a physical education, history and geography teacher in Tarbert Comprehensive School in September 1975 when I finished at the National College of Physical Education (NCPE). Tarbert was one of twelve comprehensive schools that were opened throughout the country in the late '60s and early '70s. They mainly comprised an amalgamation of a number of smaller schools in an area and they offered a broad curriculum with a wide choice of subjects, combining the technical and academic, to suit students of all abilities. There was no money spared in these schools and they were all equipped with modern language labs, science laboratories, art rooms, a staff room, a canteen and, more importantly from a physical education and sports perspective, they had ultra modern sports halls, which were rare at the time.

I was lucky compared to most of my classmates who graduated in 1975 and who didn't have the luxury of even basic indoor facilities in the schools where they were teaching. I could offer the choice of a wide range of activities, including Gaelic football, soccer, rugby, basketball, volleyball, badminton, tennis, gymnastics and trampoline, dance, hockey, athletics and cross country. It was a PE teacher's dream and I became a very enthusiastic teacher.

Generally, the students were very enthusiastic about physical education and looked forward to their weekly PE class; in a few cases it was the only reason they came to school. There was a strict dress code and the students had to have a very good reason to be excused from their PE class. Those who didn't have an aptitude for physical education were always made to feel welcome and were encouraged to do some activity during the class. As far as I was concerned, physical education, like any other subject, was for every student in the school, and every student was entitled to enjoy participating in as many activities as possible.

The ladies basketball team in 1978.
Front row left to right: Maureen Hayes, Bridie
Brennan, Breda Lavery, Coleen McElligott,
Mary Curtin, myself.
Back row left to right: Miriam Joyce, Johanna
O'Connor, Patricia Griffin, Margaret Deenihan,
Ann Collins.

I also started up school teams for both boys and girls in Gaelic football, basketball, soccer and athletics. Training for these teams usually took place after school hours and for the eight years that I was teaching in Tarbert Comprehensive I rarely left before 8pm. During that period we won both Kerry and Munster Colleges competitions in Gaelic football, and post-primary competitions in ladies basketball. The first year I taught in the school we won the Russell Cup (Kerry Colleges U15 Championship), defeating my alma mater, St. Michael's College, in the final.

Johnny O'Flaherty, my old teacher and coach, had been trying to win this competition for a number of years; I remember being on the losing team in a final while at St. Michael's College. Johnny couldn't understand how a team in their first year of the competition could succeed in winning it. We went on to win the Russell Cup again in 1977 but failed in our bid for three-in-a-row, losing in 1978 to St. Michael's. The members of that U15 team went on to win the Kerry Colleges County Cup and a number of Munster Colleges B and C competitions. They lost by just one point to St Brendan's College, Killarney, in the Dunloe Cup (Kerry Colleges U16) and the semi-final of the O'Sullivan Cup.

During my period in Tarbert Comprehensive I had the pleasure of training and coaching a number of very talented footballers who later went on to represent their county and clubs at different levels. Among them were John Kennedy who won three All-Ireland medals with Kerry in the mid '80s; Ciaran Culhane who played full-back for Kerry seniors in 1991, losing to

Tarbert Comprehensive School U15 football team and the Russell Cup.
Front row left to right: Jimmy Mulroy (teacher), James Lavery, Timmy Mackessy, Eamonn Walsh, Pa Foley, Seamus Beaton (captain), Dan Kennelly, JJ McElligott, Seán Dalton, Liam Liddy, Patrick Kelly, Liam Foley, Eddie Mangan, Finbar Carrig (assistant trainer).
Back row left to right: Tom Mac Eoin (principal, RIP), John Murphy, Eddie Scanlon, Joe Bunce, Maurice McEllistrim, Gerry Fitzmaurice, Eddie Kearney, Matthew Kelly, Eddie Sheehy, Mike Foley, TJ Reidy, myself (trainer).

Down in the All-Ireland semi-final; Mike Kissane and James Doherty who both played on the Kerry minor team; Tom Quaid and Liam Long who played with the Limerick senior football team. Obviously it was a very proud moment for me when I led Kerry to victory in the 1981 Munster final, but it was no less thrilling when the Kerry minor team, which included three of my pupils – John Kennedy, James Doherty and Mike Kissane – beat Cork in the Munster final that day.

One of the most rewarding periods of my life was the time I spent at Tarbert Comprehensive School, from 1975 to 1983. Apart from a most supportive principal (the late Tom Mac Eoin), and vice-principal (Joe Sullivan), there was an excellent teaching staff at the school. I struck up a fruitful friendship with Christy Killeen from Miltown Malbay in county Clare, who started

With teachers and pupils of Nano Nagle Special School in Lixnaw in September 1981.
Front row left to right: Nora O'Brien, John Martin O'Brien, Eoin Kiely, Michael Hussy, Annemarie Gentleman, Tom Lane, Tom Scanlon, John Savage, Geraldine Sheehan, Maurice McCarthy, Breda O'Sullivan, Josie Lyons, Eoin Carey. Middle row left to right: Myself, Sr Clare, Kathleen Harrington, Ann Lanigan, Susan S. Dunne, James Moore, Paul O'Connor, Elizabeth O'Connor, Michael O'Leary, Bridie Murphy, Sr Louise. Back row left to right: Willie Moore, Orla Mahony, Ann Lynch, Elizabeth O'Connor, PJ Fleming, John Lyons, Una Horan, Margaret O'Brien, Patrick Doody, Margaret Enright.

teaching in Tarbert in 1977. Not only did he become involved with helping me in the training and coaching of the school teams, I also got him involved with the underage teams in Finuge. Over the years he has made a significant contribution to the Finuge club at all levels and is the current vice-chairman.

During my time teaching at Tarbert, I also gave physical education classes at Nano Nagle Special School in Lixnaw. I found this work very fulfilling and I developed some lasting friendships with the pupils I met there. I am convinced that physical education and movement training can play a critical role in special needs education.

During the winter and spring periods of those years, I gave keep fit classes in the sports hall, usually on Monday night for men and Tuesday night for women. Traditionally there was very little organised sport for women in that part of the county, so they embraced their new-found experience in the sports hall enthusiastically. Even 30 years later when I meet many of these women they still remember fondly the great fun and enjoyment we had at those classes.

After winning the Sam Maguire Cup in 1979, with Tim Kennelly and Tom Mac Eoin (principal).

No doubt, the fact that I was a regular member of the Kerry team from 1975 to 1983 made me popular among the students. I was involved in seven All-Ireland finals over those years, winning five.

I found that, in ways, being a physical education teacher complemented my Gaelic football training. I always participated in the physical education classes and the after-school training sessions with the school teams. Whether it was doing press-ups, sit-ups, sprints, long runs or skill training, it helped my overall fitness. However, I did find in the early years of my teaching career that, because of the after-school hours and the time I spent training the local underage team in Finuge, I lost some of the edge and motivation for my own game: I often came home totally exhausted after spending up to 12 hours in the school.

In 1977, to give me more time for my classroom subjects, the principal appointed a second PE teacher, Sue Ellen McKenna, who was an excellent hockey, dance and gymnastics teacher. History and geography had been my two favourite subjects when I was going to St. Michael's College so I enjoyed

231

teaching them. There is no doubt that the knowledge I gained from teaching both subjects helped me later with my political career. Teaching modern Irish history, in particular, gave me a very good insight into the establishment of our State and its institutions.

I AM convinced that I would have continued to teach in Tarbert until retirement but for events that transpired in the Dáil on 5 November 1982, when a vote of no confidence in the Charles Haughey-led government was successful. On that morning I was at school coaching basketball when a local Fine Gael activist, Frank Quilter, came into the gymnasium and called me aside. He told me that he was travelling to Dublin for a meeting, that the Government would fall that day and that there would be a general election. He added that there was a widespread belief among Fine Gael activists in the constituency that I would be the only person who could win a seat for the party in Kerry North.

A number of people had previously suggested that I get involved in politics, but I didn't take them too seriously. Before the February election that year, I had been approached by senior figures of the Fine Gael party to put my name forward for the nomination. Having no ambition to become a politician at that stage, I told them that my focus was on winning the five-in-a-row with Kerry that September.

After Frank Quilter's approach, I went to the staffroom for the 11am coffee break. During the course of conversation with my colleagues, I told them of Frank's visit and his suggestion. Jim Kenny, the careers guidance teacher, was particularly enthused and advised me to *carpe diem* – seize the moment.

I called to John B. Keane's bar on my way home from school and sought his advice. He was a close friend of my father's for years; they were both passionate GAA men and Fine Gael supporters. The first man to call to our house when my father died in 1974 was John B. Keane. Because of my trust in him, John B.'s advice would be crucial to my decision whether or not to seek a nomination. His first reaction was one of surprise that I should even consider going into politics. He advised me that politics was a tough game, that your own party members could be the most negative and hurtful

With John B. Keane in the town park in Listowel, February 1998.

towards you. He said that it certainly would affect my family life as I'd be expected to attend a lot of social occasions, involving many late nights, and would have to be at the beck and call of constituents at all times.

Everything he told me that evening about politics was true, as I have discovered since. However, having given me such frank advice, he assured me that if I decided to run that he would propose me at the convention that Saturday evening in the Parklands Hotel in Tralee and that he would back me 100% for as long as he would live or I would stay in politics. As we were parting, he quoted me a celebrated line from his play *Sive*: 'If you decide to run "give it your best, your almighty best".' I did and I continue to do so.

But for John B.'s support I doubt that I would have sought a nomination. The first day I went canvassing he was with me and in the May 2002 election, just two weeks before he died, he insisted that he would canvass the main street of Listowel with me. I have never met anyone as discerning as John B.

Mary (left), then chairperson of Tralee YFG, with Monica Barnes in 1983.

when it came to summing people up; he was as much a philosopher of life as a writer and he had a profound influence on me both in sports and politics. I regret that I didn't listen more to him.

Later that evening of 5 November I was doing a keep-fit class with a group of women in Horan's Hotel in Tralee when Patsy McKenna, a local Fine Gael activist, rang me. He said he wanted to meet me after the class with Mary Dowling, a local teacher and daughter of John Dowling, the former Kerry footballer; I agreed and we met at Horan's restaurant. Mary was accompanied by her sister Antoinette. I had met her briefly a few times previously but this was the first time that I spoke to her. I gathered that Patsy and other members of the Fine Gael organisation felt that both Mary and I would make the ideal ticket for the election and Patsy was very forceful about this during our conversation. Little did I realise that Mary and I would get married four years later. Finbar Fitzpatrick, national organiser for Fine Gael at the time, said that I had married the one person who could take the Dáil seat from me.

After that meeting I returned to John B. Keane's pub in Listowel to meet Tom Quilter and Jeremiah O'Carroll, two local Fine Gael activists and friends of mine. I realised that I had to have the support of the former TD, Gerald Lynch, if I were to have any chance of winning the nomination, so the three of us went to meet him at Maureen Keane's bar. Gerald advised me that he would be backing Phil Healy, another local man, if he decided to seek the nomination: I made it clear to both Phil and Ger that I wouldn't run if that were the case. Phil, who still had some doubts, said that he would call me at school the following day at noon to confirm his decision.

I went to the school office just before noon, praying at that stage that Phil would run. When Mary O'Sullivan, the school secretary, who was related through marriage to the Fianna Fáil TD, Tom McEllistrim (RIP), asked me who was running for Fine Gael, I replied that I would tell her after I'd received a phone call. Phil duly phoned and confirmed that he decided not to seek the nomination following advice from his wife, Mary (RIP). Turning to Mary O'Sullivan, I said, 'You may now be looking at the candidate'. She was flabbergasted and I remember her saying, 'Do you know what you are letting yourself in for?' I had no idea.

After being declared elected in the June 1997 general election, at the CYMS Hall, Denny Street, Tralee, left to right: Jim Harmon (RIP), Tim Kennelly (RIP), myself, Bobby O'Connell and Leo Griffin (in front).

Sporting Policy and Activities
in Leinster House

1983–Present

ON THE NIGHT of the convention, 7 November 1982, the Parklands Hotel in Tralee was thronged with over 400 delegates from all parts of the constituency. Some really outstanding people were nominated to be selected as one of the two candidates to contest the forthcoming election, including the outgoing candidate Robert Pierse, who had run earlier that year in the February general election. Robert, grandnephew of Michael Collins and acknowledged as one of the leading solicitors in the country, was an excellent candidate. Had I known beforehand, I would certainly not have opposed him at the convention because he deserved another chance to win a Dáil seat.

John B. made a memorable speech and really sold me to the delegates. His punchline was that if I were the candidate that 'I would cut through the opposition like a scythe though switchgrass'. I made no effort to pretend I knew all the answers to the problems facing the people at that time. However, I did say that if I were selected as a candidate I'd be prepared to give the same commitment to politics as I did to playing with Kerry over the previous 12 years. John B.'s speech and my own contribution must have convinced the delegates because I was selected, together with Tralee native Bernie Gannon, as a joint ticket to contest the election for Fine Gael.

The result was announced at about 2am the following morning and I was told that I had to speak outside the hospital church in Listowel after 7am Mass. After a few hours sleep, I got up, told my mother that I was running for the election and set off to make my first speech in Listowel. I had no PA system and was in no way prepared for the speeches I had to make that morning at a number of local churches. The first man to arrive at the church was Robert Pierse. He shook hands with me and said that I was after doing both his wife and family a huge favour. He handed me all his waterproof clothing, including boots, umbrellas and caps that he had for the campaign and he introduced me at all the church gates that morning, confirming his full support for me.

We were joined by Gerald Lynch, who was TD for Kerry North from 1969 to 1977. He was very unlucky to lose his seat in 1977 and again in the June 1981 election, losing by just 140 votes on both occasions. Gerald was related to my family on his mother's side, the Stacks, and my father was one of his key supporters. This show of solidarity by both Gerald and Robert on that first morning gave me a great start and I hit the ground running.

The government had sent out word to their councillors and candidates that Garret FitzGerald was vulnerable on the question of allowing a referendum on the Right to Life of the Unborn if he were elected Taoiseach. This was thrown at us by a Fianna Fáil councillor in front of Knockanure church at the third Mass we attended that morning. Gerald Lynch requested the microphone to reply to him. He reminded the councillor that neither he nor Councillor Pierse could be accused of not being pro-life because, between them, they had 20 children – 10 each: that put an end to that argument.

I remember getting ready to address the people after the last Mass in Listowel when Joe Halpin, a very close friend of mine, emerged from the church to set up his lorry for the Fianna Fáil speakers. As he was passing me he said, 'An awful morning for this craic' – and then, when he saw me on the trailer with a microphone in my hand, he asked, 'What are you doing with that mic?' At that stage he had no clue that I was the candidate. I responded by saying that I was getting ready to make a speech. 'For that f***ing crowd?' Joe said. 'Yes,' I replied, 'and what's more, Joe, I am the candidate.' He froze on the spot and, looking up to the sky, he ran his fingers through his curly hair and said, 'Jesus Christ, boy, are you off your f***ing head?' I often think of Joe's reaction and there are times when I would agree with him: being a politician is not always easy.

No doubt, one of the chief reasons that I was asked to run for politics was because of my profile as a Kerry footballer, especially as captain of the four-in-a-row team. The constituents certainly had no problem recognising me in the election posters thanks to the photograph of the four-in-a-row Kerry team that was in every pub and in most homes in the constituency. I was received very warmly in every household, such was the respect and admiration for that team. However, positive and reassuring though their reception was, it did not translate sufficiently into votes and I failed by 144 votes to win a seat. In fact, during the campaign it was used against me that I was only a footballer and had nothing else to offer.

Having lost the Dáil election I ran for the Seanad and was generally given a very positive reception around the country from the Fine Gael councillors. However, some of them resented the fact that I was parachuted into the party because I was a footballer and felt that I was not entitled to a Seanad seat which, in any case, I failed to win.

Presenting Garret FitzGerald with a specially commissioned bronze piece by local artist and urban councillor Tony O'Callaghan (RIP), in Finuge in 1985.

I remember I was doing a keep-fit class with a group of women in the convent sports hall in Listowel when I got a call from Finbar Fitzpatrick telling me to come to Dublin that night because Garret FitzGerald wanted to see me. After the class I got into my car and drove to Dublin and was offered a seat in the Senate by Garret as one of his eleven nominees. I was delighted to accept but didn't get too carried away, knowing that I now had to justify Garret's confidence in me. Instead, I got, as they would say in football, 'stuck in' immediately.

After having taken the seat in the Seanad on 27 February 1983, I was appointed Fine Gael Party's spokesman on youth and sport, a portfolio which really suited me, coming as I did from a teaching and sporting background. During my years in the Seanad I took advantage of every opportunity to promote sport and physical education. I introduced a motion on 20 June 1984 in which I outlined my vision for sport, including the establishment of a

239

The people who got me into politics: John B. Keane, Garret FitzGerald and Mary Keane, in 1983.

National Sports Assembly to co-ordinate the development of sport in Ireland. Such an assembly could actively encourage the amalgamation of single sports clubs into multi-sports clubs, especially in urban centres sharing the same facilities: we haven't quite reached that stage yet in this country. I also suggested establishing a 'Sports House' to act as a centre of administration for the national governing bodies of Irish sport (NGBs) where facilities and personnel would be shared. Plans are now well advanced for the provision of this type of facility on Campus Ireland at Abbottstown, Dublin.

I also referred to the country's Health Bill, pointing out in my speech to the Seanad that expenditure on our medical services continues to increase at an alarming rate, apparently without any real gains in community health status. I suggested the following: 'Improvement will be only achieved by preventative measures and principally by motivating individuals to take a responsible attitude to their own health, particularly in regard to diet and physical activity.' I ended my contribution by saying that progress 'requires enthusiasm, optimism, leadership, good management and financial resources. All these elements, apart from the financial resources, are generally in place. Therefore I recommend as a top priority that every effort be made to secure additional financial resources from the government and commercial sector'.

When replying to the motion, Minister of State at the Department of Education with special responsibility for Sport, Deputy Donal Creed, said: 'Experience as a minister with responsibility for sport has brought me to the conclusion that a more comprehensive form of funding for sport is required. In this context I have for some time now been pursuing the question of the establishment of a National Sports Lottery. Many previous ministers with responsibility for sport spoke about the need and the desirability of having such a lottery. However, I am pleased to be able to advise the house that I have now succeeded in having the lottery proposal brought to government and I am optimistic that a favourable outcome will be forthcoming.' From a sports funding point of view, this was a momentous statement by Minister Creed and he did deliver.

IN October 1984, the government undertook to establish a National Lottery in their White Paper *Building on Reality*. The National Lottery Bill was introduced into the Seanad on 3 July 1986 by Minister Jim O'Keeffe. While welcoming the Bill, I expressed reservations about Section (5) which stated:

(a) Moneys paid into the central fund pursuant to Section (8) of this Act shall be applied for: the purposes of such one or more of the following and in such amounts, as the government may determine from time to time, that is to say, sport and other recreation, national culture (including the Irish language), the arts and the health of the community

(b) and such (if any) other purposes, and in such amounts, as the government may determine from time to time.

I expressed concern about Subsection (b) in particular because it left Lottery funds open for any government to use to support any purpose other than sport – and this happened subsequently. I strongly pointed out that the proceeds from the National Lottery should be solely for sport and for the development of recreational facilities and the arts. Regarding the reference to the health of the community in Section 5(a), I said:

> I would regard sport and the provision of recreational facilities as intrinsic to the health of the community. The amount of money spent in this country on curative medicine compared to preventative measures is totally disproportionate. In countries such as Australia and Canada where they have a very high awareness of the health benefits of sport and physical fitness, a positive correlation has been found through a number of surveys between the amount of money you spend on sport and the health benefits for the individual and the community.

The National Lottery went on to become a huge success and has resulted in €800,500,297 being allocated under the Sports Capital Programme for sport and recreation since 1987. About €30,825,589 of that amount has been allocated specifically to clubs and sports organisations in Kerry, with an amount of €11,225,374 being allotted to GAA projects in Kerry between 1998 and 2008.

I WAS first elected in February 1987 to Dáil Éireann, from where I continued to pursue sporting issues and, after the 1989 election, I was appointed my party's spokesperson on youth and sport. In order to increase the awareness of the importance of physical education and the lack of provision of it, I carried out a national survey on physical education provision in our primary school system in 1990. This survey showed that 75% of our schools had no indoor facilities for physical education classes and that very little physical education was actually taking place in our primary schools. In the introduction to the report on the survey findings, I pointed out that:

> Postural defects and obesity are increasing in our children. Both of these serious health problems are linked to lack of exercise. Children classified as

Campaigning for the general election in February 1987: Taoiseach Garret FitzGerald meeting former Kerry football captains, John Dowling, Johnny Walsh, myself, Tim Kennelly, and Gus Cremin in Tralee. Also in picture are Eamonn Barry and Dennis Stack (behind Garret), and my lifelong friend and supporter, Leo Griffin.

obese are usually obese in adolescence. Various research papers have shown that it is possible to reduce the level of obesity in primary school children by having a well-balanced physical education programme in the primary school at least on three occasions every week. Extra physical education at the expense of other classroom subjects does not produce deterioration in academic performance.

In fact, studies reveal that, where students undergo daily physical education programmes, they are more self-confident, disciplined, happier, healthier, fitter and with an increase in academic performance in most cases. It can be concluded from scientific research that the pursuit of a healthy lifestyle and the transmission of positive attitudes towards one's physical wellbeing should be encouraged at an early age and reinforced through a formal education experience in the primary school.

243

Following the survey, I organised a conference on physical education for primary school teachers in the Burlington Hotel in Dublin, which attracted a huge attendance and was addressed by some of the top physical education experts in the country. I later carried out a similar survey in our post-primary schools. It was obvious from this survey that physical education was being squeezed out because of the points system. At the time, the survey results received considerable media attention which did, I believe, have some effect on decision-makers. Following the publication of both surveys I wrote an article for the *Irish Independent* in 1992 which stated:

Children today are living in a society characterised by sedentary living patterns, emotional stress, poor diet and a lack of physical activity. Collectively, these factors are having a serious detrimental effect on them. Few children walk, run or cycle to school now. Most go by bus or car. When they come home from school they either sit down and study or watch TV or videos. We have become a 'video' society. There is no doubt but that we

Myself and Olwyn Enright TD at the launch of the 2005 national survey on physical education findings.

are dealing with a medical timebomb. We are now producing a generation of young people with under-developed hearts, poor posture and a weak muscle structure.

As a nation we have no notion of the consequences of having children grow into adulthood with such low fitness levels. If our children are not exercising at home, our schools must then take on that responsibility. However, the startling fact is that physical education is almost non-existent in most of our primary schools because of increasing pressure on the timetable from other subjects and the increasingly intense points race for third level places.

A follow-up national survey which I did in primary schools in 2005 confirmed that not much had changed regarding the level of provision of physical education in our primary schools, due particularly to lack of indoor facilities.

IN July of 2007, Enda Kenny appointed me as defence spokesperson on his front bench and, as a result, I became a member of the Joint Committee on Justice, Defence and Women's Rights. As part of the committee's work programme, I suggested that we produce a report on the possible role of the Defence Forces in promoting fitness and wellbeing in our schools and wider community. The committee agreed and appointed me as rapporteur. The report was published in December 2010 and came to the following conclusion:

> The Defence Forces have a range of resources, both personnel and facilities, which could be used to assist in combating the problem of childhood obesity, inactivity and poor posture, while also helping to improve the general fitness of the community. If these resources are to be used, this committee would strongly suggest that the Defence Forces should be formally tasked by government with filling a role in this area. This would mean that the provision of support would not be dependent on the goodwill of local level Defence Forces personnel but would be part of the organisation's mission.

I got considerable help in drawing up this report from Dr. Noel Richardson (former trainer of the Kilkenny hurling team), Captain Michael McDonough and Professor Niall Moyna of DCU. I was also fortunate to have excellent US interns during the period I was researching the report, including Kevin Craig, Julie Leider, John Newdick, and Sarah Zinc. They did very detailed research into the role of the Defence Forces in promoting physical education in schools and community fitness in countries like the US, UK, France and Canada. Hopefully the report will not be allowed to gather dust and the recommendations will be implemented in time.

Another welcome development is the involvement of national sports organisations such as the GAA, FAI and IRFU in primary schools. These organisations are putting development officers into schools and providing expert coaching in the basics for their respective sports. However, we still need a national, well-balanced physical education programme in our primary school system, one that looks after the needs of every child in the system on a regular basis throughout their entire primary school period.

IN 1993, I was appointed by John Bruton to his front bench as spokesperson on trade and tourism (the Minister for Tourism at the time was Charlie McCreevy). I made a big issue of sport tourism and promoting Ireland for activity holidays, particularly walking and golf. An issue arose about access to land in counties Clare and Wicklow, especially for walkers. Farmers were concerned that if people got injured on their land they could be liable for prosecution. In April 1993, I introduced a Private Members Bill, the Protection of the Occupiers of Lands Bill, which was defeated in the Dáil later that year. My Bill would have protected landowners against any litigation from people who were on their land without their permission. The Minister for Equality and Law Reform, Mervyn Taylor, later introduced a similar bill, the Occupiers of Land Bill, which became law in 1995.

THE late Deputy Tony Gregory introduced a motion to ban live hare coursing in June 1993 following the killing of a number of hares at coursing meetings around the country. The motion split the Fine Gael party. The front bench voted to support the motion and I had to do major lobbying within the parliamentary party to have this decision reversed. I made sure that all of the rural TDs were present for the vote in order to win party support to vote against Deputy Gregory's motion. I drew up a Private Members Bill to make muzzling of greyhounds compulsory and to introduce tighter veterinary controls.

At the time when I mentioned the introduction of the muzzle to the Irish Coursing Club they were not over-enthusiastic with the proposal as members felt that the muzzle could lead to neck injuries in greyhounds. However, the government took on my proposal and introduced a Bill making the wearing of the muzzle mandatory for hare coursing. This has proven to be very successful and, as I said at the time, has taken the blood out of the sport. I feel that this has saved the pastime which is very popular in many parts of rural Ireland and especially in North Kerry.

IN December 1994 the Fianna Fáil/Labour coalition government collapsed and, rather than seeking a dissolution of the Dáil, the then Taoiseach, Albert Reynolds, provided Fine Gael/Labour/Democratic Left with an opportunity to form a new government, which they succeeded in doing. The new government was referred to as the 'Rainbow Government'. John Bruton became Taoiseach and he appointed me Minister of State at the Department of Agriculture, Food and Forestry. I was hoping to be appointed to the Ministry of Sport, but Bernard Allen was given this position and, I must say, he did an excellent job during his period in office.

I was delighted that the Greyhound Racing Authority, Bord na gCon, was part of my brief in agriculture as this presented a unique opportunity for me to make a positive contribution to an industry very close to the heart of a large section of the North Kerry community. The process of change was already in motion under my predecessor, Brian O'Shea, TD, the then chairman of Bord na gCon Kevin Heffernan, and chief executive Seán Collins.

The greyhound fraternity acknowledged that radical decisions had to be made if the downward cycle, which the industry had suffered over the

Left: With Kerry officials of the Department of Agriculture while I was Minister of State – we were known as the 'Kerry Mafia'. Front left to right: Myself and my private secretary Siobhán Stack. Back left to right: Dermot Murphy, Tom Carroll, Jerome O'Shea (former Kerry footballer), Michael Dowling.

Right: At a fundraising event at the Kingdom Greyhound Stadium in Tralee with Billy Keane, Tommy Stack and Seán Kelly in 1997 for the Seanchaí Centre in Listowel.

previous 10 years, was to be reversed. For years the industry suffered from lack of investment and, as a result, facilities became dilapidated and, consequently, not attractive or saleable to the wider public. However, a change of policy by government meant that exchequer funding was provided for Bord na gCon. This enabled the board to approve the Shelbourne Park Project which included the provision of a grandstand, restaurant, hospitality suites, new kennels and full bar facilities, at a total cost of £2.5m. This became the flagship for the industry and the results were spectacular, with attendances and tote betting both showing remarkable increases.

The Shelbourne Park example influenced me to demand a similar type of development for Tralee. Before I took charge of the greyhound industry, £160,000 had been approved for stand facilities for Tralee. However, I was not prepared to accept a second class facility for Tralee and insisted that Bord na gCon come up with a more comprehensive proposal. After initial

apprehension they wholeheartedly supported the expanded project and the money was provided by the Department of Agriculture. This new £1.8m investment is not only enjoyed by the local patrons, but is now an important part of the county's tourism infrastructure, attracting thousands of visitors over the summer months. It has also become a centre for major fundraising events for local charities, including Kerry General Hospital.

I was also pleased to have been involved in the initial stages in the decision to build a new greyhound stadium in Cork. It was obvious that the existing track had too many limitations for future development and there was also the problem of car parking. This was the first new greyhound stadium to be built in Ireland since the late 1950s and it is a state-of-the-art facility.

I was most fortunate to serve with two excellent chairmen of Bord na gCon during my term of office, Kevin Heffernan and Pascal Taggart, who both contributed enormously to the revival of the industry. Kevin Heffernan, a

Left to right: Michael Field (CEO, Bord na gCon), myself, Kate Kennelly (promotions manager, Kingdom Greyhound Track, Tralee), Pascal Taggart (chairman, Bord na gCon) and Ruth Rogers (board member) in 1997.

friend since my football days, was responsible for laying the foundation for the subsequent success of the industry during his tenure as chairman of Bord na gCon from 1994–1995.

When Kevin decided to step down as chairman, I identified Pascal Taggart as his successor. I had known Pascal from meeting him at Shelbourne Park and Croke Park over the years and knew that he was a committed greyhound man and, more importantly, a very successful businessman. In order for the industry to grow, I felt that we needed someone with his business acumen.

When he was appointed chairman in late 1995, Pascal certainly made his presence felt. He devoted a considerable amount of time to the industry and was forever present at Shelbourne Park, adopting a hands-on approach. During the Taggart era, major progress was made in the greyhound industry, especially in the provision of new facilities and sanded tracks. Greyhound

Left to right: Pascal Taggart, myself, Patsy Byrne, Dolores Ruth and Seán Kelly at the Greyhound of the Year awards in 1996.

stadia all over the country attracted increased attendances, especially younger people. I am very proud of the fact that I appointed a man of his calibre who was so instrumental to the growth of the greyhound industry in this country.

IN February 2001, Michael Noonan took over from John Bruton as leader of Fine Gael. He appointed me spokesperson on sport and his advisor on Northern Ireland. The big topic of debate at the time in Irish sport was the provision of a new stadium at Abbotstown in Blanchardstown. In October 1998, the then Taoiseach, Bertie Ahern, announced that the government had decided to commission a feasibility study for the 'development of a stadium for the new century'. A consortium of consultants, headed by Price Waterhouse Coopers, was appointed to carry out the study. The FAI, in the meantime, announced that it intended to build its own 45,000 seater stadium at Tallaght at an estimated cost of £65 million, with the result that there were plans for two new stadia. At the same time, Croke Park was in the process of being rebuilt, with the Cusack Stand and Canal End completed and the new Hogan Stand under construction.

On 25 January 2000 the government accepted the consultants' recommendation on the provision of a new stadium and the Taoiseach announced the decision to go ahead with the project at a press conference, describing it as a vital piece of infrastructure with a projected cost of £230 million, and that, apart from £50 million donated by JP McManus, the project would be funded by the taxpayer.

Bernard Allen TD, the then Fine Gael spokesperson on sport, claimed in the Dáil on 8 March 2000 that the cost of building the stadium would be more in the region of £500 million and that the country simply could not afford this. In response, the then Minister for Sport, Dr. Jim McDaid, said that even though there may be additional cost, and that the costs may be underestimated or overestimated, 'We will go ahead with it because the country needs a national stadium'. On 24 February 2001 Minister McDaid unveiled a master plan for Abbotstown, including the 80,000 seater stadium and an aquatic centre.

In order to convince an increasingly sceptical media and sporting public, the government realised that it had to get the FAI and GAA on-side. The IRFU had bought into the project from the outset and on 9 March 2001 the FAI decided to abandon its plans for Eircom Park at Citywest and support the national stadium project at Abbotstown. The FAI was promised a direct incentive of £27 million and revenue from corporate box and advance ticket sales. With the IRFU and FAI now firmly on-side, the next challenge for the Taoiseach was to win the support of the GAA.

A motion to change Rule 42 to open up Croke Park for other sports, including soccer and rugby, was on the agenda for the annual GAA Congress on 7 April 2001. On 3 April the Taoiseach offered the GAA £60 million towards the re-development costs of Croke Park as an inducement to playing some of its premier games in Abbotstown. This inducement may have influenced the fate of the motion which was narrowly lost at Congress, with

176 voting for and 89 voting against; just failing by two to get the necessary two-thirds majority. Obviously if Croke Park were available for rugby and soccer, there simply would not be a case for providing an 80,000 seater stadium a few miles away at such a considerable expense to the taxpayer.

Immediately after the GAA decision on Rule 42, Campus & Stadium Ireland Development Ltd (CSID), which had been set up to spearhead the project, sent the outline bid documentation to the six international consortia who expressed an interest in bidding for the Abbotstown (Design, Build and Maintain, Operate and Finance – DBMOF) contract.

After the government decision to go ahead with the Abbotstown project, I introduced a motion in the Dáil during private members' time on 1 May 2001 requesting the government to abandon the project based on cost and location. Despite the fact that the government had the numbers to vote down the motion, Minister McDaid, in his reply to my motion, did give a commitment to appoint consultants to review the overall cost of the proposed stadium. The Department of Tourism, Sport and Recreation entered into an agreement with High-Point Rendel Ltd, a London-based consultancy company, on 26 June 2001 to undertake an independent overview of the cost of developing the proposed stadium and Sports Campus Ireland at Abbotstown.

The ensuing independent report confirmed that the project cost had exploded to an estimated £1.1 billion, compared to the original £280 million for the sports stadium alone. The report specified eight separate areas where there had not been enough planning and research, including funding and the use of facilities. The report was the nail in the coffin for the 80,000 seater stadium. An unnamed government minister was reported in the *Irish Independent* on 1 February 2002 as saying, 'We went in to the wilderness of Abbotstown with this project without a road map'.

Following the defeat of the motion, I was asked by Michael Noonan to produce a policy document setting out the party's alternative strategy to the sports stadium at Abbotstown. I published our sporting policy, *A Sporting Chance*, on 12 December 2001. It was a broad-ranging policy document and was designed to promote sport 'for the many, not just the few'. Apart from proposals for high performance sport, that is, supporting our elite athletes, it also included proposals for a major emphasis on physical education in both primary and post-primary schools, with particular focus on primary schools. As every child has to go through the primary school system, this is where most get their first chance to get involved in organised games.

The policy document also dealt with increasing the involvement of women in sport and making sporting opportunities more accessible for people with disabilities and for elderly people. It was a well-researched document and I spent a considerable amount of time writing it and thinking it through. The policy document recommended that the government abandon plans for the proposed stadium on the grounds of cost and location. It stated that, if returned to government:

> Fine Gael will enter into discussion with the GAA with a view to providing the necessary funding to further enhance Croke Park, including the completion of construction work and the provision of a top class playing surface. Hopefully the GAA, in return, will allow for the occasional soccer or rugby international game with a seating requirement of up to 80,000 spectators. Fine Gael favours the upgrading of Lansdowne Road to a 45,000 all-seater stadium for both soccer and rugby.

The president of the GAA at the time, Seán McCague, issued a damning repudiation of the policy. His statement went as follows:

> I am amazed that any political party, particularly a major political party such as Fine Gael, should signal their intention to attempt to manipulate GAA policy and signal their apparent intention to interfere with the management and administration of the Association for their own political agenda and expediency. This is even more perplexing when they never had discussions with the Association in regard to the formulation of their current published policy on sport and never had any discussions with us relative to their vision and vista for support for the development of sport and its infrastructure, including Gaelic games in the new Millennium. Indeed, the content of the Fine Gael policy document has been formulated and put in the public domain without any input from our Association or without us being afforded even the courtesy of prior sight of the document.

When I was contacted by RTÉ, informing me of Mr. McCague's statement, I was totally taken aback. First of all, there was no attempt in our policy document to exert any pressure on the GAA to open Croke Park. Secondly, I couldn't see how entering into discussions with the GAA and stating that, in return for funding to complete the refurbishment of Croke Park, the GAA might allow the occasional rugby and soccer game to be played there, could be seen as an attempt to manipulate GAA policy.

I also had made a number of efforts to contact GAA headquarters to arrange a meeting to discuss the policy document and, despite acknowledging my letters, there was no further follow-up. Even the day before the launch of the policy document, I left a number of messages for certain individuals to brief them on my proposals but got no response. To be fair to Seán McCague he apologised to me sometime afterwards when I visited Croke Park with Michael Noonan. He had not been aware of the efforts that I had made to seek a meeting with GAA headquarters

Maybe I took it too personally, but I suppose when I had given so much of my life to the GAA, as a player, coach/trainer and selector, coupled with the fact that I saw this as my own policy document and because I spent so much time working on it, I just didn't expect this broadside from the organisation of which I felt so much a part.

Karl MacGinty writing in the *Irish Independent* was also scathing of the policy document:

> At its pitiful core is Fine Gael's proposal to abandon Sports Campus and Stadium Ireland, offering us dream-world in its place. They suggest that current sporting needs would be best satisfied by the upgrading of Lansdowne Road to a 45,000 all-seater stadium. Fair enough in theory but anything up to a decade away in practice. The agreement of the IRFU would have to be sought, followed by funding (£200m?) design, and then, most difficult of all, planning permission.
>
> Where would our National Rugby and Soccer teams play during demolition and reconstruction and what of those occasions when the new facilities would not be big enough to satisfy demand? 'Simple' say Fine Gael. The narrow defeat of the motion to repeal Rule 42 at GAA Congress last spring clearly

demonstrates a willingness among the GAA fraternity to allow other sporting organisations use Croke Park for major games, they argue, adding both the FAI and the IRFU could then negotiate for the use of Croke Park.

Karl was right when he predicted that it would take ten years to achieve, but it materialised. The new stadium is there at Lansdowne Road and the GAA did open Croke Park to rugby and soccer, albeit only for the period while the new stadium was being built.

At the time of the publication of my proposal, neither the FAI, nor the IRFU, nor some elements within the GAA wanted this arrangement, but it happened, and I am convinced that it was the right solution. Thanks to the enlightened GAA delegates who voted for the opening of Croke Park and to Seán Kelly, the then president, for getting the motion before Congress, the country was saved from a monumental embarrassment. Can anyone imagine Irish rugby and soccer supporters travelling to Cardiff or Old Trafford for Ireland's home games? It would have cost the country a fortune in lost revenue and it would also have shown us in a very bad light around the sporting world. I can only imagine the reports on TV with images of the Irish supporters streaming out through our sea ports and airports and an empty Croke Park with seagulls flying around it.

I am confident that, in the future, rugby and soccer will again be played in Croke Park for games requiring a capacity of more than 50,000 spectators. The development of the new stadium at Lansdowne Road generated 800 jobs during construction. The sports capital grant of €191m invested by the government may seem to be a lot of money but, in real terms, the cost to government was under €40m when the taxes and VAT from the construction returned to the exchequer are taken into account.

RULE 21, banning participation by members of the Royal Irish Constabulary and British Defence Forces in Gaelic games, had a long history in the GAA constitution. It dates back to the 1886 decision by the UK government directing the then RIC to keep GAA members under surveillance. The ban on British soldiers and RIC members was lifted in 1893 and re-introduced in 1903.

After the Good Friday Agreement in 1998, the then president of the GAA, Joe McDonagh, called a special Congress to remove Rule 21. However, his attempts to have it removed provoked very strong resistance, from the Northern counties in particular. It was decided at the special Congress to postpone a decision on the Rule and revisit it following the publication of the Patten Report.

When the SDLP and the Catholic Church backed the new Police Service of Northern Ireland (PSNI), which replaced the RUC and encouraged young nationalists to join, I was asked to comment by RTÉ on the removal of Rule 21. Prior to this, any time I was asked to give my views on Rule 21, I always responded by saying that it should be left up to the County Boards of the Northern counties as they knew best and had firsthand experience of harassment of GAA players and officials.

However, following the Good Friday Agreement, the Patten Report on policing and the Weston Park agreement, I genuinely felt that the time had come to remove the ban on PSNI members who wanted to play Gaelic games or become members of the Association. The GAA, I felt, would now be seen as a sectarian organisation if Rule 21 wasn't removed from its constitution.

It took the Patten Commission years of negotiations with the political parties in Northern Ireland and both governments to finally agree on the naming and structure of the new police force. In the Republic, the proposal to set up a new police force had the backing of Fianna Fáil, Fine Gael and Labour, with the backing in the North of the SDLP, the Alliance Party, the Ulster Unionist Party and the main churches. Sinn Féin and Ian Paisley's Democratic Unionist Party rejected the new structure.

I was aware of the high level of interest among young Irish nationalists, north and south of the border, in joining the new force. The removal of Rule 21 would certainly make it easier for them. Because of my GAA background and the fact that I was my party leader's advisor on Northern Ireland, I was asked to comment on a regular basis on the removal of the Rule. From July to November 2001, I was continuously appearing in Northern Ireland newspapers, calling for the removal of Rule 21. As a result, I got a number of calls, emails and letters from GAA activists across Northern Ireland, some supportive of my stance, but others very much opposed, which I understood.

Following the acceptance by the SDLP and the Catholic Church of the new proposed policing structures, including the change of name from the RUC to PSNI, there was renewed pressure on the GAA to remove the ban. It was obvious if future PSNI recruitment were to be 50% nationalist, that many of these recruits would be Gaelic players from the nationalist areas. Being barred from playing with their local club would be a major disincentive to join the PSNI. The president of the GAA, Seán McCague, took the initiative and called a special Congress on 17 November 2001 to deal with Rule 21. It was removed from the GAA constitution by a large majority at the Congress.

With the support of the SDLP, the Catholic Church and the GAA, young Catholics began to join the PSNI in significant numbers. They formed a GAA club but found it very difficult to get any team to play them in Northern Ireland, mainly because of the Sinn Féin opposition in strong nationalist areas. They had to come down to Dublin to play the gardaí in a Gaelic football match.

One evening in the Dáil during May 2003, I met Eugene O'Sullivan from Cahersiveen who was Minister John O'Donoghue's driver and organiser of the match for the PSNI against the gardaí. We referred to the match during our conversation and I suggested I would try to get a Dáil team to play the PSNI. There was a core group of TDs and senators who had played in a number of rugby and soccer games over the years, and they all agreed to make themselves available for the match. Other TDs also volunteered that evening.

The match took place on Tuesday, 17 June 2003, at Kilmacud Crokes GAA club grounds in Stillorgan. It became controversial when Sinn Féin called for the match to be called off, stating that the PSNI 'should not be granted the kind of respectability such an event would confer'; the party also protested at the entrance to the ground before the match. There was heavy security at Kilmacud that evening and there was also a bomb scare earlier that day, which disrupted the club's summer camp programme. Nevertheless, it was a most enjoyable game, even if the age profile of the Dáil team was considerably older than the very young PSNI squad.

The Dáil team included MJ Nolan (FF), Enda Kenny (FG), Simon Coveney (FG), John Deasy (FG), Damien English (FG), Joe McHugh (FG), Conor Lenihan (FF), Tony Dempsey (FF), Seán Power (FF), John Browne (FF), Michael Kitt (FF), Jack Wall (Labour), Neil Blaney (FF), Frank Feighan (FG), and myself.

I only played for the final ten minutes as I had been injured two weeks previously at Old Trafford playing against a Westminster XI. TDs and senators made a major effort to be present for the game and, in so doing, they made a very positive statement of support for the PSNI. The Fianna Fáil, Fine Gael and Labour parties all contributed to the cost of the reception for both teams afterwards. The PSNI captain that evening was Peadar Heffron from Randalstown in county Antrim. He was lucky to escape with his life when his car was blown up outside his house in January 2010 and I understand he is making a steady recovery.

Myself and Peadar Heffron (captain of the PSNI team).

I am delighted that the PSNI members are now more accepted in GAA circles in Northern Ireland and fully supported by the Sinn Féin and DUP parties, indicative of a new maturity in Northern Ireland politics.

Like all games that the Oireachtas participate in, be it rugby, soccer or, in this case, Gaelic football, it was a total cross-party effort and I was very proud of the fact that members of the Oireachtas from all parties were prepared to send out a strong signal that the PSNI GAA club deserved to be recognised and treated like all other GAA clubs in Ireland.

DURING my eight years teaching physical education at Tarbert Comprehensive School I developed an understanding and appreciation of the importance of participation in sport by women. Despite the fact that Ireland has produced many outstanding female athletes, support for women's sport in this country is still lagging behind most other countries. In recent years our women – including Sonia O'Sullivan, Gillian O'Sullivan and, more recently, Derval O'Rourke, who won the silver medal in the hurdles at the 2010 European Championships – have out-performed our men in major international sporting events.

In order to highlight this general lack of support I arranged a seminar entitled 'Women in Sport' at the Burlington Hotel in February 2003 which attracted a large attendance and the message went out loud and clear to all present and the media that we didn't have a sports culture of practised equality in terms of equal opportunities for boys and girls, women and men, with regard to participation in sport in this country.

In 2004 I published a report entitled 'Women in Sport', with the help of Gina Menzies and Katie Liston, on behalf of the Joint Committee on Arts, Sport, Tourism, Community and Gaeltacht Affairs. The report highlighted the barriers to female involvement in sport, and included recommendations for further action on how females can participate more fully in all aspects of sporting activity in Ireland. It was obvious from the submissions received that female involvement at all levels of sport and physical activity was substantially less than that of men, and that young girls drop out of recreational and sport activities earlier than young males.

The very poor media coverage of female sporting events was also highlighted. This lack of coverage has meant that marketing and sponsorship of female sports have been difficult to secure. The experience on the ground was that it was significantly harder to secure local sponsorship for events and activities for girls than for boys. The girls generally have to do bag packing in the local supermarket while the boys don't. It was also obvious that female athletes at the elite level were having problems getting sponsorship. Either they were not getting it at all, or they were being offered significantly less than their male counterparts.

The lack of media coverage for women's sport certainly makes it less attractive for the sponsors. On my advice, the committee invited the sports editors of the *Irish Independent*, PJ Cunningham, and *The Irish Times*, Malachy Logan, to make presentations to the members. While both sports editors acknowledged the disparity in coverage between male and female sports, they also highlighted that sports editors frequently struggle with newspaper editors for the allocation of adequate space for sports generally. In this regard Mr. Logan argued that 'it would be a foolhardy editor who decided to reduce the coverage of a popular sport simply to enhance the coverage of a female event with a small playing base, and an even smaller degree of support'. This was obviously the nub of the problem. *The Irish Times* subsequently introduced the monthy Women in Sport Award, which was one of the proposals in the Oireachtas report.

The government did respond to the report and the seminar to some extent and ringfenced €750,000 in the 2004 budget for initiatives that would encourage more female participation in sport. This was repeated in the 2005 budget when the figure was increased to €1.5 million. I was delighted in 2005 that the Women in Sport initiative was established by the Irish Sports Council to address the clear gender gap in sports participation (only 34% of women participate regularly compared to 52% of men). €10 million was invested under this programme from 2005 to 2009, and a further €1.5 million was invested in governing bodies and sport partnership in 2010. I feel that the Joint Committee report and the Burlington seminar both influenced the ISC to introduce this initiative. However, despite these improvements, I still feel that we have a long way to go in order to create a level playing pitch for women in sports.

THERE are over one thousand people working in Leinster House. As far back as 1990 I started a campaign for the provision of a fitness centre for TDs and senators and the staff of the House. Eventually this happened in 2006. The fitness centre is well used by the staff. Unfortunately it is not used as much as I had hoped by the TDs and senators, and even myself. I am a firm believer in providing fitness programmes and facilities for employees; I have organised two national seminars on corporate fitness, in Croke Park in 2003 and the Dublin Conference Centre in 2010, directed at the country's major employers in both the private and public sectors. It makes good economic sense to invest in the fitness and health of employees. In return employers will get more productivity from their workforce, there will be less absenteeism and a lower burnout rate of key workers: a fitter workforce is a happier and more productive one. I intend to continue this campaign in the years ahead. Within the Oireachtas I intend to introduce a fitness programme with Senator Eamon Coughlan for all members and staff of Leinster House in 2012.

The most organised sporting activity in the Dáil is golf but, because of the time commitment, I have never become involved. Over the years, however, I have been involved in the rugby team, where I now play at out-half, having played in the forwards until recently. We usually play an annual game against Westminster to coincide with the Ireland v England match, a tradition dating back to 1991 when the first match between the two parliaments took place.

Since then, apart from the annual game against Westminster, we have participated in a special Parliamentarians' Rugby World Cup Tournament to coincide with the Rugby World Cup. We played in South Africa in 1995, England in 1999, Australia in 2003 and France in 2007. Games are competitive and involve guest players. Sometimes these guest players are still playing serious club rugby and can make the game rather risky for the generally less fit politicians. MJ Nolan from Carlow was responsible for getting the rugby team off the ground and was the captain for a number of years. I took over captaincy from MJ before passing it on to Simon Coveney, who played rugby at secondary school and also with Garryowen.

I was captain of the team for the 1999 World Cup in the UK. In the final game we played Westminster and I remember one incident in particular from that match. The great Welsh rugby player, JPR Williams, was a guest player with

Myself with F.W. de Klerk, former prime minister of South Africa, at the Parliamentarians' World Cup in Cape Town in 1995.

Westminster. Roy Bell, our scrum half, and I tackled him simultaneously. He was not at all pleased and certainly felt the impact. When we got off the ground, I said to Roy, 'Mike Gibson is avenged!' Back in JPR's international playing days, he took Mike Gibson out of a game in Lansdowne Road with a short arm tackle when Gibson kicked a ball forward and a certain try looked on the cards. I have enjoyed the rugby games over the years and, arising from them, I have made genuine friends, both in and outside the Dáil.

In South Africa for the Parliamentarians' Rugby World Cup Tournament. Included are, left to right: Barry Keohane (guest), Billy Kelliher (TD), Batt O'Keeffe (TD) Michael Creed (TD), Jerry Reynolds (TD), MJ Nolan (TD), myself, Nelson Mandela, Tom Kitt (TD), Rossa O'Donnell (guest), Seán Power (TD), Michael Begley (guest), Brian Cowen (TD), Willie Brennan (guest), Michael Aherne (TD), Pat Coakley (guest), Owen Faherty (manager), Charlie O'Malley (guest), Dr. Leo Dillon (guest), Bob Shackleton (guest), Bob Jeffers (guest), John Ennis (guest), Paddy Jordan (guest), Senator Eddie Bohan, Alan Weinrib (guest), Mattie Geraghty (guest), Leo Grogan (guest), Tony Morrin (guest), Paddy Browne (guest).

We travelled to Australia for the 2003 Rugby World Cup and I availed of the opportunity to visit the grave of my uncle, Father Paddy Deenihan, who had died at a very young age in 1933 and who was buried in Queenbeyan, near Canberra. I also used the visit to get some valuable information with respect to the development of sports stadia, especially Homebush Bay outside Sydney. As the trip coincided with resumption of the Dáil in September 2003, the deputies who were on the trip were attacked by the media and even by some of our own colleagues despite the fact that we had paid our own way and were representing our parliament.

Over the years I have also organised a number of memorable soccer games – one against the Scottish Parliament in Trinity College, to support the joint Ireland-Scottish bid for the UEFA Cup, and another against an FAI and a media selection in aid of the 2004 tsunami victims. We also played a memorable soccer match in Old Trafford against Westminster.

When my friend Tommy Horan (Tralee) asked me to get an Oireachtas team to play the King's Inn in a hurling match I was delighted to accept the challenge. This was the first hurling team ever to represent the King's Inn and also the first for the Oireachtas. We played in the Kilkenny colours and with the help of Senator John Paul Phelan's friends, we gave the King's Inn lads a bit of a lesson.

Apart from the Gaelic football game the Oireachtas played against the PSNI in 2003, we also played a very entertaining game against the GAA sports journalists, organised by John O'Shea for GOAL, before the Kilmacud Crokes All-Ireland Sevens final in 1994. I remember one incident from the game involving myself and John O'Shea. I fielded a high ball and John came in to take me out of it when I landed on the ground. However, he came off second best and I kicked the ball over the bar from about 40 yards out to the resounding applause of the large crowd watching the game.

The Oireachtas team that played the Scottish parliament at Trinity College, Dublin, November 2001.
Front row left to right: Seán Power, Frank Feehan, myself, Richard Bruton, Fergal Browne, Paul Gogarty.
Back row left to right: Damien English, Billy Kelliher, Tom Kitt, Simon Coveney, John Paul Phelan, John Deasey, Barry Andrews, MJ Nolan, Neil Blaney, Joe McHugh.

The Dáil versus Westminster at Old Trafford, left to right: Shay Byrne (usher), myself, Dermot Ahern, Paddy Crerand (referee), Michael Kitt, Richard Bruton, Paul Gogarty, in 2003.

The Oireachtas hurling team, February 2006.
Front row left to right: Tony Dempsey, Frank Feehan, Michael Ahern, JP Phelan, Frank Fahey.
Back row left to right: Paul Kehoe, Neil Blaney, myself, Tom Kitt, Barry Andrews.

The Oireachtas team that played against the GAA sports journalists in Kilmacud, 1994.
Front row left to right: Michael Ahern (Cork), myself, Michael Kitt (Galway), Willie Penrose (Westmeath).
Back row left to right: Billy Kelleher (Cork), John Farrelly (Meath), Tom Kitt (Dublin), Michael Creed (Cork),
Gerry Reynolds (Leitrim), Kilmacud, September 1994.

IN June of 2009, Gordon Flannery, who had recently moved to Listowel, called to see me at my weekly Saturday clinic in the Listowel Arms Hotel, seeking my support for the establishing of a charity running group called the Kerry Crusaders. His late brother, Howard, who owned the Maid of Erin pub in Listowel for a number of years, had set up a similar group in Clare called the Clare Crusaders. I didn't realise then that I would end up running the Dublin City Marathon that October (well, I ran the first 13 miles and walked/ran the second half, in a time of 5hrs 4mins).

After the event, that great champion of Irish running, Frank Greally, challenged me to get an Oireachtas team to participate in the 2010 Dublin City Marathon. I sent out an email and 15 responded; a team of 11 eventually participated in the event for charities of their choice.

We started training on Wednesday, 27 January 2010, running just one side of Merrion Square; over the following months we gradually increased the

266

The Oireachtas team that took part in the 2010 Dublin City Marathon.
Front row left to right: Lucinda Creighton TD, Mary Upton TD, Senator Fidelma Healy Eames, Senator Cecelia Keavney, Senator Nicky McFadden.
Back row left to right: James Reilly TD, Damien English TD, Senator Briain Ó Domhnaill, Minister Barry Andrews, Frank Feighan TD, myself.

distance we covered. By July we were running or walking as far as the Stillorgan flyover, and over the summer recess we followed the *Irish Runner* marathon training schedule, devised by Listowel man Brendan O'Shea.

I prepared for the marathon as if it were an All-Ireland final, following a strict diet and making sure to drink six to eight pints of water daily in the week before the event. I finished in a very relaxed state in 4hrs 22mins 30secs. Having prepared properly for the event, I really enjoyed it and it was a worthwhile experience. However, I doubt if I will do it again. For the past four years, I have organised an all-party Oireachtas annual charity hill walk. This has proven to be very popular and has always been well supported by my political colleagues.

My most recent sporting event in the Dáil was a charity game between an Oireachtas selection against a Martin McHugh sports journalists selection in Croke Park on 8 October 2011 to mark the 125th anniversary of the CIE GAA club. I was delighted that 25 parliamentarians, many of whom had never

On the Comeragh Mountains, left to right: Paudie Coffey, Senator Rónán Mullen, Senator Catherine Noone, myself and Caoimhghín Ó Caoláin TD, July 2011.

John O'Keeffe, Enda Kenny TD, Senator Paul Coughlan, myself and Eamon Breen at the start of the Ring of Kerry Charity Cycle in July 2010.

played competitive football previously, took part in the game, and that Senator Eamonn Coghlan was also a participant. No doubt I will continue to be involved in organising similar charity events for the remainder of my tenure in Leinster House.

AS I am approaching 60 years of age I intend, in the future, to concentrate on hillwalking and cycling. For the past three years, I have participated in the Ring of Kerry Charity Cycle, which is one of the largest mass participation cycle events in the country. I train with former county footballer, Eamon Breen, and longtime friend Pat Joe Sullivan, and we really push each other over the roads of North Kerry. Cycling is less severe on the joints and very beneficial for the cardiovascular system and I would highly recommend it to individuals when they retire from contact sport. I also intend to take up golf seriously whenever I retire from politics.

Mary and myself having a run on
Ballybunion Beach, November 2011.

(Photo: Dillon Boyer)

Conclusion

SPORT HAS PLAYED a key role in my life. Being a participant rather than a spectator, I've always been a keen competitor and have enjoyed pitting myself against others, both on the playing pitch and the running track. I still retain those competitive instincts and continue to enjoy a challenge. Team sports taught me the value of co-operation, impressing on me the primacy of the team over individual performances. It was a lesson I benefited from, both as a teacher and as a politician.

The indispensible role of the coach to a team's success was brought home to me by Mick O'Dwyer. I witnessed at first hand his leadership qualities, his charismatic way with players, his ability to motivate, to respond to setbacks and, when required, to make unpopular decisions.

He was a role model whose qualities I have tried to emulate in my own career, both in and out of sport.

My participation in sport has kept me fit and healthy and has given me a very positive outlook on life, and has helped me cope with its ups and downs. I've always enjoyed and continue to be an advocate of the outdoor life. Whether I'm hillwalking on the Reeks in Kerry or cycling around the Ring of Kerry, I feel at one with nature and uplifted by the beauty of the landscape.

I tried to pass on the discipline and respect for authority that I acquired from sport to my students as a teacher, and to the various teams I coached over the years. Involvement in sport was perhaps the best preparation I could have had for my career in politics. It cultivated essential qualities, including commitment, patience, perseverance, resilience and the ability to work with others.

Sport has been good to me.

Acknowledgements

I would like to acknowledge the contribution made by my mother, Mary Ellen, to this book. When she passed away in October 2009, Patricia, my sister, discovered a significant archive of my inter-county career in her house. As I have often said in public, mothers are the greatest archivists. She also collected photographs over the years which I have used in this book. I would also like to acknowledge the contributions of the following people who assisted me in various ways to complete this publication:

Frank O'Carroll, Dr Michael Finnerty, Dr Paul Rouse, Dr Ciara Meehan, Eugene McGee, Pat Flanagan, Dr John Chute, JJ Barrett, Michael Lynch (county librarian), Mike Brennan (MD Kerryman Ltd), Kerry Kennelly, Anne Kearney (head of library services, *Irish Examiner*), Billy Keane, Gabriel Fitzmaurice, Don MacMonagle, Dillon Boyer, Brendan Landy, Philip Tyndall, Dominic Lee, Michelle Cooper Galvin, Kevin Coleman, Karen Collins, Gina Menzies, Kevin Craig (intern), Mark Reynolds (archivist, Croke Park), the director and staff at the National Library of Ireland, Seán Wight (RIP), Patricia Deenihan, Bernadette Lee (personal secretary), Mike Foley and Mike Browne (Listowel constituency office), my drivers Jim O'Mahony and Albert Barrett, and my wife Mary, for being so patient while I was writing the book.

Appendix A

TEAM SELECTIONS

Team selections I have played with and against at inter-county minor, U21, senior championship, National League, and inter-provincial levels:

Minor

Munster Minor Semi-final
Askeaton, 1970
Kerry 2-10; Waterford 0-4
Kerry: P. O'Mahoney, D. Healy, J. Clifford, J. Deenihan, M. O'Sullivan, G. O'Keeffe, M. O'Connor, J. Long, D. O'Connor, C. O'Connell, P. Lynch, J. Power, J. Dillon, J. Egan, D. Moore.
Waterford: T. Hunt, P. O'Sullivan, D. Flynn, P. Norris, L. O'Brien, M. Hanrahan, D. Twomey, T. Casey, T. Moore, J. Galvin, PJ Ryan, E. Curley, H. Kelleher, D. Power, M. Kiely.

Munster Minor Final
Killarney, 26 July 1970
Kerry 4-9; Cork 1-11
Kerry: P. O'Mahoney, B. O'Shea, G. O'Keeffe, J. Deenihan, D. Healy, M. O'Sullivan, M. O'Connor, J. Long, P. Lynch, C. O'Connell, P. Brosnan, G. Power (capt), G. Dillon, J. Egan, J. Murphy. Subs: S. Clifford, D. Moore.
Cork: J. Kiely, B. Murphy, L. O'Flynn, S. Coughlan, D. Burns, M. O'Doherty, M. McCarthy, S. Fitzgerald, J. Lynch, D. Allen, M. Lynch, D. Crowley, B. Field, T. Callanan, P. Lonergan. Subs: M. Corbett, D. O'Sullivan, K. Aherne.

All-Ireland Minor Championship Semi-final
Croke Park, 3 August 1970
Kerry 2-10; Derry 0-11
Kerry: P. O'Mahoney, B. O'Shea, J. Clifford, J. Deenihan, D. Healy, M. O'Sullivan, G. O'Keeffe, P. Lynch, J. Long, C. O'Connell, P. B. Brosnan, G. Power, G. Dillon, J. Egan, J. Murphy. Subs: G. Browne for G. Dillon.
Derry: M. McFeely, M. Brennan, P. McGuckian, B. McGuckian, N. McGlone, L. O'Hara, P. Burke, E. Laverty, M. Moran, S. Mullan, M. O'Neill, P. McCloskey, P. Lennon, B. Kelly, S. Mullan. Subs: E. R. O'Neill for P. McCloskey, S. O'Neill for N. McGlone.

All-Ireland Minor Championship Final
Croke Park, September 1970
Galway 1-8; Kerry 2-5
Galway: J. Higgins, S. Cloonan, A. Marren, S. Kemple, PJ Burke, M. Geraghty, J. Corcoran (capt), P. Silke, T. O'Connor, J. Lardner, M. Rooney, M. Burke, I. Barrett, M. Walsh, J. Tobin.

Subs: J. Meehan for M. Walsh.

Kerry: P. O'Mahoney, B. O'Shea, J. Clifford, J. Deenihan, D. Healy, M. O'Sullivan, G. O'Keeffe, P. Lynch, S. Long, C. O'Connell, P. B. Brosnan, G. Power (capt), J. Murphy, J. Egan, G. Dillon. Subs: T. McEllistrim for B. O'Shea, D. Moore for J. Murphy.

All-Ireland Minor Final (replay)
1970
Galway 1-11; Kerry 1-10
Galway: J. Higgins, S. Cloonan, A. Marren, S. Kemple, PJ Burke, M. Geraghty, J. Corcoran (capt), P. Silke, T. O'Connor, I. Barrett, M. Rooney, J. Lardner, M. Burke, J. Meehan, J. Tobin. *Kerry*: P. O'Mahoney, B. O'Shea, J. Clifford, J. Deenihan, D. Healy, M, O'Sullivan, G. O'Keeffe, P. Lynch, J. Long, C. O'Connell, J. Egan, G. Power (capt), P. Brosnan, S. Fitzgerald, D. Moore. Subs: M. O'Connor, R. Casey.

Under 21

Munster Final
Cork Athletic Grounds
Cork 3-9; Kerry 2-3
Cork: B. O'Brien, B. Murphy, M. Doherty, S. Looney, D. Cogan, J. Coleman, P. McMahon, D. Aherne, B. Twomey, T. Murphy, D. Curran, B. Daly, D. Allen, D. Barron, B. Cogan. *Kerry*: J. Crean, J. Deenihan, J. O'Keeffe, P. O'Shea, T. O'Donnell, P. Lynch, D. Kavanagh, N. O'Sullivan, J. Long, P. Horan, M. O'Sullivan, J. Walsh, D. Coffey, J. Egan, G. Power. *Referee*: S. O'Connor.

Munster Final
Fitzgerald Stadium, August 1972
Kerry 1-11; Cork 2-7
Kerry: J. Crean, M. Murphy, J. Deenihan, D. O'Keeffe, S. O'Donovan, P. Lynch, G. O'Keeffe, J. O'Keeffe, J. Long, J. Coffey, J. Egan, J. Walsh, M. O'Shea, M. Ferris, G. Power. *Cork*: B. O'Brien, J. Corcoran, M. Doherty, G. O'Sullivan, N. Crowley, B. Murphy, C. Hartnett, J. Coleman, J. Lynch, S. Murphy, D. Barron, D. Curran, J. Barry-Murphy, S. Coughlan, D. Allen. *Referee*: S. Moloney.

All-Ireland Semi-final
Newbridge
Kerry 0-13; Kildare 0-6
Kerry: J. Crean, S. Donovan, J. Deenihan, D. O'Keeffe, M. Murphy, P. Lynch, G. O'Keeffe, J. O'Keeffe, M. McEllistrim, G. Power, J. Coffey, J. Walsh, M. O'Shea, M. Ferris, J. Egan. Subs: P. Horan for M. O'Shea.
Kildare: M. Moore, C. Kelly, D. Dalton, P. Gavin, T. Cullen, P. Murphy, P. Swords, R. O'Sullivan, H. Doyle, B. Geraghty, T. Herbert, D. Coogan, P. Deering, B. Doherty, B. Maloney. *Referee*: S. Campbell (2 minutes) for J. Martin.

1972 U21 All-Ireland Final
Croke Park
Galway 2-6; Kerry 0-7

Kerry: J. Crean, S. Donovan, J. Deenihan, D. O'Keeffe, M. Murphy, P. Lynch, G. O'Keeffe, J. O'Keeffe, N. Sullivan, M. McEllistrim, M. Sullivan, J. Walsh, P. Horan, M. Ferris, G. Power.

Galway: M. Noonan, J. Waldron, J. Dillon, B. Costelloe, P.J. Burke, M. Geraghty, S. Stephens, M. Walsh, M. Rooney, P. Burke, T. Naughton, M. Burke, J. Lardner, F. Rushe, J. Tobin.

U21 All-Ireland Semi-final
Tralee, 1973
Kerry 3-11; Offaly 2-6

Kerry: P. O'Mahoney, B. Harmon, J. Deenihan, B. O'Shea, G. O'Keeffe, G. Power, K. O'Donoghue, J. Long, P. O'Shea, J. Coffey, M. O'Sullivan, M. Sheehy, N. Brosnan, J. Egan, M. Shea.

Offaly: T. McNamara, E. Mulhall, M. Wright, W. O'Connor, J. Mulligan, S. Lowry, M. Currans, M. Brennan, M. Fitzgerald, C. Quinn, E. Lowry, R. Molloy, R. O'Loughlin, B. Collins, M. Devine.

Referee: J. Martin.

U21 All-Ireland Final
Ennis, 1973
Kerry 2-13; Mayo 0-13

Kerry: P. O'Mahoney, B. Harmon, J. Deenihan, B. O'Shea, G. O'Keeffe, G. Power, K. O'Donoghue, J. Long, P. Lynch, J. Coffey, M. O'Sullivan, P. O'Shea, M. O'Shea, J. Egan, M. Sheehy.

Mayo: S. Langan, P. Cunningham, S. Reilly, J. O'Mahony, G. Feeney, C. Moynihan, J. Culkin, R. McNicholas, G. Farragherty, M. Gannon, E. Webb, R. Bell, E. Ralph, D. McGrath, M. Flannery.

Referee: M. Spain.

Senior Championship

Munster SFC
17 June 1973
Kerry 3-11; Tipperary 0-5

Kerry: E. Fitzgerald; D. O'Sullivan, P. O'Donoghue, J. Deenihan, T. Prendergast, D. Crowley, G. O'Keeffe, D. Kavanagh (0-1), J. O'Keeffe (0-1), B. Lynch (0-1), M. O'Sullivan (2-1), E. O'Donoghue (0-1), J. Egan (0-1), M. O'Dwyer (1-6), J. Walsh. Subs: L. Higgins for B. Lynch, G. Power for G. O'Keeffe.

Tipperary: J. O'Donoghue, D. O'Gorman, E. Webster, N. Byrne, P. O'Connell, D. Bourke, P. O'Donoghue, V. O'Donnell, S. Kearney, L. Myles, D. Strang, C. O'Flaherty (0-1), B. Hall, J. Kehoe (0-2), J. Cummins (0-2). Subs: P. Moroney for V. O'Donnell.

Munster SFC Final
Cork, 15 July 1973
Cork 5-12; Kerry 1-15

Cork: B. Morgan (capt), F. Cogan, H. Kelleher, B. Murphy, K. J. O'Sullivan, J. Coleman, C. Hartnett, D. Long, D. Coughlan, W. Field, D. Barron, D. McMarthy, J. Barry-Murphy, R. Cummins, J. Barrett.

Kerry: E. Fitzgerald; D. O'Sullivan, P. O'Donoghue, J. Deenihan, T. Prendergast, D. Crowley, G. O'Keeffe, J. O'Keeffe (0-1), D. Kavanagh (1-0), B. Lynch (0-3), M. O'Sullivan, E. O'Donoghue (0-1), J. Egan (0-3), M. O'Dwyer (0-6), J. Walsh (0-1). Subs: L. Higgins for M. O'Sullivan, M. Ó Sé for T. Prendergast, M. Gleeson for E. O'Donoghue.

Muster SFC
Clonmel, 15 June 1975
Kerry 3-13; Tipperary 0-9

Kerry: P. O'Mahoney, P. Ó Sé, G. O'Keeffe, J. O'Keeffe, B. O'Shea, M. O'Sullivan, T. Kennelly, G. Power, G. O'Driscoll, D. Moran, B. Lynch (0-5), P. McCarthy, P. Spillane (0-3), J. Egan (2-3), R. Prenderville (1-0), M. Sheehy (0-2). Subs: J. Bunyan for G. O'Driscoll, J. Deenihan for B. O'Shea.

Tipperary: J. O'Donaghue, E. O'Gorman, E. Webster, N. Byrne, S. Kearney, V. O'Donnell, M. McDermott, J. Kehoe, P. Fanning, J. Treacy, G. Stapleton, C. O'Flaherty (0-4), L. Myles (0-3), M. Keating (0-2), G. McGrath. Subs: J. Keane for G. McGrath, T. McGrath for J. Treacy.

Munster SFC Final
Killarney, 13 July 1975
Kerry 1-14; Cork 0-7

Kerry: P. O'Mahoney; G. O'Keeffe, J. O'Keeffe, J. Deenihan, P. Ó Sé, T. Kennelly, G. Power; P. Lynch, P. McCarthy (0-1); B. Lynch (0-4), M. Sheehy (0-4); M. O'Sullivan (0-1), J. Egan (0-2), J. Bunyan, P. Spillane (1-1). Subs: D. Moran (0-1) for P. Lynch, G. O'Driscoll for B. Lynch.

Cork: B. Morgan; B. Murphy, H. Kelleher, M. O'Doherty, K. J. O'Sullivan, K. Kehilly, C. Hartnett; D. Long, D. McCarthy; D. Allen (0-3), S. Coughlan, A. Murphy (0-1), J. Barry-Murphy, D. Barron (0-1), R. Cummins (0-2). Subs: D. Hunt for M. O'Doherty, J. Coleman for O'Sullivan, J. Barrett for A. Murphy.

All-Ireland SFC Semi-final
Croke Park, 10 August 1975
Kerry 3-13; Sligo 0-5

Kerry: P. O'Mahoney, G. O'Keeffe, J. O'Keeffe, J. Deenihan, P. Ó Sé, T. Kennelly, G. Power (0-1); P. Lynch (0-4), P. McCarthy, B. Lynch (0-2), M. Sheehy, M. O'Sullivan (0-1), J. Egan (2-2), J. Bunyan, P. Spillane (1-1). Subs: G. O'Driscoll (0-2) for M. Sheehy, D. Moran for G. O'Driscoll.

Sligo: T. Cummins, R. Lipsett, J. Brennan, A. Caffrey, M. Brennan, B. Murphy, P. Henry, J. Stenson, T. Colleary, M. Laffey, M. Hoey (0-3), F. Henry, D. Kearins, M. Kearins (0-2), J. Kearins. Subs: D. Connolly for M. Laffey, B. Wilkinson for J. Kearins, T. Carroll for R. Lipsett.

All-Ireland SFC Final
Croke Park, 28 September 1975
Kerry 2-12; Dublin 0-11
Kerry: P. O'Mahoney, G. O'Keeffe, J. O'Keeffe, J. Deenihan, P. Ó Sé, T. Kennelly, G. Power,
P. Lynch, P. McCarthy, B. Lynch (0-3), D. Moran (0-2), M. O'Sullivan, J. Egan (1-0),
M. Sheehy (0-4), P. Spillane (0-3). Subs: G. O'Driscoll (0-1) for M. O'Sullivan.
Dublin: P. Cullen, G. O'Driscoll, S. Doherty, R. Kelleher, P. Reilly, A. Larkin, G. Wilson,
B. Mullins (0-1), B. Brogan, A. O'Toole, T. Hanahoe, D. Hickey, J. McCarthy, J. Keaveney
(0-6), P. Gogarty (0-2). Subs: B. Doyle (0-1) for B. Brogan, P, O'Neill for J. McCarthy,
B. Pocock (0-1) for P. Reilly.

Munster SFC
Dungarvan, 20 June 1976
Kerry 3-17; Waterford 0-6
Kerry: P. O'Mahoney, G. O'Keeffe, J. O'Keeffe, J. Deenihan, P. Ó Sé, T. Kennelly, G. Power,
P. Lynch, P. McCarthy, B. Lynch (1-2), D. Moran (0-2), M. O'Sullivan (0-2), J. Egan (0-2),
M. Sheehy (1-4), P. Spillane (1-5). Subs: S. Walsh for D. Moran.
Waterford: T. Fleming, N. Hayes, R. Aherne, N. Cashin, J. Moloney, J. Glavin (0-1), W. Moore,
T. Moore (0-1), R. Dunford, D. Conway (0-1), J. Hennessy (0-2), E. O'Halloran (0-1),
S. Aherne, P. Clancy, V. Kirwan. Subs: K. O'Connor for J. Moloney, M. Power for N. Hayes,
P. Keating for K. O'Connor.

Munster SFC Final
Pairc Uí Chaoimh, 11 July 1976
Kerry 0-10; Cork 0-10
Kerry: P. O'Mahoney, G. O'Keeffe, J. O'Keeffe, J. Deenihan, P. Ó Sé, T. Kennelly, G. Power,
P. Lynch, P. McCarthy (0-2), B. Lynch, D. Moran, M. O'Sullivan, J. Egan, M. Sheehy (0-5),
P. Spillane (0-2). Subs: S. Walsh (0-1) for B. Lynch, J. Walsh for M. O'Sullivan.
Cork: B. Morgan, S. O'Sullivan, B. Murphy, D. O'Driscoll, J. Coleman, T. Creedon, K. Kehilly,
D. Long (0-2), D. McCarthy, C. O'Rourke, S. Coughlan (0-1), B. Field (0-2), J. Barry-Murphy
(0-1), D. Barron (0-1), D. Allen (0-2). Subs: S. Murphy (0-1) for B. Field, K. Collins for
D. McCarthy.

Muster SFC Final (replay)
Pairc Uí Chaoimh, 25 July 1976
Kerry 3-20; Cork 2-19 (after extra time)
Kerry: P. O'Mahoney, G. O'Keeffe, J. O'Keeffe, J. Deenihan, P. Ó Sé, T. Kennelly, G. Power,
P. Lynch, P. McCarthy, D. Moran, M. O'Sullivan (1-2), P. Spillane (1-3), B. Lynch, M. Sheehy
(0-11), J. Egan (0-1). Subs: S. Walsh (1-3) for M. O'Sullivan.
Cork: B. Morgan, S. O'Sullivan, B. Murphy, B. O'Driscoll, J. Coleman, T. Creedon, K. Kehilly,
D. Long (0-1), D. McCarthy (0-1), C. O'Rourke (0-4), D. Allen (0-1), S. Murphy (0-5),
J. Barry-Murphy (1-3), D. Barron (0-3), S. Coughlan (1-0). Subs: K. Collins for S. O'Sullivan,
B. Fields (0-1) for C. O'Rourke. Extra time: C. O'Rourke for Coughlan, C. Murphy for B. Fields,
K. Murphy for T. Creedon.

All-Ireland SFC
Croke Park, 8 August 1976
Kerry 5-14; Derry 1-10

Kerry: P. O'Mahoney, G. O'Keeffe, J. O'Keeffe, J. Deenihan, P. Ó Sé, T. Kennelly, G. Power, P. Lynch, P. McCarthy, M. O'Sullivan (0-1), D. Moran (0-1), P. Spillane (0-2); B. Lynch (0-3), M. Sheehy (3-3), J. Egan (0-2). Subs: S. Walsh (1-1) for P. McCarthy, G. O'Driscoll (1-0) for B. Lynch.

Derry: J. Somers, L. Murphy, T. Quinn, P. Stevenson (1-0), G. Bradley, A. McGurk, M. Moran, T. McGuinness (0-1), G. McElhinney, B. Kelly (0-4), M. Lynch (0-2), F. McCluskey (0-1), A. McGuckian, L. Diamond (0-1), J. O'Leary (0-1). Subs: B. Ward for A. McGuckian, M, McAfee for L. Murphy, P. Chivers for G. McElhinney.

All-Ireland SFC Final
Croke Park, 26 September 1976
Dublin 3-8; Kerry 0-10

Dublin: P. Cullen, G. O'Driscoll, S. Doherty, R. Kelleher, T. Drumm, K. Moran, P. O'Neill, B. Mullins (1-1), B. Brogan (0-1), A. O'Toole (0-1), T. Hanahoe (0-1), D. Hickey (0-1), B. Doyle, J. Keaveney (1-2), J. McCarthy (1-1). Subs: F. Ryder for T. Hanahoe, P. Gogarty for B. Doyle.

Kerry: P. O'Mahoney, G. O'Keeffe, J. O'Keeffe, J. Deenihan, P. Ó Sé, T. Kennelly, G. Power, P. Lynch, P. McCarthy, D. Moran (0-2), M. Sheehy (0-3), M. O'Sullivan (0-1), B. Lynch (0-1), J. Egan (0-1), P. Spillane (0-2). Subs: C. Nelligan for P. O'Mahoney, S. Walsh for P. McCarthy, G. O'Driscoll for M. O'Sullivan.

Munster SFC
Tralee, 3 July 1977
Kerry 3-14; Tipperary 0-9

Kerry: P. O'Mahoney, J. Deenihan, P. Lynch, G. O'Keeffe, D. Moran, T. Kennelly, G. Power (0-1), P. Ó Sé (0-3), S. Walsh (0-3), J. Long, P. Spillane (1-0), B. Walsh (2-3), J. O'Keeffe (0-1), J. Egan (0-3). Sub: T. O'Keeffe for D. Moran.

Tipperary: J. O'Shea; A. O'Mahony, E. Webster, J. Kane, M. O'Riordan, V. O'Donnell, B. O'Neill, A. Cahill, G. McGrath (0-5), P. Morrissey, G. Stapleton, T. McGrath (0-1), S. Kearney (0-1), H. Mulhare (0-1), D. Ryan (0-1). Subs: M. McKeogh for G. Stapleton, D. McGrath for E. Webster.

Munster SFC Final
Killarney, 24 July 1977
Kerry 3-15; Cork 0-9

Kerry: P. O'Mahoney, J. Deenihan, J. O'Keeffe, G. O'Keeffe, D. Moran, T. Kennelly, G. Power, P. Ó Sé, J. O'Shea (0-2), J. Egan (1-0), P. Lynch (0-1), P. Spillane (1-3), B. Walsh (0-5), S. Walsh (1-1), M. Sheehy (0-3).

Cork: B. Morgan, S. Looney, T. Creedon, B. Murphy, D. O'Grady, J. Coleman, K. Kehilly, D. Long (0-2), S. Coughlan (0-3), M. Mullins, D. McCarthy, S. Murphy, D. Allen (0-1), J. Barry-Murphy (0-1), S. O'Shea (0-2). Sub: S. O'Sullivan for S. Looney.

All-Ireland SFC Semi-final
Croke Park, 21 August 21 1977
Dublin 3-12; Kerry 1-13
Dublin: P. Cullen, G. O'Driscoll, S. Doherty, R. Kelleher, T. Drumm, K. Moran, P. O'Neill,
B. Mullins, F. Ryder, A. O'Toole (0-4), T. Hanahoe (0-3), D. Hickey (1-1), B. Doyle (0-1),
J. Keaveney (0-3), J. McCarthy (1-0). Subs: B. Brogan (1-0) for F. Ryder, P. Gogarty for
J. McCarthy.
Kerry: P. O'Mahoney, J. Deenihan, J. O'Keeffe, G. O'Keeffe (0-1), D. Moran, T. Kennelly,
G. Power, P. Ó Sé, J. O'Shea, J. Egan (0-2), P. Lynch (0-1), P. Spillane, B. Walsh, S. Walsh
(1-2), M. Sheehy (0-7). Subs: T. Doyle for B. Walsh, P. McCarthy for J. O'Shea.

Munster SFC
Killarney, 18 June 1978
Kerry 4-27; Waterford 2-8
Kerry: C. Nelligan, J. Deenihan, J. O'Keeffe, D. Moran, P. Ó Sé, T. Kennelly, P. Lynch, J. O'Shea,
J. Mulvihill (0-2), G. Power (0-3), T. Doyle (0-3), P. Spillane (2-5), J. Egan (0-5), S. Walsh,
M. Sheehy (2-8). Sub: M. O'Sullivan for S. Walsh.
Waterford: T. Hunt, S. Flavin, M. Coffey, N. Hayes, D. Conway, S. Breen, J. Walsh,
R. Dunford (0-2), F. Murphy, T. Casey (0-2), B. Fleming (2-0), J. Hennessy, T. Keating (0-1),
M. Hackett (0-1), J. McGrath (0-1). Sub: P. Keating (0-1) for J. Walsh.

Munster SFC Final
Pairc Uí Chaoimh, 16 July 1978
Kerry 3-14; Cork 3-7
Kerry: C. Nelligan, P. Lynch, K. O'Keeffe, J. Deenihan, P. Ó Sé (0-1), T. Kennelly, D. Moran,
J. O'Shea, S. Walsh, G. Power (1-0), T. Doyle (0-2), P. Spillane (0-4), J. Egan (0-2), E. Liston,
M. Sheehy (2-5). Sub: P. McCarthy for J. O'Shea.
Cork: B. Morgan, B. Murphy, G. Desmond, K. Murphy, J. Coleman, T. Creedon (0-1),
B. McSweeney, D. McCarthy, C. Ryan, D. Allen (2-2), D. Barron, S. Murphy, J. Barry-Murphy
(1-0), R. Cummins (0-3), J. Barrett. Subs: J. Kerrigan for K. Murphy, D. Linehan (0-1) for
S. Murphy, V. Coakley for J. Coleman.

All-Ireland SFC
Croke Park, 13 August 1978
Kerry 3-11; Roscommon 0-8
Kerry: C. Nelligan, P. Lynch, J. O'Keeffe, J. Deenihan, P. Ó Sé, T. Kennelly, D. Moran,
J. O'Shea (0-1), S. Walsh, G. Power (1-2), T. Doyle, P. Spillane (1-2), J. Egan (0-1), E. Liston
(0-1), M. Sheehy (0-4). Subs: P. McCarthy for T. Doyle, M. O'Sullivan for P. McCarthy,
P. O'Mahony (1-0) for D. Moran.
Roscommon: G. Sheerin, H. Keegan, P. Lindsay, T. Heneghan, E. McManus, T. Donnellan,
D. Murray, D. Earley (0-1), J. O'Gara (0-1), J. O'Connor (0-4), M. Freyne, S. Kilbridge,
L. O'Gara, T. McManus, M. Finneran (0-2). Subs: P. Cox for L. O'Gara, M. McDermott for
S. Kilbride.

281

All-Ireland SFC Final
Croke Park, 24 September 1978
Kerry 5-11; Dublin 0-9
Kerry: C. Nelligan, J. Deenihan, J. O'Keeffe, M. Spillane, P. Ó Sé, T. Kennelly, P. Lynch,
J. O'Shea (0-1), S. Walsh, G. Power (0-1), D. Moran, P. Spillane (0-1), M. Sheehy (1-4),
E. Liston (3-2), J. Egan (1-2). Sub: P. O'Mahony for J. Deenihan.
Dublin: P. Cullen, G. O'Driscoll, S. Doherty, R. Kelleher, T. Drumm, K. Moran, P. O'Neill,
B. Mullins, B. Brogan (0-1), A. O'Toole, T. Hanahoe, D. Hickey, B. Doyle, J. Keaveney (0-8),
J. McCarthy.

Munster SFC
Milltown Malbay, 1 July 1979
Kerry 9-21; Clare 1-9
Kerry: C. Nelligan, J. Deenihan, J. O'Keeffe, M. Spillane, P. Ó Sé, T. Kennelly, P. Lynch,
J. O'Shea (0-2), V. O'Connor (1-2), G. Power (2-2), T. Doyle (0-5), P. Spillane (3-3),
M. Sheehy (1-4), E. Liston (2-2), J. Egan (0-1).
Clare: A. Burke, T. Tubridy, P. Begley, P. Garry, N. Roche, S. O'Doherty, M. Keigh, P. Nealon,
N. Normoyle (0-1), T. Curtin, J. McGrath (0-1), M. Downes (0-3), S. Moloney (0-4),
V. Casey (1-0), P. Ó Sé. Subs: M. Flynn for A. Burke, A. Maloney for P. Ó Sé.

Munster SFC Final
Killarney, 23 July 1979
Kerry 2-14; Cork 2-4
Kerry: C. Nelligan, J. Deenihan, J. O'Keeffe, M. Spillane, P. Ó Sé, T. Kennelly, P. Lynch,
J. O'Shea, V. O'Connor, G. Power (2-4), T. Doyle (0-1), P. Spillane (0-5), M. Sheehy (0-3),
E. Liston, J. Egan. Subs: D. Moran for T. Doyle, S. Walsh (0-1) for D. Moran.
Cork: B. Morgan, T. Creedon, K. Kehilly, B. Murphy, J. Crowley, C. Ryan, J. Coleman,
V. Coakley, J. Courtney (0-1), P. Kavanagh, D. Barron, D. McCarthy, J. Barry-Murphy (1-0),
D. Allen (1-2), C. Kearney (0-1). Subs: S. Murphy for V. Coakley, S. O'Sullivan for J. Coleman,
T. O'Reilly for P. Kavanagh.

All-Ireland SFC
Croke Park, 12 August 1979
Kerry 5-14; Monaghan 0-7
Kerry: C. Nelligan, J. Deenihan, J. O'Keeffe, M. Spillane, P. Ó Sé, T. Kennelly, P. Lynch,
J. O'Shea, V. O'Connor (0-1), G. Power (1-0), S. Walsh (0-2), P. Spillane (0-1), M. Sheehy (3-5),
E. Liston (1-1), J. Egan (0-3). Subs: D. Moran (0-1) for P. Ó Sé, G. O'Keeffe for J. Deenihan,
T. Doyle for E. Liston.
Monaghan: P. Linden, E. Hughes (0-1), S. Hughes, F. Caufield, P. Kerr, S. McCarville, E. Tavey,
G. McCarville, H. Clerkin (0-1), A. McArdle, D. Mulligan, K. Treanor, K. Finlay (0-4),
T. Moyna, B. Brady (0-1). Subs: G. Finnegan for A. McArdle, PJ Finlay for T. Moyna.

All-Ireland SFC Final
Croke Park, 16 September 1979
Kerry 3-13; Dublin 1-8
Kerry: C. Nelligan, J. Deenihan, J. O'Keeffe, M. Spillane, P. Ó Sé, T. Kennelly, P. Lynch, J. O'Shea, T. Doyle, D. Moran, P. Spillane (0-4), M. Sheehy (2-6), E. Liston (0-1), J. Egan (1-1). Sub: V. O'Connor for J. O'Keeffe.
Dublin: P. Cullen, M. Kennedy, M. Holden, D. Foran, T. Drumm, F. Ryder, P. O'Neill, B. Mullins, B. Brogan, A. O'Toole (0-1), T. Hanahoe (0-2), D. Hickey (0-2), M. Hickey, B. Doyle (0-3), J. McCarthy. Subs: J. Ronayne (1-0) for M. Kickey, G. O'Driscoll for J. McCarthy, B. Pocock for A. O'Toole.

Munster SFC Final
Pairc Uí Chaoimh, 6 July 1980
Kerry 3-13; Cork 0-12
Kerry: C. Nelligan, T. Kennelly (0-1op), J. O'Keeffe, M. Spillane, P. Ó Sé, G. O'Keeffe, D. Moran, J. O'Shea, S. Walsh, G. Power (1-2), T. Doyle (0-1), P. Spillane (0-5), M. Sheehy (0-3), E. Liston (2-1), J. Egan (0-1). Sub: V. O'Connor for J. O'Shea.
Cork: B. Morgan, S. O'Sullivan, K. Kehilly, J. Evans, J. O'Sullivan, T. Creedon (0-2), J. Kerrigan, C. Ryan (0-1), C. Collins, S. Murphy, D. Allen (0-5), T. Dalton (0-1), J. Barry-Murphy, J. Allen, D. Barry. Subs: T. O'Reilly (0-2) for S. Murphy, M. Healy for S. O'Sullivan, V. Coakley for J. O'Sullivan.

All-Ireland SFC
Croke Park, 24 August 1980
Kerry 4-15; Offaly 4-10
Kerry: C. Nelligan, G. O'Keeffe, J. O'Keeffe, M. Spillane, P. Ó Sé, T. Kennelly, D. Moran (0-1), J. O'Shea, S. Walsh, G. Power (0-2), T. Doyle (0-2), P. Spillane (2-2), M. Sheehy (1-3), E. Liston (0-1), J. Egan (1-4). Sub: J. Deenihan for S. Walsh.
Offaly: M. Furlong, M. Wright, S. Lowry, E. Mulligan, S. Darby, R. Connor, L. Currams, T. Connor, G. Carroll (2-1), A. O'Halloran, K. Kilmurray, P. Fenning, M. Connor (2-9), V. Henry, J. Mooney. Subs: C. Conroy for V. Henry, T. Fitzpatrick for A. O'Halloran.

All-Ireland SFC Final
Croke Park, 21 September 1980
Kerry 1-9; Roscommon 1-6
Kerry: C. Nelligan, J. Deenihan, J. O'Keeffe, P. Lynch, P. Ó Sé, T. Kennelly, G. O'Keeffe, J. O'Shea (0-1), S. Walsh, G. Power (0-1), D. Moran, P. Spillane (0-1), M. Sheehy (1-6), T. Doyle, J. Egan. Sub: G. O'Driscoll for G. Power.
Roscommon: G. Sheerin, H. Keegan, P. Lindsay, G. Connellan, G. Fitzmaurice, T. Donnellan, D. Murray, D. Earley (0-1), S. Hayden (0-1), J. O'Gara (0-1), J. O'Connor (1-2), A. Dooley, M. Finneran (0-1), T. McManus, E. McManus. Subs: M. Dolphin for A. Dooley, M. McDermott for S. Hayden.

Munster SFC
Listowel, 28 June 1981
Kerry 4-17; Clare 0-6

Kerry: C. Nelligan, J. Deenihan, J. O'Keeffe, P. Lynch, P. Ó Sé (0-1), T. Doyle, M. Spillane, J. O'Shea (0-1), T. Spillane (0-1), G. Power, D. Moran (0-1), P. Spillane (0-3), M. Sheehy (0-6), E. Liston (3-3), J. Egan (1-1). Subs: B. O'Sullivan for J. O'Keeffe.

Clare: A. Burke, T. Tubridy, D. O'Doherty, M. Keogh, P. Garry, M. Murray, N. Roche (0-1), N. Normoyle, T. Bonfil, P. McNamara (0-2), J. McGrath (0-1), M. O'Reilly, P. Burke, G. Fitzpatrick (0-2), T. Killeen. Subs: S. Moloney for T. Killeen, S. O'Doherty for P. Garry.

Munster SFC Final
Killarney, 19 July 1981
Kerry 1-11; Cork 0-3

Kerry: C. Nelligan, J. Deenihan, J. O'Keeffe, P. Lynch, P. Ó Sé, T. Doyle, M. Spillane, J. OShea (0-1), T. Spillane, G. Power, D. Moran, P. Spillane (0-3), M. Sheehy (1-5), E. Liston (0-1), J. Egan (0-1).

Cork: B. Morgan, M. Healy, K. Kehilly, J. Evans, M. Moloney, C. Ryan, J. Kerrigan, T. Creedon (0-1), C. Collins, D. Barry (0-1), S. Hayes, T. Dalton, F. O'Mahony, D. Allen (0-1), D. Barron. Subs: M. Creedon for B. Morgan, J. Lynch for S. Hayes.

All-Ireland SFC
Croke Park, 9 August 1981
Kerry 2-19; Mayo 1-6

Kerry: C. Nelligan, J. Deenihan, J. O'Keeffe, P. Lynch, P. Ó Sé, S. Walsh, M. Spillane, J. O'Shea (0-1), T. Doyle (0-1), G. Power (1-0), D. Moran (0-3), P. Spillane (0-3), M. Sheehy (0-6), E. Liston (1-2), J. Egan (0-3). Sub: T. Kennelly for G. Power.

Mayo: M. Webb, M. Gavin, A. Egan, A. Garvey (0-1), H. Gavin, T. Kearney, M. O'Toole, J. Lyons (0-1), W. Nally, J. P. Kean, W. J. Padden, M. Carney (0-1), E. McHale (1-0), J. Burke (0-1), J. McGrath (0-2). Subs: G. Feeney for A. Egan, J. Maughan for M. Carney.

All-Ireland SFC Final
Croke Park, 20 September 1981
Kerry 1-12; Offaly 0-8

Kerry: C. Nelligan, J. Deenihan, J. O'Keeffe, P. Lynch, P. Ó Sé (0-1), T. Kennelly, M. Spillane, J. O'Shea (1-0), S. Walsh (0-1), G. Power (0-1), D. Moran (0-2), T. Doyle (0-1), M. Sheehy (0-5), E. Liston, J. Egan (0-1). Subs: P. Spillane for J. Egan (67 mins), G. O'Keeffe for M. Spillane.

Offaly: M. Furlong, M. Fitzgerald, L. Connor, C. Conroy, P. Fitzgerald, R. Connor, L. Currams, T. Connor (0-1), P. Dunne, V. Henry, G. Carroll, A. O'Halloran, M. Connor (0-4), S. Lowry (0-2), B. Lowry (0-1). Subs: J. Mooney for T. Connor, J. Moran for V. Henry.

League Games 1972–1973

Round 1
Roscommon, 29 October 1972
Kerry 0-9; Roscommon 0-8
Kerry: E. Fitzgerald, D. O'Keeffe, D. Crowley, J. Deenihan, M. Gleeson, J. O'Keeffe,
M. O'Sullivan, L. Higgins, P. Lynch, J. Saunders, P. Griffin, J. Walsh, J. Egan, D. Kavanagh,
G. Power.
Roscommon: J. Neill, H. Keegan, P. Lindsay, T. Heneghan, T. Regan, J. Kerrane, D. Watson,
G. Beirne, T. Hunt, J. Mannion, D. Earley, J. Finnegan, M. Flanagan, M. Frayne, J. Kelly.
Referee: L. Maguire.

Round 2
Tralee, 12 November 1972
Longford 0-11; Kerry 0-8
Longford: J. Moloney, K. Canavan, S. Ryan, M. McGrath, E. Smith, S. Mulvihill, J. P. Reilly,
J. Hannify, F. Sheridan, T. Mulvihill, P. Burke, F. Farrell, S. Lee, S. Donnelly, V. Daly.
Kerry: E. Fitzgerald, J. Deenihan, P. O'Donoghue, D. O'Keeffe, P. Lynch, D. Kavanagh,
G. O'Keeffe, M. O'Connell, J. O'Keeffe, J. Walsh, P. Griffin, E. O'Donoghue, J. Saunders,
L. Higgins, G. Power.
Referee: F. Halbert.

Round 3
Cork, 26 November 1972
Kerry 1-13; Cork 1-8
Kerry: E. Fitzgerald, D. O'Sullivan, P. O'Donoghue, D. Crowley, J. Deenihan, G. O'Keeffe,
G. Power, E. O'Donoghue, P. Lynch, B. Lynch, P. Griffin, J. Walsh, D. Kavanagh, F. Russell,
M. O'Dwyer.
Cork: B. Morgan, P. Barry, M. Doherty, B. Cummins, K. J. O'Sullivan, T. Murphy, C. Hartnett,
D. Hunt, D. Long, D. Allen, D. McCarthy, F. Cogan, J. Barrett, D. Barron, D. Coughlan.
Referee: S. O'Connor.

National League Final
Croke Park, 6 May 1973
Kerry 2-12; Offaly 0-14
Kerry: E. Fitzgerald, D. O'Sullivan, P. O'Donoghue, J. Deenihan, J. O'Keeffe, D. Crowley,
M. O'Shea, D. Kavanagh, J. O'Keeffe, B. Lynch, L. Higgins, E. O'Donoghue, J. Egan,
M. O'Dwyer, J. Walsh.
Offaly: M. Furlong, S. Lowry, M. Ryan, M. O'Rourke, E. Mulligan, L. Coughlan, M. Wright,
W. Bryan, S. Evans, P. Fenning, K. Kilmurrey, A. McTague, M. Connor, J. Smith, J. Cooney.
Referee: J. Moloney.

League Games 1973–1974

Round 1
Aughrim, 14 October 1973
Kerry 6-13; Wicklow 2-5
Kerry: J, Bambury, D. Crowley, J. Deenihan, B. O'Shea, G. O'Keeffe, J. O'Keeffe, G. Power,
J. Long, P. Lynch, B. Lynch, J. Coffey, M. O'Sullivan, J. Walsh, J. Egan, S. Fitzgerald.
Wicklow: B. Finnegan, B. Dignam, G. Synnott, P. Behan, M. Behan, M. McNamee, M. Finn,
M. Coffey, J. Darcy, S. Keogh, B. Carthy, L. O'Loughlin, O. Doyle, P. Clarke, J. Dowling.
Referee: P. Kelly.

Round 2
Tralee, 28 October 1973
Kerry 1-14; Roscommon 2-5
Kerry: P. O'Mahoney, D. Crowley, J. Deenihan, S. Fitzgerald, G. Power, J. O'Keeffe, G. O'Keeffe,
P. Lynch, J. Long, J. Walsh, M. O'Sullivan, E. O'Donoghue, J. Coffey, J. Egan, M. Sheehy.
Roscommon: P. White, G. Mannion, P. Lindsay, T. Regan, D. Watson, H. Keegan, J. Kerrane,
G. Byrne, J. Mannion, D. Earley, M. Freyne, T. Donlon, J. Kelly, O. Hanley, T. Henegan.
Referee: J. Dennigan.

Round 3
Longford, 12 November 1973
Kerry 1-16; Longford 0-9
Kerry: P. O'Mahoney, D. Crowley, J. Deenihan, S. Fitzgerald, G. Power, J. O'Keeffe, G. O'Keeffe,
P. Lynch, J. Long, J. Walsh, M. O'Sullivan, E. O'Donoghue, J. Coffey, J. Egan, M. Sheehy.
Longford: M. Esler, J. Smith, S. Ryan, T. Kiernan, E. Smith, S. Mulvihill, M. McElvaney,
J. Flynn, F. Sheridan, P. Brady, P. Bourke, T. McGrath, J. Hughes, V. Daly, B. Barden.
Referee: P. Collins.

Round 4
Killarney, 26 November 1973
Cork 1-6; Kerry 0-8
Cork: B. Morgan, F. Cogan, H. Kelleher, B. Murphy, K. J. O'Sullivan, J. Coleman, C. Hartnett,
D. Coughlan, D. Long, N. Kirby, R. Cummins, G. Lynch, J. Barry-Murphy, D. Barron,
J. Barrett.
Kerry: P. O'Mahoney, D. Crowley, P. O'Donoghue, J. Deenihan, G. Power, J. O'Keeffe,
G. O'Keeffe, P. Lynch, J. Long, J. Walsh, J. Egan, M. O'Sullivan, B. Lynch, M. O'Dwyer,
E. O'Donoghue.
Referee: J. Maloney.

Round 5
Tullamore, 9 December 1973
Kerry 5-7; Offaly 1-11
Kerry: P. O'Mahoney, D. O'Sullivan, P. O'Donoghue, J. Deenihan, G. O'Keeffe, D. Crowley,

J. O'Keeffe, N. O'Sullivan, J. Long, B. Lynch, M. O'Sullivan, G. Power, M. Sheehy, S. Fitzpatrick, J. Egan.
Offaly: M. Furlong, M. Wright, M. Ryan, M. O'Rourke, E. Mulligan, W. Bryan, M. Heavey, S. Evans, S. Lowry, P. Fenning, K. Kilmurray, S. Darby, S. Conney, E. Lowry, M. O'Connor.
Referee: P. Kelly.

Round 6
Cashel, 17 February 1974
Kerry 3-14; Tipperary 0-10
Kerry: P. O'Mahoney, D. O'Sullivan, P. O'Donoghue, J. Deenihan, G. Power, D. Crowley, A. O'Keeffe, J. Long, J. O'Keeffe, B. Lynch, M. O'Sullivan, J. Walsh, J. Egan, S. Fitzgerald, M. Sheehy.
Tipperary: J. O'Donoghue, J. Keane, D. Egan, E. O'Gorman, A. O'Mahony, E. Webster, P. O'Donoghue, M. Kiely, J. Cummins, S. Conway, M. Keating, J. Whyte, S. Kearney, S. Meade, J. Kehoe.
Referee: S. O'Connor.

League Games 1974–1975

Round 1
Tullamore, 20 October 1974
Offaly 0-8; Kerry 0-7
Offaly: M. Furlong, S. Lowry, J. Smith, M. O'Rourke, E. Mulligan, M. Ryan, S. Grogan, K. Claffey, P. Fitzgerald, K. Kilmurrey, D. Kelly, T. McTague, J. Cooney. S. Evans, W. Bryan.
Kerry: P. O'Mahoney, P. Ó Sé, J. O'Keeffe, J. Deenihan, G. Power, T. Kennelly, G. O'Keeffe, P. Lynch, G. O'Driscoll, D. Moran, M. O'Sullivan, M. Sheehy, B. Lynch, J. Bunyan, J. Egan.
Referee: J. Moloney.

Round 2
Killarney, 11 November 1974
Kerry 0-8; Dublin 0-8
Kerry: P. O'Mahoney, P. Ó Sé, J. O'Keeffe, J. Deenihan, G. Power, T. Kennelly, M. Murphy, P. Lynch, G. O'Driscoll, B. Lynch, P. Spillane, D. Moran, M. O'Sullivan, PJ McIntyre, M. Sheehy.
Dublin: P. Cullen, G. O'Driscoll, S. Doherty, R. Kelleher, P. Reilly, A. Larkin, G. Wilson, B. Mullins, B. Donovan, A. O'Toole, T. Hanahoe, B. Doyle, J. McCarthy, J. Keaveney, P. Gogarty.
Referee: F. Halbert.

Round 3
Cork, 7 December 1974
Kerry 1-12; Cork 1-6
Kerry: P. O'Mahoney, P. Ó Sé, J. O'Keeffe, J. Deenihan, M. Murphy, T. Kennelly, G. O'Keeffe,

G. O'Driscoll, D. Moran, B. Lynch, M. O'Sullivan, G. Power, J. Egan, J. Bunyan, M. Sheehy.
Cork: B. Morgan, B. Murphy, H. Kelleher, M. O'Doherty, K. J. O'Sullivan, K. Kehilly,
C. Hartnett, D. McCarthy, D. Barron, D. Long, S. Coughlan, T. Murphy, J. Barry-Murphy,
D. Hunt, D. Coughlan.
Referee: B. Cross.

Round 4
Roscommon, 2 February 1975
Kerry 1-9; Roscommon 0-9
Kerry: P. O'Mahoney, P. Ó Sé, J. O'Keeffe, J. Deenihan, M. O'Sullivan, T. Kennelly, G. O'Keeffe,
G. O'Driscoll, P. Lynch, B. Lynch, J. Egan, G. Power, P. Spillane, J. Bunyan, M. Sheehy.
Roscommon: J. McDermott, T. Henegan, P. Lindsay, G. Mannion, P. O'Callaghan, H. Keegan,
T. Regan, J. O'Gara, G. Beirne, J. Finnegan, M. Freyne, M. McNamara, F. Brandon, D. Earley,
J. Kelly.
Referee: M. Spain.

Round 5
Tralee, 2 March 1975
Kerry 3-8; Kildare 1-3
Kerry: P. O'Mahoney, P. Ó Sé, J. O'Keeffe, J. Deenihan, M. Sullivan, T. Kennelly, G. O'Keeffe,
G. O'Driscoll, P. Spillane, B. Lynch, P. Lynch, G. Power, J. Egan, J. Bunyan, M. Sheehy.
Kildare: O. Crinnigan, S. Malone, P. Kelly, D. Dalton, J. Delaney, E. O'Donoghue, T. Smullen,
P. Managan, T. Herbert, J. O'Connell, H. Hyland, J. McKeown, L. Shinneys, M. McKeever,
W. Moloney.
Referee: J. Dennigan.

League Play-off
Croke Park, 23 March 1975
Meath 0-11; Kerry 0-6
Meath: R. Giles, M. Collins, J. Quinn, B. Murray, P. Smith, P. Reynolds, PJ O'Halloran,
J. Cassels, M. Ryan, E. O'Brien, K. Rennicks, P. Traynor, M. Kerrigan, C. Rowe, O. O'Brien.
Kerry: P. O'Mahoney, P. Ó Sé, J. O'Keeffe, J. Deenihan, M. O'Sullivan, T. Kennelly, G. O'Keeffe,
S. O'Donovan, D. Moran, B. Lynch, P. Spillane, G. Power, J. Egan, J. Bunyan, M. Sheehy.
Referee: G. Fagan.

League Games 1975–1976

Round 1
Tralee, 26 October 1975
Kerry 1-9; Offaly 0-9
Kerry: P. O'Mahoney, B. O'Shea, G. O'Keeffe, J. Deenihan, P. Ó Sé, T. Kennelly, G. Power,
P. McCarthy, S. Walsh, D. Moran, J. Long, P. Spillane, J. Egan, M. Sheehy, G. O'Driscoll.
Offaly: M. Furlong, M. Ryan, J. Smith, M. O'Rourke, R. Connor, M. Wright, N. Clavin,

S. Lowry, E. Mulhall, S. Darby, G. Hickey, P. Fenning, S. Darby, C. Dunne, M. Connor.
Referee: F. Halbert.

Round 2
Croke Park, 9 November 1975
Dublin 2-11; Kerry 0-13
Dublin: P. Cullen, G. O'Driscoll, S. Doherty, R. Kelleher, P. Reilly, P. O'Neill, B. Pocock, B. Mullins, L. Egan, A. O'Toole, T. Hanahoe, D. Hickey, B. Doyle, J. Keaveney, P. Gogarty.
Kerry: P. O'Mahoney, B. O'Shea, G. O'Keeffe, J. Deenihan, P. Ó Sé, T. Kennelly, G. Power, P. McCarthy, G. O'Driscoll, B. Lynch, M. O'Sullivan, J. Egan, M. Sheehy, P. Spillane.
Referee: H. Reilly.

Round 3
Killarney, 24 November 1975
Kerry 1-9; Cork 2-6
Kerry: P. O'Mahoney G. O'Keeffe, J. O'Keeffe, J. Deenihan, P. Ó Sé, T. Kennelly, G. Power, P. McCarthy, D. Moran, B. Lynch, M. Sheehy, M. O'Sullivan, J. Egan, G. O'Driscoll, P. Spillane.
Cork: B. Morgan, S. O'Sullivan, H. Kelleher, B. Murphy, K. Collins, T. Creedon, K. Kehilly, D. Long, D. McCarthy, J. McCarthy, D. Allen, S. Murphy, W. Field, J. Barry-Murphy, C. Murphy.
Referee: B. Cross.

Round 4
Tralee, 7 December 1975
Kerry 3-11; Roscommon 2-8
Kerry: P. O'Mahoney, G. O'Keeffe, J. Deenihan, P. Ó Sé, B. O'Shea, T. Kennelly, G. Power, P. McCarthy, D. Moran, G. O'Driscoll, M. Sheehy, M. O'Sullivan, J. Egan, W. Murphy, P. Spillane.
Roscommon: G. O'Dowd, H. Keegan, P. Lindsay, T. Heneghan, K. Kerrane, D. Watson, T. O'Regan, G. Beirne, J. Mannion, M. Fenton, E. McManus, M. Freyne, J. Finnegan, P. Cox, J. Kelly.
Referee: J. Dennigan.

League Play-off
Cork, 7 March 1976
Kerry 1-5; Cork 2-6
Kerry: P. O'Mahoney, G. O'Keeffe, J. O'Keeffe, J. Deenihan, P. Ó Sé, T. Kennelly, G. Power, D. Moran, G. O'Driscoll, B. Lynch, M. Sheehy, M. O'Sullivan, J. Egan, P. Lynch, P. Spillane.
Cork: B. Morgan, S. O'Sullivan, H. Kelleher, B. Murphy, K. Collins, T. Creedon, K. Kehilly, D. Long, D. McCarthy, J. Coleman, C. O'Rourke, S. Coughlan, J. Barry-Murphy, D. Barron, D. Allen.
Referee; J. Landers.

League Games 1976–1977

Round 2
Tralee, 24 October 1976
Kerry 0-12; Dublin 0-7
Kerry: C. Nelligan, P. Ó Sé, J. O'Keeffe, J. Deenihan, D. Moran, T. Kennelly, G. Power,
J. Long, J. O'Shea, G. O'Driscoll, P. Lynch, P. Spillane, M. Sheehy, S. Walsh, J. Egan.
Dublin: N. Bernard, G. O'Driscoll, S. O'Doherty, R. Kelleher, T. Drumm, K. Moran, P. O'Neill,
B. Mullins, B. Brogan, A. O'Toole, T. Hanahoe, D. Hickey, B. Doyle, J. Keaveney, J. McCarthy.
Referee: J. Dennigan.

Round 4
Galway, 21 November 1976
Kerry 2-9; Galway 1-8
Kerry: C. Nelligan, G. Leahy, J. O'Keeffe, J. Deenihan, D. Moran, A. O'Keeffe, G. Power,
G. O'Driscoll, J. Long, V. O'Connor, P. Lynch, P. Spillane, T. Doyle, S. Walsh, J. Egan.
Galway: G. Mitchell, TJ Gilmore, J. Dillon, M. Judge, P. O'Neill, J. Hughes, I. Barrett,
W. Joyce, D. Smith, B. Corbett, J. Connolly, L. Samman, J. Tobin, J. Duggan, G. McManus.
Referee: R. Barry.

League Semi-final
Croke Park, 3 April 1977
Kerry 2-13; Roscommon 0-9
Kerry: C. Nelligan, J. Deenihan, J. O'Keeffe, G. Leahy, P. Ó Sé, T. Kennelly, G. Power,
J. O'Shea, D. Moran, S. Walsh, M. Sheehy, P. Spillane, B. Walsh, T. O'Regan, J. Egan.
Roscommon: G. O'Dowd, J. Kerrane, P. Lindsay, T. Henegan, T. Donnellan, M. Freyne,
T. Regan, M. McDermott, G. Beirne, M. Menton, D. Earley, J. O'Gara, J. O'Connor,
T. McManus, E. McManus.
Referee: P. Kelly.

League Final
Croke Park, 17 April 1977
Kerry 1-8; Dublin 1-6
Kerry: C. Nelligan, J. Deenihan, J. O'Keeffe, G. Leahy, P. Ó Sé, T. Kennelly, G. Power,
J. O'Keeffe, J. O'Shea, S. Walsh, D. Moran, M. Sheehy, B. Walsh, P. Spillane, J. Egan.
Dublin: P. Cullen, G. O'Driscoll, S. Doherty, R. Kelleher, T. Drumm, K. Moran, P. O'Neill,
B. Brogan, A. Larkin, A. O'Toole, T. Hanahoe, D. Hickey, B. Doyle, J. Keaveney, J. McCarthy.
Referee: J. Dennigan.

League Games 1977–1978
J. Deenihan did not play.

League Games 1978–1979

Round 1
Croke Park, 8 October 1978
Kerry 2-9; Dublin 0-8
Kerry: C. Nelligan, J. Deenihan, J. O'Keeffe, M. Spillane, P. Ó Sé, P. Lynch, V. O'Connor,
J. O'Shea, S. Walsh, G. Power, D. Moran, P. O'Mahony, M. Sheehy, P. Spillane, J. Egan.
Dublin: P. Cullen, G. O'Driscoll, S. Doherty, R. Kelleher, T. Drumm, D. Maher, P. O'Neill,
B. Mullins, B. Brogan, A. O'Toole, T. Hanahoe, D. Hickey, B. Doyle, J. Keaveney, J. McCarthy.
Referee: J. Geraghty.

Round 2
Tralee, 5 November 1978
Kerry 7-8; Kildare 0-7
Kerry: C. Nelligan, J. Deenihan, J. O'Keeffe, M. Spillane, P. Ó Sé, T. Kennelly, D. Moran,
J. O'Shea, G. O'Driscoll, G. Power, J. Coffey, P. Spillane, M. Sheehy, E. Liston, J. Egan.
Kildare: O. Crinnigan, M. Moore, P. O'Donoghue, F. Mulligan, M. Condon, E. O'Donoghue,
D. Reilly, J. Crofton, J. Giblin, G. Power, D. Dalton, N. Dunne, H. Hyland, P. Mangan, T. Carew.
Referee: J. Dennigan.

Round 3
Cork, 19 November 1978
Cork 3-10; Kerry 2-5
Kerry: C. Nelligan, J. Deenihan, J. O'Keeffe, M. Spillane, P. Ó Sé, T. Kennelly, V. O'Connor,
J. O'Shea, J. Mulvihill, D. Moran, J. Coffey, P. Spillane, M. Sheehy, E. Liston, J. Egan.
Cork: B. Morgan, S. O'Sullivan, K. Kehilly, B. Murphy, J. Crowley, C. Ryan, J. Kerrigan,
J. Courtney, V. Coakley, J. O'Brien, J. Barry-Murphy*, D. Allen, P. Kavanagh, D. Barron,
C. Kearney.
Referee: P. Lane.

Round 4
Tralee, 3 December 1978
Kerry 6-11; Laois 0-0
Kerry: P. O'Mahoney, J. Deenihan, J. O'Keeffe, M. Spillane, A. O'Keeffe, T. Kennelly,
J. Mulvihill, J. O'Shea, S. Walsh, T. Bridgeman, M. Sheehy, M. O'Sullivan, P. Spillane,
E. Liston, J. Egan.
Laois: M, Mulhall, S. Hunt, R. Nearney, D. Brennan, C. Browne, P. Brophy, E. Whelan, R.
Millar, J. Costelloe, M. Moore, J. Hovington, T. Prendergast, A. O'Brien, L. Brennan, J. Lawlor.
Referee: J. Deenigan.

Round 5
Killarney, 10 December 1978
Kerry 2-6; Galway 0-7
Kerry: P. O'Mahoney, J. Deenihan, M. Spillane, T. O'Keeffe, T. Kennelly, G. Casey, J. O'Shea,

S. Walsh, M. Sheehy, V. O'Connor, M. O'Sullivan, P. Spillane, E. Liston, J. Egan.
Galway: G. Mitchell, J. Dillon, TJ Gilmore, M. Judge, J. Hughes, T. Heavey, P. O'Neill,
W. Joyce, J. Duggan, P. McGettigan, L. Higgins, G. McManus, P. Lee, T. Naughton, S. Joyce.
Referee: F. Halbert.

League Quarter-final
Croke Park, 1 April 1979
Roscommon 1-12; Kerry 1-11
Roscommon: J. McDermott, H. Keegan, P. Lindsay, T. Henegan, G. Fitzmaurice,
T. Donnellan, D. Murray, D. Earley, M. McDermott, J. O'Connor, J. O'Gara, S. Kilbride,
T. McManus, M. Freyne, E. McManus.
Kerry: C. Nelligan, J. Deenihan, J. O'Keeffe, M. Spillane, P. Ó Sé, T. Kennelly, V. O'Connor,
J. O'Shea, J. Mulvihill, D. Moran, J. Coffey, P. Spillane, M. Sheehy, E. Liston, J. Egan.
Referee: S. McManus.

League Games 1979–1980

Round 1
Tralee, 7 October 1979
Kerry 1-16; Dublin 0-10
Kerry: C. Nelligan, J. Deenihan, J. O'Keeffe, P. Lynch, P. Ó Sé, T. Kennelly, M. Spillane,
V. O'Connor, J. O'Shea, T. Doyle, S. Walsh, P. Spillane, M. Sheehy, E. Liston, J. Egan.
Dublin: M. Kennedy, D. Foran, M. Holden, R. Keleher, T. Drumm, F. Ryder, J. Brogan,
J. Roynane, B. Brogan, P. Canavan, B. Mullins, P. Ellis, A. O'Toole, A. Larkin, T. Hanahoe.
Referee: J. Dennigan.

Round 2
Galway, 1 November 1979
Galway 1-7; Kerry 1-7
Kerry: C. Nelligan, J. Deenihan, J. O'Keeffe, G. O'Keeffe, V. O'Connor, T. Kennelly,
M. Spillane, J. O'Shea, S. Walsh, G. Power, T. Doyle, P. Spillane, G. O'Driscoll, E. Liston,
M. Sheehy.
Galway: W. Devlin, J. Hughes, S. Kinneavy, M.J. Judge, P. O'Neill, M. Coleman,
S. McHugh, W. Joyce, T. Naughton, B. Brennan, R. Lee, B. O'Donnell, T. Mannion,
D. Smyth, S. Joyce.
Referee: PJ McGrath.

Round 4
Killarney, 9 December 1979
Kerry 0-12; Cork 0-10
Kerry: C. Nelligan, J. Deenihan, J. O'Keeffe, M. Spillane, P. Ó Sé, T. Kennelly, P. Lynch,
J. O'Shea, V. O'Connor, D. O'Donoghue, E. Liston, G. Power, M. Sheehy, P. Spillane, J. Egan.
Cork: B. Morgan, S. O'Sullivan, K. Kehilly, M. Healy, J. O'Sullivan, C. Ryan, J. Kerrigan,

V. Coakley, T. Creedon, C. Collins, J. Barry-Murphy, D. Allen, S. Murphy, J. Allen, C. Kearney.
Referee: P. Lane.

Round 5
Tullamore, 3 February 1980
Kerry 1-9; Offaly 1-5
Kerry: C. Nelligan, J. Deenihan, J. O'Keeffe, G. O'Keeffe, P. Ó Sé, P. Lynch, M. Spillane,
J. O'Shea, V. O'Connor, G. Power, D. Moran, P. Spillane, M. Sheehy, E. Liston, J. Egan.
Offaly: M. Furlong, E. Mulligan, S. Lowry, O. Minnock, P. Fitzgerald, R. Connor,
P. McGuinness, L. Connor, S. Lalor, V. Henry, K. Kilmurray, L. Currams, P. Doyle,
M. Connor, G. Carroll.
Referee: T. Jordan.

League Quarter-final
Limerick, 23 March 1980
Kerry 1-8; Roscommon 1-5
Kerry: P. O'Mahoney, J. Deenihan, J. O'Keeffe, M. Spillane, P. Ó Sé, T. Kennelly, V. O'Connor,
J. O'Shea, S. Walsh, D. Moran, T. Doyle, P. Spillane, B. Walsh, E. Liston, J. Egan.
Roscommon: J. McDermott, T. Heneghan, P. Lindsay, G. Connellan, G. Fitzmaurice,
T. Donnellan, D. Murray, S. Hayden, J. O'Gara, S. Kilbride, D. Earley, A. Dooley, T. McManus,
M. Finneran, E. McManus.
Referee: J. Dennigan.

League Semi-final
Croke Park, 6 April 1980
Kerry 1-11; Armagh 1-6
Kerry: P. O'Mahoney, J. Deenihan, J. O'Keeffe, M. Spillane, P. Ó Sé, T. Kennelly, P. Lynch,
J. O'Shea, S. Walsh, D. Moran, T. Doyle, P. Spillane, M. Sheehy, E. Liston, J. Egan.
Armagh: B. McAlinden, D. Stevenson, J. McKerr, K. Rafferty, B. Canavan, J. McCorry,
J. Donnelly, P. Moriarty, C. McKinstry, J. Murphy, J. Smyth, P. Loughran, M. McConville,
M. Murphy, S. Devlin.
Referee: S. Aldridge.

League Final
Pairc Uí Chaoimh, 27 April 1980
Cork 0-11; Kerry 0-10
Cork: B. Morgan, S. O'Sullivan, K. Kehilly, J. Evans, J. O'Sullivan, C. Ryan, J. Kerrigan,
T. Creedon, V. Coakley, S. Murphy, D. Allen, T. Dalton, J. Barry-Murphy, J. Allen,
D. Barron.
Kerry: P. O'Mahoney, J. Deenihan (capt.), J. O'Keeffe, M. Spillane, P. Ó Sé, T. Kennelly,
P. Lynch, J. O'Shea, S. Walsh, D. Moran, T. Doyle, P. Spillane, G. Power, E. Liston, J. Egan.
Referee: T. Moran.

League Games 1980–1981

Round 1
Pairc Uí Chaoimh, 5 October 1980
Kerry 0-13; Cork 0-10
Kerry: C. Nelligan, J. Deenihan, J. O'Keeffe, P. Lynch, P. Ó Sé, G. O'Keeffe, M. Spillane,
J. Mulvihill, S. Walsh, D. Moran, T. Doyle, P. Spillane, M. Sheehy, G. O'Driscoll, J. Egan.
Cork: B. Morgan, S. O'Sullivan, K. Kehilly, J. Evans, M. Healy, M. Moloney, J. Kerrigan,
T. O'Reilly, D. Philpott, D. Barry, G. Lynch, T. Dalton, D. O'Mahony, T. Holland,
F. O'Mahony.
Referee: P. Lane.

Round 2
Tralee, 2 November 1980
Kerry 1-6; Roscommon 0-9
Kerry: C. Nelligan, J. Deenihan, J. O'Keeffe, M. Spillane, P. Ó Sé, J. Mulvihill, G. O'Keeffe,
J. O'Shea, S. Walsh, D. Moran, T. Doyle, P. Spillane, B. Walsh, E. Liston, M. Sheehy.
Roscommon: G. Sheerin, H. Keegan, P. Lindsay, G. Connellan, G. Fitzmaurice, T. Donnellan,
D. Murray, S. Hayden, J. O'Gara, E. McManus, T. McManus, J. O'Connor, A. Dooley,
D. Earley, M. Finneran.
Referee: J. Moloney.

Round 3
Lurgan, 16 November 1980
Armagh 1-17; Kerry 2-5
Armagh: B. McAlinden, J. Donnelly, J. McKerr, D. Stevenson, D. Canavan, J. Kernan,
P. Moriarty, F. McMahon, J. Loughran, S. Devlin, J. Smyth, N. Marley, J. Corvan, B. Hughes,
P. Loughran.
Kerry: C. Nelligan, J. Deenihan, J. O'Keeffe, M. Spillane, P. Ó Sé, J. Mulvihill, G. O'Keeffe,
J. O'Shea, S. Walsh, D. Moran, T. Doyle, P. Spillane, B. Walsh, E. Liston, M. Sheehy.
Referee: S. Aldridge.

Round 6
Tullamore, 1 February 1981
Kerry 3-10; Offaly 1-9
Kerry: C. Nelligan, J. Deenihan, J. O'Keeffe, M. Spillane, P. Ó Sé, T. Kennelly, P. Sheehan,
T. Doyle, S. Walsh, G. Power, D. Moran, P. Spillane, M. Sheehy, E. Liston, J. Egan.
Offaly: M. Furlong, O. Minnock, E. Lowry, C. Conroy, S. Darby, M. Wright, L. Currams,
R. Connor, L. Connor, A. O'Halloran, J. Morgan, G. Guinan, M. Connor, J. Mooney,
K. Kilmurray.
Referee: PJ McGrath.

Round 7
Tralee, 1 March 1981
Kerry 2-14; Kildare 0-6

Kerry: P. O'Mahoney, J. Deenihan, J. O'Keeffe, P. Lynch, P. Ó Sé, T. Kennelly, D. Moran, S. Walsh, G. Power, T. Doyle, P. Spillane, M. Sheehy, E. Liston, J. Egan.
Kildare: J. Donoghue, D. Reilly, J. Crofton, M. Kirwan, C. Moran, P. Glynn, B. O'Donoghue, P. Kelly, J. O'Rourke, J. Geoghegan, J. Tomkins, P. Farrell, J. Kelly, J. Kelly, L. Tomkins.
Referee: S. O'Connor.

League Games 1981–1982

Round 1
Croke Park, 15 November 1981
Kerry 1-7; Dublin 0-7

Kerry: C. Nelligan, J. Deenihan, S. Walsh, B. O'Sullivan, P. Ó Sé, T. Kennelly, M. Spillane, J. O'Shea, T. Spillane, G. Power, T. Doyle, J. Doyle, D. O'Donoghue, E. Liston, J. Egan.
Dublin: J. O'Leary, M. Kennedy, V. Conroy, D. Foran, R. Hazley, M. Holden, PJ Buckley, T. Drumm, J. Ronayne, D. Carr, B. Jordan, C. Duff, J. Thompson, A. McCaul, M. Loftus.
Referee: J. Gunning.

Round 2
Hyde Park, 22 November 1981
Roscommon 0-9; Kerry 0-6

Roscommon: G. Sheerin, H. Keegan, P. Lindsay, M. Keegan, A. Garvey, E. McManus, D. Murray, J. O'Gara, G. Fitzmaurice, G. Watson, T. McManus, J. Kelly, M. Finneran, D. Earley, A. Dooley.
Kerry: C. Nelligan, J. Deenihan, J. O'Keeffe, B. O'Sullivan, P. Ó Sé, T. Kennelly, M. Spillane, J. O'Shea, T. Spillane, J. Shannon, A. O'Donovan, J. Doyle, G. Power, S. Walsh, G. O'Driscoll.
Referee: PJ McGrath.

Round 3
Crossmolina, 29 November 1981
Mayo 0-9; Kerry 1-5

Mayo: M. Webb, M. Gavin, J. Gallagher, M. O'Toole, H. Garvin, T. Kearney, M. Connolly, D. McGrath, J. Lyons, T. O'Malley, J. Bourke, M. Carney, G. Feeney, E. McHale, T. Reilly.
Kerry: J. Deenihan, M. Keane, J. O'Keeffe, M. Spillane, P. Ó Sé, T. Kennelly, P. Sheehan, J. O'Shea, S. Walsh, T. Spillane, A. O'Donovan, D. Moran, G. Lynch, E. Liston, J. Egan.
Referee: S. Mullaney.

Round 4
Tralee, 31 January 1982
Kerry 1-11; Offaly 0-8

Kerry: C. Nelligan, J. Deenihan, J. O'Keeffe, M. Spillane, P. Ó Sé, T. Kennelly, P. Sheehan,

J. O'Shea, S. Walsh, A. O'Donovan, D. Moran, T. Doyle, G. Power, E. Liston, M. Sheehy.
Offaly: M. Furlong, M. Fitzgerald, L. Connor, C. Conroy, P. Fitzgerald, R. Connor, L. Currams, G. Carroll, P. Dunne, A. O'Halloran, M. Connor, A. Brereton, S. Lowry, J. Moran, B. Lowry.
Referee: J. Dennigan.

Round 5
Killorglin, 7 February 1982
Armagh 1-5; Kerry 0-6
Armagh: B. McAlinden, D. Stevenson, J. McKerr, J. Murphy, B. Canavan, P. Moriarty, P. Rafferty, F. McMahon, C. McKinstry, S. Devlin, J. Kernan, A. Shortt, C. McGurk, B. Hughes, P. Loughran.
Kerry: C. Nelligan, J. Deenihan, J. O'Keeffe, M. Spillane, P. Ó Sé, T. Kennelly, P. Sheehan, J. O'Shea, S. Walsh, A. O'Donovan, D. Moran, T. Doyle, G. Power, E. Liston, J. Egan.
Referee: J. Dennigan.

League Quarter-final
Croke Park, 21 March 1982
Kerry 1-11; Derry 0-5
Kerry: C. Nelligan, J. Deenihan, V. O'Connor, M. Spillane, P. Ó Sé, T. Kennelly, G. Lynch, J. O'Shea, S. Walsh, J. L. McElligott, T. Spillane, T. Doyle, G. Power, E. Liston, J. Doyle.
Derry: J. Somers, T. Moore, F. Trainor, B. Trainor, F. Johnston, J. McGuckin, G. O'Loughlin, J. Irwin, D. Barton, E. Donnelly, M. Lynch, F. McCloskey, C. McKee, P. Dougan, B. O'Neill.
Referee: J. Gunning.

League Semi-final
Croke Park, 11 April 1982
Kerry 3-14; Armagh 1-5
Kerry: C. Nelligan, J. Deenihan, J. O'Keeffe, V. O'Connor, G. Lynch, T. Kennelly, G. O'Keeffe, S. Walsh, J. O'Shea, J. L. McElligott, T. Doyle, M. Spillane, G. Power, E. Liston, T. Spillane.
Armagh: B. McAlinden, D. Stevenson, J. McKerr, J. Murphy, B. Canavan, P. Moriarty, P. Rafferty, F. McMahon, C. McKinstry, K. McGurk, J. Kernan, S. Devlin, H. Kernan, B. Hughes, P. Loughran.
Referee: P. Collins.

League Final
Killarney, 25 April 1982
Kerry 0-11; Cork 0-11
Kerry: C. Nelligan, J. Deenihan (capt.), J. O'Keeffe, V. O'Connor, G. Lynch, T. Kennelly, G. O'Keeffe, J. O'Shea, S. Walsh, J. L. McElligott, T. Doyle, G. Power, M. Spillane, E. Liston, J. Egan.
Cork: M. Creedon, M. Healy, K. Kehilly, J. Evans, M. Moloney, T. Creedon, J. Kerrigan, D. Creedon, T. O'Reilly, D. Barry, D. Allen, M. Connolly, D. McCarthy, C. Ryan, E. Fitzgerald.
Referee: S. Aldridge.

League Final (replay)
Pairc Uí Chaoimh, 23 May 1982
Kerry 1-9; Cork 0-5
Kerry: C. Nelligan, J. Deenihan (capt.), J. O'Keeffe, G. O'Keeffe, P. Ó Sé, T. Kennelly, G. Lynch, J. O'Shea, S. Walsh, J. L. McElligott, D. Moran, T. Doyle, G. Power, E. Liston, J. Egan.
Cork: M. Creedon, M. Healy, K. Kehilly, J. Evans, M. Moloney, T. Creedon, J. Kerrigan, M. Burns, D. Creedon, D. Barry, D. Allen, T. O'Reilly, D. McCarthy, C. Ryan, E. Fitzgerald.
Referee: S. Aldridge.

Railway Cup Finals 1975–1982

Croke Park, 17 March 1975
Munster 6-7; Ulster 0-15
Munster: B. Morgan (Cork), E. Webster (Tipperary), H. Kelleher (Cork), J. Deenihan (Kerry), K. J. O'Sullivan (Cork), J. O'Keeffe, G. Power (Kerry), D. Long, D. McCarthy (Cork), B. Lynch (Kerry), J. Barrett (Cork), M. O'Sullivan (Kerry), J. Barry-Murphy (Cork), S. Kearney (Tipperary), J. Egan Kerry).
Ulster: L. Turbett (Tyrone), D. Monaghan, P. McShea (Donegal), P. Mulgrew (Tyrone), P. Kerr (Monaghan), J. P. O'Kane (Antrim), E. Tavey (Monaghan), T. McGuinness (Derry), P. McGinnity (Fermanagh), F. McGuinan (Tyrone), C. McAlarney (Down), M. Carney (Donegal), P. Rooney (Down) S. Bonner (Donegal), S. O'Neill (Down).

Croke Park, 17 March 1976
Munster 2-15; Leinster 2-8
Munster: P. O'Mahoney (Kerry), E. Webster (Tipperary), B. Murphy (Cork), J. Deenihan, P. Ó Sé (Kerry), K. Kehilly (Cork), G. Power (Kerry), D. Long (Cork), D. Moran (Kerry), D. Allen (Cork), M. Sheehy, M. O'Sullivan, J. Egan (Kerry), J. Barry-Murphy (Cork), P. Spillane (Kerry).
Leinster: P. Cullen, G. O'Driscoll (Dublin), J. Conway (Laois), R. Kelleher (Dublin), J. Balfe (Kildare), S. Lowry (Offaly), K. Brennan (Laois), B. Mullins (Dublin), K. Rennicks (Meath), R. Doyle, T. Hanahoe, D. Hickey (Dublin), P. Fenning (Offaly), J. Keaveney, A. O'Toole (Dublin).

Croke Park, 27 March 1978
Munster 2-7; Ulster 2-7
Croke Park, 16 April 1978 (replay)
Munster 4-12; Ulster 0-19 (after extra time)
Munster: B. Morgan, B. Murphy (Cork), J. O'Keeffe, J. Deenihan, P. Ó Sé, T. Kennelly (Kerry), M. Murphy (Clare), G. McGrath (Tipperary), M. Quish (Limerick), P. Spillane, M. Sheehy, G. Power (Kerry), J. Barry-Murphy (Cork), S. Walsh (Kerry), J. Hennessy (Waterford).
K. Kehilly, D. Allen, D. McCarthy (Cork) and G. O'Driscoll (Kerry) played in drawn game. B. Murphy, M. Quish, J. B. Murphy, and M. Sheehy came on for replay.
Ulster: J. Somers (Derry), D. Stevenson (Armagh), P. Mulgrew (Tyrone), E. McGowan

297

(Cavan), P. Moriarty (Armagh), A. McGuirk, M. Moran (Derry), C. McAlarney (Down), P. McGinnity (Fermanagh), L. Austin (Down), E. McKenna (Tyrone), J. Kernan (Armagh), J. Byrne (Down), P. Rooney (Down), P. Traynor (Armagh). Kevin McCabe (Tyrone) and J. Smith (Armagh) played in drawn game. P. Moriarty and J. Kernan came on for replay.

Croke Park, 17 March 1980
Ulster 2-10; Munster 1-9
Ulster: B. McAlinden (Armagh), E. Hughes (Monaghan), T. McGovern (Down), F. Ward (Donegal) K. McCabe (Tyrone) P. Moriarty (Armagh), S. McCarville (Monaghan), P. McGinnitty (Fermanagh), L. Austin, C. McAlarney (Down), J. Kernan (Armagh), E. Young (Derry), P. McNamee (Cavan), P. Rooney (Down), P. Loughran (Armagh).
Munster: C. Nelligan, J. Deenihan, J. O'Keeffe (Kerry), K. Kehilly (Cork), P. Ó Sé, T. Kennelly (Kerry), T. Creedon (Cork), S. Walsh (Kerry), C. Ryan (Cork), G. Power, M. Sheehy, P. Spillane (Kerry), D. Allen (Cork), E. Liston, J. Egan (Kerry).

Ennis, 17 March 1981
Munster 3-10; Connacht 1-9
Munster: C. Nelligan, J. Deenihan, J. O'Keeffe (Kerry), K. Kehilly (Cork), P. Ó Sé, T. Kennelly, D. Moran, S. Walsh, J. O'Shea, G. Power (Kerry), D. Allen (Cork), P. Spillane, M. Sheehy, E. Liston, J. Egan (Kerry).
Connacht: M. Webb (Mayo), J. Hughes (Galway), P. Lindsay, J. McManus (Roscommon), S. McHugh (Galway), T. Donnellan, D. Murray, S. Hayden (Roscommon), M. McCorrick (Sligo), B. Brennan (Galway), J. Kent (Sligo), D. Earley, M. Finneran, A. McManus (Roscommon), M. Carney (Mayo).

Appendix B

ACHIEVEMENTS

5 All-Ireland Senior medals:
1975, 1978, 1979, 1980, 1981

4 National League medals:
1973,1974, 1977, 1982

4 Railway Cup medals:
1975, 1976, 1978, 1981

1 All-Ireland U21 medal:
1973

2 Kerry County Senior Championship medals:
1978, 1980

Higher Education Football Leagues
Division 1: 1975
Division 2: 1974

1 North Kerry Championship medal:
1987

All Star Award:
1981

Selected on Kerry Team of the Millennium 2000 at right corner-back